CW00434530

UNDERSTANDING MUSLIM

Ashgate AHRC/ESRC Religion and Society Series

Series Editors:

Linda Woodhead, University of Lancaster, UK
Rebecca Catto, University of Lancaster, UK

This book series emanates from the largest research programme on religion in Europe today – the AHRC/ESRC Religion and Society Programme which has invested in over seventy-five research projects. Thirty-two separate disciplines are represented looking at religion across the world, many with a contemporary and some with an historical focus. This international, multi-disciplinary and interdisciplinary book series will include monographs, paperback textbooks and edited research collections drawn from this leading research programme.

Other titles in the series:

Ageing, Ritual and Social Change
Comparing the Secular and Religious in Eastern and Western Europe
Edited by Peter Coleman, Daniela Koleva and Joanna Bornat

Media Portrayals of Religion and the Secular Sacred
Representation and Change
Kim Knott, Elizabeth Poole and Teemu Taira

Discourses on Religious Diversity
Explorations in an Urban Ecology
Martin D. Stringer

Social Identities Between the Sacred and the Secular
Edited by Abby Day, Giselle Vincett and Christopher R. Cotter

Religion in Consumer Society
Brands, Consumers and Markets
Edited by François Gauthier and Tuomas Martikainen

Contesting Secularism
Comparative Perspectives
Edited by Anders Berg-Sørensen

Understanding Muslim Chaplaincy

SOPHIE GILLIAT-RAY
Cardiff University

MUHAMMAD MANSUR ALI
Cardiff University

STEPHEN PATTISON
University of Birmingham

ASHGATE

Sophie Gilliat-Ray would like to dedicate her work for this book to
Mr Yousef Jameel

Mansur Ali would like to dedicate his work for this book to
Hafiz Mohammed Mujahid Ali

Stephen Pattison would like to dedicate his work for this book to
Aisha-Saara, Hanaan, and Zayd

Understanding Muslim Chaplaincy

Understanding Muslim Chaplaincy provides a lens through which to explore critical questions relating to contemporary religion in public life, and the institutionalisation of Islam in particular. Providing a rich description of the personnel, practice, and politics of contemporary Muslim chaplaincy, the authors consider the extent to which Muslim chaplaincy might be distinctive in Britain relative to the work of Muslim chaplains in the USA and other countries. This book will make a major contribution to international debate about the place of religion in public life and institutions.

This book derives from research that has depended on exclusive access to a wide range of public institutions and personnel who largely work 'behind closed doors'. By making public the work of these chaplains and critically examining the impact of their work within and beyond their institutions, this book offers a groundbreaking study in the field of contemporary religion that will stimulate discussion for many years to come about Islam and Muslims in Western societies.

Published by
Ashgate Publishing Limited
Wey Court East
Union Road
Farnham
Surrey, GU9 7PT
England

Ashgate Publishing Company
110 Cherry Street
Suite 3-1
Burlington, VT 05401-3818
USA

www.ashgate.com

British Library Cataloguing in Publication Data
A catalogue record for this book is available from the British Library

The Library of Congress has cataloged the printed edition as follows:
Gilliat-Ray, Sophie, 1969–
Understanding Muslim chaplaincy / by Sophie Gilliat-Ray, Mansur Ali and Stephen Pattison.
     p. cm. – (Ashgate ahrc/esrc religion and society series)
  Includes bibliographical references and index.
  ISBN 978-1-4094-3592-1 (hardcover) – ISBN 978-1-4094-3593-8 (pbk) – ISBN 978-1-4094-3594-5 (ebook) 1. Imams (Mosque officers)–Great Britain. 2. Imams (Mosque officers)–United States. 3. Prison chaplains–Great Britain. 4. Prison chaplains–United States. I. Pattison, Stephen. II. Ali, Mansur. III. Title.
  BP185.G55 2013
  297.6'1–dc23
                                                              2012048387

ISBN 9781409435921 (hbk)
ISBN 9781409435938 (pbk)
ISBN 9781409435945 (ebk – PDF)

Printed in the United Kingdom by Henry Ling Limited, at the Dorset Press, Dorchester, DT1 1HD

Contents

List of Figures   *ix*
List of Abbreviations   *xi*
Notes on Authors   *xiii*
Foreword   *xv*
Preface and Acknowledgements   *xvii*

Chapter 1   Chaplaincy and British Muslims   1

Chapter 2   Pastoral Care in Islam   25

Chapter 3   Chaplaincy People   43

Chapter 4   Chaplaincy Practice   71

Chapter 5   Chaplaincy Politics   99

Chapter 6   The Impact of Chaplaincy   123

Chapter 7   Muslim Chaplaincy in the United States of America   145

Chapter 8   Chaplaincy, Religious Diversity and Public Life   167

Glossary   *191*
References   *193*
Index   *203*

List of Figures

1.1	'Doing time at HM's pleasure', *The Muslim News*, June 1991	10
1.2	Latif Mir (left) and Imam Asim Hafiz (right) – the first Muslim chaplains to be appointed to an HM Magistrates and Crown Court and HM Armed Forces	17
1.3	Composition of sample, by sector	18
1.4	Composition of sample, by sector and gender	19
3.1	Shaheen Kauser, Muslim Chaplain, Bradford Teaching Hospitals NHS Foundation Trust	54
3.2	Imam Abdul Mumin Choudhury (left), Chaplain at Guy's and St Thomas's NHS Foundation Trust, in conversation with Imam Faisal Ahmed (right), Muslim chaplain at HMP/ YOI Isis & HMP/YOI Rochester	57
4.1	Imam Farid Khan, Muslim Chaplain at HMP and YOI Parc, South Wales	74
4.2	Maulana Mohammed Arshad, Head of Chaplaincy, Bradford Teaching Hospitals NHS Foundation Trust, praying with a patient	83
6.1	Cover of *A Gift for the Bereaved Parent*, written and compiled by Zamir Hussain, Birmingham Children's Hospital	128
8.1	Imam Yasar Zaman, Homerton University Hospital (left) with Muhammed Foulds (right) Head Chaplain and Imam at HMP Bristol, at the Muslim Chaplaincy project conference, Cardiff, September 2011	177
8.2	Asgar Halim Rajput, chaplain at Brunel University, London	185

List of Abbreviations

ACPE   Association for Clinical Pastoral Education
AMC   Association of Muslim Chaplains

BMC   British Muslim Chaplains

CTC   Counter Terrorism Clearance

HEI   Higher Education Institution

ISF   Islamic Seminary Foundation

MCA   Muslim Chaplains Association
MECCT   Muslim Endorsement Council of Connecticut
MIHE   Markfield Institute of Higher Education
MOJ   Ministry of Justice

NHS   National Health Service
NOMS   National Offender Management Service

PSC   Prison Service Chaplaincy
PSO   Prison Service Orders

YOI   Young Offender Institution

Notes on Authors

Maulana Muhammad Mansur Ali is the Jameel Lecturer in Islamic Studies in the School of History, Archaeology and Religion at Cardiff University. He has a PhD in Middle Eastern Studies (specialising in Hadith Studies) from Manchester University (2010), and has served as a Muslim Chaplain at Ashworth High Security Hospital. Prior to his appointment at Cardiff, he was a Research Fellow at Cambridge Muslim College.

Sophie Gilliat-Ray is Professor of Religious and Theological Studies at Cardiff University and Director of the Centre for the Study of Islam in the UK. She is the author of *Muslims in Britain: an Introduction* (2010), *Religion in Higher Education: the Politics of the Multi-faith Campus* (Ashgate, 2000) and *Religion in Prison: Equal Rites in a Multi-faith Society* (1998, with Professor James Beckford).

Stephen Pattison is Professor of Religion, Ethics and Practice and HG Wood Professor of Theology, at the Department of Theology and Religion at the University of Birmingham. He has authored *Shame: Theory, Therapy, Theology* (2000), *Seeing Things: Deepening Relations with Visual Artefacts* (2007), *Saving Face* (Ashgate, 2013) and co-edited *Values in Professional Practice* (2004) and *Emerging Values in Health Care* (2010).

Foreword

This book addresses the compelling need for formal research into and reflection on the development of Muslim involvement in chaplaincy. It is a major contribution to our discussion of beliefs and assumptions about chaplaincy, and its relevance to contemporary multi-cultural, multi-ethnic and multi-religious societies. It brings valuable insight to our understanding of the role and place of Muslim chaplains and how they face the poignant issues of care and need within the Muslim community. It explores how on the one hand they are navigating their way into an already established structure and, on the other, how they are making sense of their presence to their respective community institutions.

Muslim chaplaincy has come a long way, particularly since 2000. To begin with it was largely a locally organised affair focused on meeting the basic religious needs of prison inmates and hospital patients. In the seventies and eighties it was still mainly a volunteer effort often, of necessity, oriented more to what suited the chaplains than what suited their clients. I can remember that in the early eighties volunteer Muslim chaplains, in prison services, occasionally offered their services of Friday congregational prayer on Saturdays because they could not get time off from their jobs to do otherwise. No doubt the prisoners and the chaplains had an understanding. In the higher education sector needs were largely met from within the student Islamic Societies. A mature and religiously conversant student acted as a 'chaplain'. In some cases it was, and indeed still is, a university staff member who would perform this role. The 'professionalisation' of Muslim chaplains, particularly in sectors where they have been appointed as full/part time chaplains, is a welcome development. It has its own dynamics, as this book shows. Muslim chaplains are generally motivated by their new disciplined vocation to talk about their experience and expertise with the management of Muslim community institutions – madrassas, mosques and others. However, when they approach their communities they meet great 'elders' at the gates, greet them reverently and wait for another day to tell their success story. I hope that this experience of hierarchy, set in the Muslim community, will not become a template for Muslim chaplaincy within the prison or healthcare sectors. A new or junior chaplain should feel at ease when engaging with and asking questions about, Muslim chaplaincy, and not need to display reverence.

Muslim chaplaincy has benefited immensely from inter-faith experiences in all sectors of the work. In my experience of running the course on chaplaincy at our Institute I have often been reminded by outgoing students that their time in placement, working with the people of other faiths, was most valuable. They felt that they were welcomed and made at home. Their opinions mattered, they were trusted and valued, and this changed their outlook on the world. A few years ago a senior imam joined our course to study the theoretical and placement part of chaplaincy. On the last day of the course he took the time to call on me and said: 'I thought this would be one of those certificate courses where students attend, get a certificate and go home. What I did not realise was that the chaplaincy training experience would be a life-changing one'. He was particularly referring to his time in placement. Although he had limited exposure to working with other faiths and management systems, it had been enough to change his outlook. For sure, there are some darker areas of inter-faith chaplaincy, which this book, quite rightly, does not shy from pointing out; nonetheless, they are not pervasive. Muslim chaplains perhaps need to take more careful note of the importance of a properly respectful attitude to inter-faith chaplaincy. There will be occasions when their commitment to inter-faith work will be tested.

This is a comprehensive and superbly organised treatment of the values embodied in the Muslim chaplains' Islamic understanding of khidmah (service). It narrates how chaplains cross back and forth over the lines between the different schools of Islamic jurisprudence (fiqh) in order to overcome real-life pastoral care issues. The authors provide insights into what goes on in the minds of chaplains who are having to, as it were, work out their theology when confronted by the lived realities of day-to-day chaplaincy. These acted experiences provide a rich resource for the 'pastoral care theology' of Islam. However, as the authors duly emphasise, the lack of books and material resources in Muslim chaplaincy needs to be addressed as soon as possible. There are expanding resources in health care chaplaincy, but very few in the prison, higher education or community sectors. A significant Muslim narrative of pastoral care is scattered in the pages of Prophetic traditions and Islamic history, but this requires a keen eye, a mature mind and of course an ability to access the sources with diligence and care.

The scope of the discussion is both significant and impressive – a broad range of relevant topics are picked out, engaged with and brought together. The authors have made a major contribution to the profession and its emerging literature. The book will prove useful in many areas, Muslim chaplaincy in particular and also chaplaincy in general. It is written in an engaging and reflective style, and I urge everyone to ponder deeply the issues raised and assessed here. I congratulate its authors, particularly the two veterans in the field, Professor Stephen Pattison and Professor Sophie Gilliat-Ray . They are pioneers in the study of chaplaincy and Dr Mansur Ali is a happy addition to the illustrious team.

Dr Ataullah Siddiqui
Markfield Institute of Higher Education
August 2013

Preface and Acknowledgements

In 1970 there were no formally recognised Muslim chaplains in England and Wales. In 2013, Muslim chaplains are working in a wide range of public institutions in Britain, including prisons, hospitals, HM Courts, leisure attractions, airports, shopping centres and in a variety of educational settings. There are now an estimated 450 Muslim chaplains in England and Wales, just under half of whom are employed by HM Prison Service.

This book presents the main findings of one of the most in-depth studies of contemporary chaplaincy, and provides a lens through which to examine the changing role of religion in society by looking at the rise and nature of Muslim chaplaincy practice. At the same time, our work for this book represents one of the most thorough investigations of the work of Muslim religious professionals in the West. Many Muslim chaplains have served at some point as community-based religious leaders, and some continue in these roles alongside their work as chaplains in public institutions. As far as we are aware, there has been no other study of such a large group of Muslim religious professionals. Our research with chaplains has enabled an evaluation of some of the practical and theological challenges facing Muslim communities in Britain, and the broader accommodation of Islamic traditions within the dynamic of public life. The research conducted with Muslim chaplains based in the USA provides an important point of comparison, and allows the distinctiveness of British Muslim traditions to come into view.

In this book, we try to understand the rise, nature and practices of contemporary Muslim chaplaincy. Who becomes a Muslim chaplain, and why? What is the career trajectory of Muslim chaplains and what prior experience and training do they bring to their role? What is involved in Muslim chaplaincy practice and what kind of resources do Muslim chaplains draw upon? How do chaplains navigate their way through the power dynamics of their institutions, and to what extent have they been affected by the broader 'politics' facing Muslims in Britain more generally? Are the skills and professionalism that Muslim chaplains are acquiring as part of their work influencing ideas about religious leadership in Muslim communities, or shaping the chaplaincy profession more widely? In attempting to answer these questions we address some of the most profound issues affecting Muslim communities in Britain today.

This book is the product of a research project generously funded by the joint Arts and Humanities Research Council (AHRC) and Economic and Social Research Council (ESRC) 'Religion and Society Programme'. We are extremely appreciative of the support of the Programme Director, Professor Linda Woodhead, throughout the project. We would like to thank the commissioning panel for supporting our funding application, especially Professor Jim Beckford, a pioneer of the social scientific study of religion (especially religion in prisons). Also connected to the funding application process was Imam Dr Abduljalil Sajid, one of the longest-serving Muslim chaplains in Britain today. As a key 'stakeholder', Imam Sajid was able to offer an informed practitioner perspective on our proposal, for which we are grateful.

The success of our work has depended a great deal upon the co-operation and support of Dr Ataullah Siddiqui and the staff at Markfield Institute of Higher Education, Leicester. Part of our research sought to understand how the identity 'Muslim chaplain' is acquired by those undertaking chaplaincy training courses. By allowing us to contact former students of the 'Certificate in Muslim Chaplaincy', and by giving us permission to observe a cohort of students undertaking training in 2009, we have been able to reflect on the significance of the Markfield course, and the very important ways in which it has clearly shaped the arena of professional Muslim chaplaincy activity.

Our research benefitted from the input of four project 'consultants'. We knew at the outset that our understanding of professional Muslim chaplaincy would need to be informed by some leading practitioners who have in various ways pushed at the boundaries of chaplaincy practice, and done a great deal to further the professional development and profile of Muslim chaplains. To that end, we are extremely grateful to Maulana Yunus Dudhwala, Head of Chaplaincy and Bereavement Services at Newham University Hospital, London; Imam Asim Hafiz, Muslim Chaplain to HM Armed Forces; Maulana Sikander Pathan, Muslim Chaplain at YOI Feltham; and Asgar Halim Rajput, Muslim Chaplain at Brunel University and at Heathrow Airport. They were regular sources of advice, facts and guidance, and although we take full responsibility for any shortcomings arising from our project, nevertheless we wanted to thank you all for your engagement. During the life of the study, we also derived a great deal of support from the chaplaincy team at Bradford Teaching Hospitals NHS Foundation Trust. Maulana Mohammad Arshad and the wider chaplaincy team there deserve special acknowledgment.

At face value, the prospect of interviewing 65 Muslim chaplains in England and Wales about their work may seem relatively straightforward. We have, however, found it a complex undertaking, not least because of the considerable bureaucracy surrounding the work of chaplains in public institutions. On occasion, our struggles to access chaplains, their initial suspicions about our interests and the purpose of our work and the complex paperwork involved in gaining an entree have all been indicative of a very difficult climate for contemporary chaplaincy. This is amplified by the securitisation and counter-radicalisation policies that powerfully affect some public institutions. We are extremely grateful to Ahtsham Ali, the Muslim Advisor for the Prison Service Chaplaincy (PSC), for helping us to navigate some of the bureaucratic barriers that we faced in the early phases of our research.

For a range of administrative reasons, the research and writing of this book extended well beyond the intended time-frame. This has been beneficial, not least because of the opportunity to benefit from the insights of former members of the research team. These include Sheikh Ali Omar who worked on the project during its first year. Ali travelled the length and breadth of the country gathering interview data; we are grateful to him for the sacrifices and hard work this involved. We would also like to record our appreciation of Rehnaz Mustafa, who served as the part-time project administrator from July 2008 to March 2010. We are also grateful to Stephen Roberts who, at the time of the project, was at St Michael's Theological College in Cardiff (now at the University of Chichester). Stephen acted as a consultant and occasional team member, advising us from his experience in higher education chaplaincy and helping us to analyse some of the results of our study.

The greatest appreciation is owed to the interviewees who kindly shared their experiences and working lives with us, and who were often extremely hospitable and generous with their time. Those of you who took part in our research might remember being asked what you regarded as the qualities of a 'good' chaplain. Responses to that question included characteristics that we have very much valued in our research relationships with you, such as kindness, sincerity, forgiveness, respectfulness and patience. Thank you for embodying and sharing those qualities with us as we conducted our study.

We owe a very significant debt of gratitude to a number of organisations and individuals associated with the production of this book. Firstly, we acknowledge with great appreciation Cambridge Muslim College, who provided Mansur Ali with an opportunity to write his chapters for this book, between November 2011 and October 2012, during his Research Fellowship. Given the important role of the College in the training of Muslim religious professionals in Britain, we hope that this book will help to further the interests and objectives of the College into the future.

We would like to thank Sarah Lloyd and her colleagues at Ashgate, for making the production of this book such a straightforward process. Thank you.

In order to maximise the accessibility of the book we provide a full glossary of frequently used religious terms, but we have omitted full diacritical marks. Meanwhile, in most cases, we have simplified references to hadith literature by simply citing the relevant book of hadith (and the number) rather than referring readers to translated or secondary sources.

Muhammad Mansur Ali
Sophie Gilliat-Ray
Stephen Pattison
August 2013

Chapter 1
Chaplaincy and British Muslims

Introduction

A convicted paedophile serving a life sentence in a high-security prison wishes to convert to Islam. He wants to talk to the Muslim chaplain about his decision, and would like him to hear his declaration of faith: 'There is no God but God, and Muhammad is His Messenger'. Other prisoners are aware of the crimes committed by the prisoner. Somehow the chaplain must find credible religious arguments to persuade the other prisoners to accept this new Muslim as a legitimate member of the worldwide Muslim community (ummah) and the more local Muslim community within the prison. What Islamic resources and texts enable him to do this? How does he balance competing tensions and emotions around forgiveness and compassion, alongside anger and disgust?

Meanwhile, a newly appointed Muslim chaplain at a large further education college in the Midlands faces different dilemmas. The staff of the chaplaincy team are working together to prepare Easter gift packs for the Christian students, each pack containing a chocolate Easter egg, a prayer card with details of local church services and crosses made from palm leaves. The Muslim chaplain questions herself: by joining in with the preparation of the Easter packs and facilitating the celebrations, is she promoting a positive image of Muslim engagement in a multi-faith society, or compromising the indivisible unity of God, thereby committing a sin (shirk)? She asks a number of senior religious scholars ('ulama) for advice, but they each offer different opinions.

Muslim chaplains employed in British institutions face interesting challenges of this kind every day. These men and women, working in full-time, part-time and voluntary roles, can be found in prisons, hospitals, educational institutions, HM Courts, shopping centres and airports, while others have formal association with police forces and leisure attractions. As the examples above indicate, they often have to decide how, and to what extent, Islamic traditions and practices can be accommodated within the confines of secular, multi-faith, public institutions. Decision-making often requires an ability to think and act contextually, and in light of both institutional policies and the principles of shari'ah (Islamic legal traditions).

In some prisons or hospitals, the Muslim chaplain is perhaps the only Muslim that other staff meet on a regular basis. In such a context, Muslim chaplains can become important educators about the Islamic tradition in the public sphere. Given their acquired understanding of the dynamics and politics that shape public institutions, their need to work as part of multi-faith chaplaincy teams, and their need to deploy skills of counselling and care with a cross-section of sometimes vulnerable people, Muslim chaplains are regarded by some as role models for the kind of professional religious leadership often sought within British Muslim communities more widely. In the light of these developments, the growing involvement of Muslims in chaplaincy provides a unique lens through which to consider major contemporary issues about Islamic religious leadership, and the place of Islam in the public sphere.

But who decides to become a Muslim chaplain, and why? What skills, training or experience do they bring to their role? Given that there is no formal institutionalised tradition of pastoral care in Islam, what do Muslim chaplains actually do, and how does their practice differ according to religious school of thought, ethnic background or gender? How are Muslim chaplains navigating their way through the politics that shape their work, whether this is within their institutions, among their various professional associations or in relation to the wider politics that surround Islam and Muslims in public life? These are some of the questions that *Understanding Muslim Chaplaincy* addresses, based on the first major empirical study of Muslim chaplaincy undertaken to date.

About this Book

This book provides a rich description of the personnel, practice and politics of contemporary Muslim involvement in chaplaincy in England and Wales, based on extensive qualitative research on religious leadership and pastoral care in Islam.[1] To cover the breadth of our subject and to increase the accessibility of the book, we have kept theory and methodological discussion to a minimum. We are conscious that readers may come from a range of backgrounds, and that the interests of policymakers, Muslim chaplains and other religious professionals will be quite different to those of students or academics. It is also worth noting that much rich material from our research lies on the cutting-room floor. There are nuances and details of experiences that we would have liked to include, but have necessarily had to omit. In the following paragraphs, we briefly describe the contours of each chapter, so that readers can identify those parts of the book that will be of most interest to them.

Chapter 1 considers the emergence of Muslim chaplaincy roles within the wider context of the development of Muslim communities in Britain. The rationale for the research upon which the book is based is described, along with a brief discussion of research methods, sampling and data analysis techniques. We end by considering the major questions that are raised as a consequence of growing

---

[1]   For a range of practical and strategic reasons, we confined our empirical research in the UK to England and Wales. However, during the life of the project, we became aware of important developments in relation to Muslim chaplaincy in Scotland, which clearly warrant further research.

Muslim involvement in chaplaincy, for public institutions, for pastoral care practitioners and theorists and for Muslim communities themselves. Some readers may already be familiar with the rise and development of Muslim chaplaincy, or may be unconcerned with the details of research methodology, in which case, they should begin this book at Chapter 2.

In Chapter 2, we evaluate the evolution of Muslim involvement in chaplaincy from an Islamic theological perspective. We consider the way in which practical and spiritual care has historically been delivered in Muslim societies, via family and kinship networks, and via religious teachers and scholars. The basis for caring within Islamic societies and communities is considered in relation to key Quranic verses and hadith, alongside the example of the Prophet Muhammad himself. To date, there has been no articulate written account of the way in which Islamic traditions and scriptural sources are accommodated within contemporary chaplaincy practice. This is therefore an important chapter for situating Muslim chaplaincy within the wider Islamic tradition.

Chapter 3 reflects the first substantial discussion of empirical research findings. Here, we discuss the question of who decides to become a chaplain, and why? We reflect upon the kind of educational, religious and social capital that chaplains bring to their work, and consider the various routes by which chaplains are recruited. Additionally, we discuss how chaplaincy practice relates to career development and progression, and the place that education and training have for the acquisition of a professional identity as a chaplain. Considerations of gender are important in our evaluation; we reflect upon the way in which chaplaincy is enabling Muslim women in Britain to adopt professional religious roles.

Given that there is no tradition of institutionalised pastoral care in Islam, Chapter 4 considers what it is that chaplains actually do as they work in prisons, hospitals, HM courts or educational institutions. To what extent is their practice informed by Islamic sources, by institutional requirements, by the adaptation or 'Islamisation' of Christian pastoral care models, or perhaps a new hybrid of these and other factors? Based on ethnographic observations, focus group discussions and interview data, this chapter provides an in-depth discussion of the underlying practices that characterise the work of Muslim chaplains. We consider the tasks they perform that are distinctive to the Islamic tradition (for example facilitating Ramadan fasting), as well as duties that are shared with chaplains of other faiths, such as pastoral visiting or administration. In this case we explore what, if anything, makes their performance of this work distinctively 'Islamic'.

The degree to which Muslims are now involved in chaplaincy has had implications within public institutions, and among chaplains themselves. Chapter 5 considers the micro- and macro-politics of Muslim involvement in chaplaincy, by considering, first of all, how Muslim chaplains have navigated their way through the politics of their own institutions, and more especially their location within multi-faith chaplaincy 'teams'. How have they been incorporated into these 'teams', and what is their perception of the process? How is their work viewed by senior managers and employers, as contributing to the welfare of the organisation? Meanwhile, the macro-politics of Islam in Britain also shapes the work of Muslim chaplains. The rivalries and tensions in Muslim communities at a national level are reflected in the professional associations and interpersonal tensions among chaplains themselves. Many aspects of Islam in Britain can be seen in microcosm in the work of chaplains and the professional networks they have established to support their work. But the 'Preventing Violent Extremism' agenda of recent governments has perhaps had the most significant impact on the politics of Muslim chaplaincy, and this chapter provides a case study of how the politics of 'Prevent' have affected a distinctive group of British Muslim religious professionals.

Chapter 6 reflects on the structural location of chaplains as they work at the interface of public institutions, multi-faith chaplaincy teams and their own faith communities. Standing at the intersection of these different constituencies, they are perhaps uniquely placed to comment upon, and contribute to, the discourse surrounding the place of Muslims in Britain more widely. This chapter surveys the contribution that Muslim chaplains are playing within and beyond their institutions by considering the impact of chaplaincy practice upon 'clients', and the degree to which they value the services of Muslim chaplains. How and to what extent does the employment of Muslim chaplains 'make a difference' to the lived experience of being a British Muslim, and a sense that Islam has a recognised place within British society? How do chaplains themselves perceive the implications and impact of their work on Muslim communities in Britain, and to what extent are the skills and professionalism they are acquiring shaping patterns of religious leadership in mosques and other Islamic organisations?

Chapter 7 offers some international perspectives on Muslim involvement in chaplaincy, and argues that the growth (or not) of Muslim chaplaincy roles, whether in England and Wales, in the United States or in Europe, is a direct reflection of socio-political forces and complex religious histories. Based on a short period of empirical research in the United States, this chapter will consider what makes Muslim involvement in chaplaincy in England and Wales both similar to, and different from evolving models of chaplaincy in other parts of the world, especially the USA.

In Chapter 8, we explore how Muslim chaplaincy appears to be both similar to, and different from the work of Christian chaplains. How have Muslims been influenced by Christian models of pastoral care, and the undergirding principles that shape the working of public institutions, such as equality and diversity? The final chapter also provides scope to explore the implications of Muslim chaplaincy work as practiced in multi-faith contexts. What kind of social and religious capital do Muslim chaplains acquire as a consequence of their experiences of religious diversity, and how might these various forms of capital have significance for religion in public life more broadly?

The Growth and Development of Muslim Chaplaincy

A chaplain is an individual who provides religious and spiritual care within an organisational setting. Although this role has evolved from within the Christian churches, the term 'chaplain' is now increasingly associated with other faith traditions. Chaplains may be qualified religious professionals, or lay people, and while religious and pastoral care might be central to their role, the increasing complexity of many large public organisations has led to an expansion in the range of their activities.

Chaplaincy has a long history in British hospitals (Pattison 1994; Swift 2009), prisons (Priestly 1985), the military (Snape 2005) and industry (Fuller and Vaughan 1986), as well as many other sectors (Legood 1999a). The Christian churches have so far dominated this sphere of work; in England, the appointment of Anglican chaplains in particular, usually in the most senior post, has been an extension of the established character of the Church of England (Davie 1994). The 1952 Prison Act stipulates the appointment of an Anglican chaplain, whilst fulfilling the requirements of the Patients Charter of 1991, usually means the appointment of at least one Anglican chaplain in hospitals. Prison and hospital chaplaincy posts are publicly funded through taxes, and whilst the 'sending churches' endorse the qualifications and competence of chaplains from Christian denominations, they are the employees of the institutions in which they work. Other institutions also have a long history of employing chaplains (especially the military), while over the last 50 years chaplaincy has been developing in education and industry (agriculture, sports, fire services, leisure, shopping, airports, to name a few). These posts are usually funded either by religious communities, or by employing institutions. Over time, various Christian dominations, Jews and, more recently, members of other world religions have been drawn into chaplaincy work, and this has raised complex questions about the status of religion in the law and in public institutions (Beckford and Gilliat 1998). In many ways, chaplaincy provides a unique opportunity to observe various aspects of religion in Britain, in microcosm, especially in relation to increasing religious diversity.

This is especially the case in relation to the Muslim population in Britain which grew substantially following the migration of large numbers of South Asians to Britain in the post-Second World War period (Gilliat-Ray 2010b). Many of these migrants were drawn to Britain because of the abundance of unskilled and semi-skilled employment in large manufacturing centres, such as London, Birmingham and northern towns and cities such as Leeds, Bradford and Manchester. As a consequence, Muslims are unevenly distributed around the UK, and some parts of Britain have very small (or non-existent) Muslim populations. Despite this, Muslims now comprise the second largest faith group in Britain overall, and approximately 4.8 per cent of the UK population. The employment of Muslim chaplains has often been a pragmatic and necessary way of ensuring that the religious rights of Muslim patients or prisoners are adequately fulfilled. Other institutions might employ Muslim chaplains for other strategic reasons, such as the wish to attract overseas (Muslim) students in the case of higher education institutions, or to increase the representation of ethnic minority personnel, in the case of the military.

Various academic studies in recent decades have begun to document the growth of Muslim involvement in institutionally based religious provision in Britain, either directly or indirectly. One of the first and most substantial pieces of research was undertaken in the mid-1990s at the University of Warwick.[2] This work was centrally concerned with the role played by Anglican chaplains in facilitating arrangements for members of other faiths in English prisons and hospitals. Part of the research involved gathering data from 'visiting ministers' of other faiths, including Muslims, in order to establish the extent to which existing arrangements were satisfactory. Publications arising from this work provided a catalyst for substantial policy changes (especially in HM Prison Service) (Beckford and Gilliat 1998) and, later, new research on religion in prisons and other public institutions, often with a particular emphasis on the situation of Muslims and Islam (Beckford 1998; Beckford 2001; Beckford et al. 2005; Hunt 2011; Marranci 2009; Siddiqui 2007; Spalek and Wilson 2001; Tarleton et al. 2003). In more recent years, there has been an increasing political interest in the work of Muslim chaplains, fuelled by Preventing Violent Extremism policies. This has led to the production of a number of controversial reports about the recruitment and qualifications of Muslims engaged as chaplains in Britain (Brandon 2009; Mughal 2010).

Meanwhile, an academic interest in Muslim involvement in chaplaincy and pastoral care for Muslims in public institutions has been growing across Europe (Becci 2011; Furseth and Kuhle 2011), in the United States (Abu-Ras 2010; Ammar et al. 2004; Edward Jones 1989; Hamza 2007; Khoja-Moolji 2011; Lahaj 2009) and to a lesser extent in Australia (Cooper 2008). What becomes evident through these publications is that the development of Muslim involvement in chaplaincy often reflects national policies about religion in public life, and historic church-state arrangements. The gradual incorporation of Muslims into chaplaincy roles around the world has also contributed to an evolving perception that chaplaincy is no longer a distinctively Christian activity. Chaplaincy is now a 'multi-faith' endeavour.

It is difficult to place an exact timeline against the development of Muslim involvement in chaplaincy in Britain in particular, because of the extent of regional and institutional variation. The demography of particular localities and the politics of different institutions have usually determined the extent to which Muslims have become incorporated into chaplaincy over time. Despite this caveat, in general it would be fair to say that early Muslim involvement in prison or hospital pastoral care in Britain, especially from about the 1970s up to and including the 1990s, tended to be haphazard, locally organised and largely focused upon meeting the

---

[2]   'The Church of England and Other Faiths Project', funded by the Leverhulme Trust and the Church of England, 1994–96, conducted by Professor James Beckford and Dr Sophie Gilliat.

basic religious needs of patients or inmates, such as ensuring the provision of halal food, making suitable arrangements for prayer facilities and enabling the celebration of Eid festivals.

Those Muslims involved in prison or hospital visiting were often termed 'visiting ministers'. Their work was often voluntary, and usually confined to several hours per week, if that. Sometimes visiting ministers were mosque-based imams, but because many imams working in Britain in the 1970s or 1980s could not speak adequate English, it was not unusual for visiting ministers to be so-called 'community leaders', this term often applying to Muslim (usually male) professionals with good standing in the locality, or within a particular mosque community. It was also common for the term 'visiting minister' to be applied to existing institutional staff members, such as Muslim doctors, or simply well-meaning members of a Muslim congregation who had time to spare and a reasonable fluency in English. The term 'visiting minister' was therefore applied to individuals with a wide range of backgrounds, and their designation as 'visiting ministers' fully conveyed the fact that, generally speaking, they had only a marginal involvement in the life of the institution. They were 'on call' when necessary, but were rarely able to make strategic decisions, or to shape the context in which they were working (Spalek and Wilson 2001).

The 1990s was a critical decade for change. There were still many Muslim 'visiting ministers' going into prisons and hospitals, but some institutions were starting to advertise full or half-time posts for 'Muslim Chaplains' (especially in the health care setting), and a new Muslim professional religious role was slowly coming into being. The transition from 'visiting minister' to 'Muslim chaplain' was brought about by a range of contextual factors all coming together to make the emergence of 'Muslim chaplaincy' possible. The driving forces for change came from a number of different sources, both within and outside Muslim communities.

Firstly, within public institutions in the UK, there was a growing expectation of better service quality and standards for the general public in their engagement with government departments. In health care, the 1991 Patient's Charter prioritised the religious and spiritual needs of all patients, regardless of their faith tradition. The Charter laid down patients' rights to care, standards and targets for health care providers to achieve and ways of assessing the performance of the National Health Service (NHS). The first of the nine National Charter Standards stated in the Patient's Charter specifies 'Respect for privacy, dignity and religious and cultural beliefs'. As a consequence, religious care provision was no longer confined to what chaplains provided; it became incumbent on every NHS employee to show respect for patients' religious beliefs. Crucially, no distinction was made between the standards of respect demanded for Christian and non-Christian beliefs (Beckford and Gilliat 1996). This Charter directive required hospitals and other health care settings to facilitate the provision of adequate facilities and personnel, and it was clear that meeting the requirements of the Charter demanded a new multi-faith approach. In those parts of the country with large local Muslim communities, fulfilling the requirements of the Charter began to mean the full-time, part-time or sessional employment of a Muslim chaplain.

The book *Religion in Prison: Equal Rites in a Multi-Faith Society* (Beckford and Gilliat 1998) outlined the history and development of Prison Service chaplaincy, especially in terms of the increasing and often contentious provision of facilities and personnel for members of other faiths. Just as in the health care setting, during the 1990s the Prison Service was under similar political, social and legal pressures to adopt a more multi-faith approach to its chaplaincy provision. The rapidly increasing and growing over-representation of Muslim prisoners was also a catalyst for progress. It became increasingly obvious that new resources would have to be devoted to the employment of Muslim religious professionals if one of the few rights of prisoners – to practice their religion and to receive appropriate pastoral and religious care – was to be met.

In both hospital and prison settings, then, the combined growth in the Muslim patient and prison population, and the increasing complexity of the issues associated with this growth, meant that personnel were increasingly needed on a full-time or part-time basis, particularly in some parts of the country. The issues were beginning to extend beyond simply advising on basic religious needs, and performing a role that was largely an extension of what a mosque-based imam might do. Christian chaplains and institutional managers began to recognise that Muslim chaplains could usefully do far more than simply lead Friday prayers and make arrangements for religious festivals. A more active and informed Muslim professional input was required to advise on a whole range of issues. And so, from the top down, and both locally and nationally, new posts were created, facilitating the development of 'Muslim chaplaincy'. As part of this incremental shift from 'visiting minister' to 'Muslim chaplain', new postholders increasingly began to recognise that they would need to work within the assumptions that govern public life and institutions, especially ideas around equal opportunities, respect for diversity and non-proselytism. Chaplaincy has taught chaplains simultaneously both individualism and corporatism.

The development of Muslim chaplaincy was stimulated in the prison context by the employment of a new 'Muslim Advisor' at the Prison Service Chaplaincy Headquarters in 1999. This role meant that the often serious lack of provision for Muslim inmates in terms of access to religious support, halal meals and Friday prayers could be proactively addressed at a national level. The first incumbent of this post, Maqsood Ahmed, also instituted a centralised vetting system for potential Muslim chaplains, thus ensuring that new chaplaincy posts were only offered to those with appropriate credentials and counter-terrorism clearance (Birt 2006: 699). In 2003, the Prison Service renamed its Muslim 'visiting ministers', conferring upon them the title 'Muslim Chaplain' (Beckford et al. 2005); this enabled female Muslim chaplains to gain professional recognition alongside their male counterparts.

The NHS has made slower progress with the appointment of Muslim chaplains, but the decision by the Department of Health to set aside funding to support the new employment and training of chaplains from minority faith groups helped to secure new posts in mid-2000. This has recently been supported by the organisation of an annual 'Muslim Healthcare Chaplaincy Training Course', jointly organised by the Muslim Council of Britain (MCB) and the Department of Health. However, financial pressures within the public sector from 2010 onwards have made the funding of chaplaincy vulnerable, and chaplains of all faiths – including Muslims – are often fearful for their long-term job security.

A second important driving force for the emergence of Muslim chaplaincy in Britain has been the increasing maturation and confidence of Muslim communities themselves. During the 1990s there was a growing awareness and recognition of social needs and problems. Whereas difficulties and sensitive issues had often been ignored by Muslim communities, by the 1990s the British Muslim press, such as *The Muslim News* and *Q News*, were starting to report on problems of marital breakdown and domestic violence, substance abuse, the need for a stronger 'home-grown' religious leadership and so on. Perhaps as a response to this more open community debate, a range of British Muslim organisations were formed to directly tackle some of the social problems within communities, and especially to support the needs of young people. Against this background, the work of Muslim chaplains, especially in the reform and rehabilitation of Muslim offenders, had greater legitimacy and support because they were clearly tackling questions and challenges that were now being openly debated within Muslim communities more widely. And so, in June 1991, *The Muslim News* devoted an entire page to the rising Muslim prison population, the opening of the first mosque in a British prison (at HMP Wandsworth) and the work of one of the first Muslim imams/chaplains in Britain, Dr Ijaz Mian, who was at the time visiting Muslim inmates in a number of prisons on a full-time basis (Dhalla 1991).

Another important contextual factor that made the development of Muslim chaplaincy possible, and which reflected the developmental progress of Muslim communities in Britain, was the growing availability of suitable personnel to take up the new chaplaincy posts. A new generation of British born, English-speaking students were starting to graduate from their lengthy period of training in British Islamic seminaries (dar ul-uloom), particularly those established by the Deobandi school of thought in the 1970s and 1980s (Birt 2006; Gilliat-Ray 2006).[3] Although they had received no formal training in the techniques of pastoral care and counselling, they were knowledgeable in their faith, they could speak English and often a range of other community languages, and the newly emerging chaplaincy posts offered well-paid career prospects. Thus some of the first appointments of Muslim chaplains in both the prison and health contexts were among individuals

---

[3]   The Deobandi 'school of thought' is associated with a South Asian Islamic reform movement, founded in 19th century India to preserve and protect Islamic traditions from the influence of colonial rule. Although there is internal diversity within this movement, it is distinctive for its educational and religious philosophy which places an emphasis on Hanafi fiqh and preservation of Islamic traditions (Geaves 2012; Metcalf 1982; Metcalf 2002).

The Muslim News 21 - 06 - 91 / 08 - 12 - 11   5

Doing time at HM's pleasure

Muslim prisoner numbers on the up

Prison visiting is not for the timid or easily offended. Dr Ijaz Mian, an imam based in South London, spends most of his time visiting the growing number of Muslims detained at Her Majesty's pleasure. *Musadiq Dhalla* accompanied him on one of his visits recently.

Britain's prisons are sturdy structures, burgeoning from an increased population. Currently, there are just under 45,000 prisoners held in England and Wales, down from the peak figures of the mid-1980s. But while prisoner numbers have been falling in the past five years, the number of Muslim prisoners has been rising. No figures are available as to the exact number of Muslim prisoners, although each prison does log the religious status of inmates, in case of death, where funeral rites may need observing. The Home Office keeps records of the total prison population, but does not collate the religious affiliation of prisoners centrally. The Muslim prisoner population is estimated to be about 5,000 and it is a population that has needs.

For Dr Ijaz Mian, formerly a lecturer in genetics, and now an imam based at the Lewisham and Kent Islamic centre, prison visiting has become somewhat of an occupation. Visiting prisoners is not for the timid or the easily offended. It is a task that offers little succour. "I visit prisons because I am interested in *da'wah* (propagation), to show the people the right way". *Da'wah* words these may be, but for Dr Mian the task is more complicated. In theory he is talking to the converted who live in an artificial world.

to convert to Islam. This "food factor" was of serious concern to the Christian chaplains and the authorities began placing restrictions. Prisoners wishing to convert to Islam could still do so and attend all the classes and prayers, but they would not be given any halal food for three months. After this period prisoners would be assessed to see whether their conversion had been faithful. Unfortunately, there are no figures to see whether the restrictions stemmed the flow of converts. Dr Mian adopts a philosophical approach to the "food factor". "It is not necessarily a good thing that people should convert to Islam because of the provision of better food, but since they are then in our company we are able to show them the many facets of Islam."

Dealing with the authorities presents an interesting challenge. There are two levels - the prison officers ("the screws") who work at the ground level and the governors. According to Dr Mian, the former can sometimes be difficult to deal with. "Prison officers do not have knowledge of other religions and often they are not clear about the Home Office's aims for the prison service. Imams are viewed as interfering in their work." Governors, on the other hand, are more accommodating to the needs of the imam. He recalls problems he has faced from

Muslim community to contribute. Funds have been coming, but slowly. Care of Muslim prisoners is not very high on the resource agenda and the attitude of those "on the outside" to those "on the inside" is a source of disappointment to Dr Mian. "Muslims are ignorant of the needs of prisoners.

Given the number of prisons in the country and the rising number of Muslim inmates, visitors like Dr Mian are seemingly fighting a losing battle if support is not forthcoming from the community. "This is not the job for one man. When I go to the prisons my priority is listening. I may not always

The number of Muslims in prison is on the up, with about 5,000–6,000 being detained or sentenced at any one time, writes *Musadiq Dhalla*.

No actual figure is available, according Dr Mashuq Ibn Ally, director of Islamic Studies, University of St David's University College, University of Wales, but the year-on-year observations indicate rising numbers. "The rise in the numbers is inevitable given the lack of equal opportunities and socio-economic pressures Muslims face. The deprivation and exploitation leads to the black market," says Dr Ally. Most of the crimes are of corruption, theft and in some instances, murder and rape. Dr Ally cautions on taking a too negative view of the numbers because it creates a false picture of the level of criminality within the community.

Although each prison logs the religious affiliation of each prisoner, no central collation of the data is carried out. "Collating the data on the number of Muslim prisoners is important for the community to assess the degree of provision they should give. In order the rights of the inmates will also be recognised." He says that reforming prisoners should be the ultimate aim and the educational courses within prisons should be geared for this.

The Centre for Islamic Studies is planning to undertake some collation of prisoner numbers as part of a larger study of care of Muslims, covering subjects in prisons under

Dr Mian, playing a sophisticated mediating role between the authorities and the inmates
    (Photo: The Muslim News)

Figure 1.1   'Doing time at HM's pleasure', *The Muslim News*, June 1991

from the Deobandi school of thought, and graduates of British Islamic seminaries. As we shall see shortly, the predominance of Muslim chaplains that reflect this particular 'school of thought' has sometimes been interpreted negatively. But seen against the background of the gradual development of British Muslim institutions, any over-representation of Deobandis among the professional chaplaincy community is a reflection of the economic, religious and social capital of a particular group of Muslims in Britain in the late 1970s and early 1980s.

The development of the 'Certificate in Muslim Chaplaincy' provided by Markfield Institute of Higher Education (MIHE) in Leicester from 2003 reflects another important social and educational landmark for the Muslim community in Britain in its engagement in chaplaincy. The course provides students with a basic grounding in chaplaincy skills and knowledge, and the opportunity to do a supervised placement under the direction of an experienced chaplain. The emergence of this course, in consultation with Christian churches and chaplaincy bodies has been another important impetus for progress by giving current and prospective chaplains the opportunity for in-service training. As we shall see shortly, there are some important parallels between the MIHE course and the Islamic Chaplaincy Program at Hartford Seminary in Connecticut, in the USA.

There is now a sufficient critical mass of part-time and full-time Muslim chaplains in Britain for a distinctive professional identity to be emerging, and this has found expression in the foundation of a number of associations. The 'Association of Muslim Chaplains' was established in 2004 (to support graduates of the MIHE course) and the 'Muslim Chaplains Association' was formed in May 2007 to represent the interests and professional development of Muslim prison chaplains. This most recent development was predicted by Beckford and his team in their study of Muslims in British and French prisons back in 2005 (Beckford et al. 2005: 241). Chaplaincy is now starting to become a career option for those Muslims in Britain who aspire to serve their community within the context of a public institution, and there is a sense of greater Muslim 'ownership' of chaplaincy than was previously conceivable among part-time 'visiting ministers' back in the 1990s (Beckford et al. 2005: 239). More recently, the Association of Muslim Chaplains in Education (AMCed) has been established to support the work of Muslim chaplains working in further and higher education institutions.

A third significant driver for growing Muslim involvement in chaplaincy has been the emergence of new or more inclusive national chaplaincy structures and committees that give Muslims, and members of other faiths, a voice for articulating their ideas and their concerns, and for engaging in long-term planning. The 'Islam Resource Group' within the College of Health Care Chaplains, or the Multi-Faith Group for Health Care Chaplaincy are good examples, alongside an equivalent kind of body in the Prison Service Chaplaincy. Where Muslims were often marginal in national debates about chaplaincy, from about the year 2000 onwards, new or more inclusive structures made it possible for the contribution and perspectives of Muslims to be given greater recognition. Muslim chaplains and Muslim organisations have started to become partners in national discussion, giving them a legitimate voice and a sense of real long-term inclusion.

These important contextual factors within public institutions, within Muslim communities, and within national chaplaincy structures, in a society increasingly aware of ethnic and religious diversity, have made the emergence of Muslim chaplaincy possible. But state funding has also been an important part of the dynamic. In a context where there were few substantive paid professional positions available for Muslim religious scholars, apart from those based in mosques and Islamic centres, the growth of chaplaincy opportunities will have seemed like an attractive emergent possibility. The felicitous convergence of factors outlined here required the catalyst of state funding to enable the transition from volunteer, to part-time, to increasingly full-chaplaincy roles for Muslims in Britain.

But this development arguably has a significance that extends beyond particular public institutions. Muslim involvement in institutional chaplaincy provides a framework and an opportunity for the growing inclusion of Muslims in the public life of society more generally, and the research upon which this book is based has sought to explore the extent to which these possibilities are becoming evident.

The Muslim Chaplaincy Research Project: An Introduction

In 2007, two major academic research councils (Arts and Humanities Research Council – AHRC, and the Economic and Social Research Council – ESRC) announced the launch of a joint programme of funding to enable research on 'Religion and Society'. Given the growth of Muslim involvement in chaplaincy during the early 2000s onwards, as described above, this funding scheme provided an ideal opportunity to undertake a significant piece of original empirical research which might begin to map and evaluate these developments. Thus in 2008, a multidisciplinary team of researchers began work on a 28-month project based at Cardiff University. The team comprised Sophie Gilliat-Ray (Religious Studies/ Sociology of Religion), Stephen Pattison (Practical Theology/Pastoral Care) and a full-time Research Assistant Ali Omar (Islamic Studies/chaplaincy). Mansur Ali, who replaced Ali Omar, brought expertise in Islamic Studies (especially in Hadith Studies) and classical Arabic, as well as previous experience as a Muslim chaplain working in a high-security hospital near Liverpool.

Being the first major study of Muslim chaplaincy, many of our research questions were necessarily framed around the mapping of people, practices and contexts. Thus, we asked: Who decides to become a Muslim chaplain, and why?; What does chaplaincy practice involve for Muslims?; How do Muslim chaplains navigate their way through the politics that shape their work, both within and outside their institutions?; How does their work 'make a difference', either within their institutions, or in Muslim communities beyond? In order to answer these questions, extensive qualitative fieldwork research was undertaken between November 2008 and January 2011. This involved in-depth interviews, 'shadowing' of chaplains in the workplace, observation of Muslim chaplaincy training courses and focus-group discussions with the 'clients' and employers of chaplains. In the following sections, we describe our research methods and data analysis techniques in more depth. Some readers may wish to omit these sections and move directly to the Conclusion.

Methodology and Methods

Our project rested upon the collection of qualitative data using a variety of methods, including interviewing, shadowing, participant observation, focus groups and collection of relevant documents and reports. But prior to the fieldwork phase, the development of professional Muslim chaplaincy associations and educational training programmes provided important points of reference for the design and methodology of the project. For example, our funding application made explicit reference to a formal Memorandum of Understanding drawn up between Cardiff University and Markfield Institute of Higher Education (MIHE), the provider of an entry-level training programme for Muslim chaplains in Britain. The involvement of some key personnel from MIHE from the outset (especially Dr Ataullah Siddiqui) was highly significant for the progress of the project. For example, by accessing past students of its 'Certificate in Muslim Chaplaincy' on our behalf, and by allowing us to observe a cohort of students undertaking the programme during 2009, we have been able to reflect on how, and in what ways, training and education contributes to an acquired sense of identity as a professional Muslim chaplain. Some of the students we observed shared their course placement reports with us, and some were also interviewed.

The emergence of sector-specific associations for Muslim chaplains during the mid-2000s was also significant for our study. Not only did these associations point to the 'professionalisation' of Muslim chaplaincy, but it was clear our project would benefit from consultation with, and advice from, chaplains leading some of these associations. By November 2008, we had identified a number of key 'gatekeepers', mostly already known to one or more members of the research team. They provided essential insights into the development of the Muslim chaplaincy profession, and made suggestions about chaplains whom we might contact for interview.

Identifying and accessing potential chaplains to interview occurred via a number of routes, in addition to the professional Muslim chaplaincy associations, and the MIHE course. For example, while securing formal approval for the project via the Ministry of Justice (MOJ) and the National Offender Management Scheme (NOMS), we sought guidance from the Muslim Advisor in the Prison Service Chaplaincy Headquarters, Ahtsham Ali. This resulted in a list of suggested interviewees within the Prison Service, some of whom we did indeed contact for interview. A small number of chaplains were also selected having been participants in the 'Church of England and Other Faiths Project' (University of Warwick, 1994–96), thereby enabling some long-term evaluation of how the shift from 'visiting minister' to 'Muslim chaplain' had affected particular individuals.

In addition to the approval required from the MOJ and NOMS for access to prison chaplains, our project paperwork was reviewed by key personnel in the National Health Service (NHS). This resulted in exemption from the necessity to gain formal ethical approval for the study. However, some local hospitals did require Research and Development permission (which was granted, in these cases), and when we sought to 'shadow' prison chaplains over consecutive days, we had to undergo Counter Terrorism Clearance (CTC), also granted. Ethical approval for our study was secured via the Cardiff University School of Social Sciences Ethics Committee, based on the preparation of information sheets, consent forms and so on. However, as we moved from the interviewing to the shadowing phase of data gathering, we decided to supplement these documents with a set of written protocols, explaining in more detail what 'shadowing' would actually involve. This included a requirement for chaplains to explain our presence to those whom we were meeting during the day, seeking *their* consent for us to be present. Prior to undertaking this on-site ethnographic fieldwork, we asked chaplains to read the 'shadowing protocols', and to initial and date their original signed consent form.

When the fieldwork phase of the project was getting underway, relevant databases were searched in the hope of finding useful material to inform and guide the qualitative interviewing and 'shadowing' work. Although there are a number of well-established journals in the field of healthcare chaplaincy in particular (for example *The Scottish Journal of Health Care Chaplaincy*, *The Journal of Health Care Chaplaincy*, *Journal of Religion and Health*), the academic field of 'chaplaincy studies' more generally is still in its infancy, and much of the research has been, and continues to be produced by academically inclined practitioners, chaplains who have undertaken academic action-research projects as part of their work (Autton 1969; Cobb and Robshaw 1998; Phillips 1970; Speck 1988; Swift 2009). Searches of relevant bibliographic databases, such as Web of Knowledge and Sociological Abstracts, revealed the paucity of literature by non-practitioners engaged in research about chaplains and chaplaincy. There was an especially deafening silence about the politics and practicalities of research methodology, particularly in relation to qualitative studies, a significant exception being some discussion of auto-ethnography by a British Anglican chaplain (Swift 2009). We could locate only one relevant article reflecting ethnographic research about chaplaincy written by a *non-practitioner* of chaplaincy (Norwood 2006), but *none* which might guide our research with Muslim chaplains to any degree.[4] In light of that, some of the publications arising from the project which relate specifically to methodology make significant contributions to the evolving field of chaplaincy studies research (Gilliat-Ray 2010a; Gilliat-Ray 2011).

The Muslim Chaplaincy project fieldwork involved semi-structured recorded interviews with 65 chaplains in a range of sectors, as well as follow-up shadowing of a small number of chaplains in their places of work.[5] In the project proposal, the rationale for an individual researcher to shadow an individual chaplain was explained in terms of its potential to understand the actual performance of pastoral work in practice rather than relying entirely upon chaplains' verbal descriptions of their work as part of an interview (Atkinson and Coffey 2002; Atkinson et al. 2003). It was a way of 'triangulating against information gathered through other means' (Tjora 2006: 430). The shadowing phase was of critical importance: 'most knowledge is stored in action rather than words … [so we] have to comprehend meaning as it emerges in practice' (Gilliat-Ray 2011; Hastrup 1995: 82). Shadowing provided an opportunity to gain a contextualised understanding of Muslim chaplaincy practice as a lived reality, glimpsing the various ways in which it is performed by male and female chaplains, among those with differing levels of experience, from different religious 'schools of thought' and working in different kinds of institution. In addition to our interviews with practitioners, we also talked to 'stakeholders', individuals who had influential national level administrative

---

[4] Quraishi's reflections on conducting qualitative research with Muslim prisoners in England and Wales was relevant (Quraishi 2008), but his interaction with imams is part of a much broader discussion about fieldwork in prisons.

[5] All the interviews were fully transcribed, either by our project administrator, or via an agency whose staff had signed the Official Secrets Act. 'Way with Words' undertakes transcription work for a number of government departments where data protection and confidentiality are paramount. We stored our data on fully encrypted devices (for example an 'IronKey' USB memory stick, and via PGP encryption on laptops).

roles in relation to the employment of Muslim chaplains, or who had been involved in, or had observed the development of Muslim chaplaincy work over a long period of time.

Where previous research access to Muslim 'visiting ministers' or Muslim chaplains (in the Prison Service) in England and Wales has usually depended upon a Christian chaplain playing a mediating facilitative role (Beckford and Gilliat 1998; Beckford et al. 2005; Quraishi 2008), we were able to identify and contact Muslim chaplains directly. This in itself reflects the shift from 'visiting minister' to 'Muslim chaplain', and the increasing autonomy, visibility and independence that Muslim chaplains have acquired in the last decade. Indeed, we might go further and regard this as part of a significant redistribution of power, prestige and authority in chaplaincy.

Interview transcripts were supplemented by field notes, written during and after each interview or period of shadowing. These notes provided a description of the day's events, a record of significant incidents, observations and conversations. They also provided a space for the research team to record impressions, ideas and questions for follow-up.

Sampling Strategies

It would have been impossible to select an interview sample that was entirely representative. There is no census of Muslims working in chaplaincy from which we could draw a statistically accurate sample. However, certain criteria governed the selection of participants and these were intended to ensure that we captured the diversity within the Muslim chaplaincy population as far as possible. For example, we wanted to ensure we spoke to chaplains from different schools of religious thought, to women as well as men, to religious scholars and to those with less formal religious training and to those who were serving in different types of institution within a specific sector. For example, among those serving in HM prisons, we ensured that this included Young Offender Institutions, remand prisons, women's prisons, a private prison, as well as prisons reflecting different security levels. Our sample of health care chaplains included those working in mental health services, as well as acute hospitals. We were also at pains to ensure our sample included those with differing levels of experience in chaplaincy, across the sectors. Consequently, we spoke to some chaplains with less than six months experience, while others had been working as chaplains for over 15 years. Thus, we felt better able to reflect on some of the major social and political changes that have taken place in the development of Muslim chaplaincy over time, as well as the ways in which individual chaplains have developed their pastoral skills as a consequence of experience, and in response to influences such as career training opportunities, multi-faith teamwork and the ethos of public service.

Some of our chaplains were categorised as 'mixed-sector'. This meant that they were working in at least two different chaplaincy sectors, simultaneously.

This usually involved a prison-hospital combination, but there were others (such as education and airport). The insights from these mixed-sector chaplains were valuable in helping us to think about the degree to which Muslim chaplains are developing sector-specialisation, and managing the switch from a pastoral role in one institution (usually a hospital) to a similar role in another (usually a prison), often during the course of the same working day.

Establishing what the overall size of our sample should be, and then how it should be sub-divided to capture the diversity of experience within the Muslim chaplaincy profession, we were guided by a number of principles about proportions. For example, we knew that HM Prison Service was employing just over 200 Muslim chaplains around the time of our research (full-time male n=41; part-time male n=68; co-ordinating male n=7; sessional male n=90; sessional female n=12).[6] Meanwhile, the National Health Service was employing about 80 (with another 80 in voluntary/honorary roles). Establishing the number of chaplains across the education sector is difficult, because of the autonomy of these institutions, the lack of a central administrative infrastructure and, in some cases, the rather vague arrangements by which particular individuals take on chaplaincy roles. For example, some Muslim chaplains in education are principally employed as lecturers or support staff, and undertake pastoral work as an informal extension of these positions. However, based on Clines' research on higher education chaplaincy in 2008 (Clines 2008: 13), he established that there were 41 Muslim chaplains in the sector (full-time n=1; part-time n=5; voluntary n=35). In our research, we estimated that there were about three or four more chaplains in further education, and one employed in a school. This makes for an approximate total of about 50 Muslim chaplains in education, at the time of our study.

In 2005, the Ministry of Defence appointed civilian chaplains from Muslim, Hindu, Sikh and Buddhist traditions for the first time, so we knew there was one Muslim chaplain in the military. Likewise, during the course of our work, we came to know about a Muslim employed as a chaplain in a Magistrates and Crown Court, and another in a major retail park/shopping centre.

As a consequence of our desktop research, the information provided to us by the Prison Service Chaplaincy Headquarters and the Muslim Council of Britain Healthcare Chaplaincy office, and allowing for some possible increases in the number of education chaplains since Clines' research in 2008, the overall number of serving Muslim chaplains in England and Wales is probably about 425–450 in total: our sample of 65 means that we spoke to about 15 per cent of all Muslim chaplains in England and Wales. Clearly, a larger project would have enabled us to speak to more, but time and budgetary constraints naturally limited the overall scope of the study.

Sub-dividing our sample was a more complex undertaking, because we had to balance numerous considerations. Sector was clearly important, but so too was gender, school of thought and so on. Based on the overall number of Muslims

---

6   Figures were correct at 6/12/2010. Figures for sessional male chaplains are variable.

Figure 1.2   Latif Mir (left) and Imam Asim Hafiz (right) – the first Muslim chaplains to
                 be appointed to an HM Magistrates and Crown Court and HM Armed Forces

employed by the Prison Service, to have been proportionate, our sample should, technically, have been comprised of about 50 per cent of prison chaplains, with the remaining 50 per cent from other sectors. However, we made a decision to reduce slightly the proportion of prison chaplains in our sample (to 42 per cent), in order to ensure that we had scope to include the growing opportunities for Muslim women in NHS chaplaincy, and to incorporate the recent appointment of individual Muslims in other sectors (military, HM Courts and retail). Likewise, the 'mixed-sector' chaplains were important for our work, as were the very variable circumstances that shape the roles and employment status of educational chaplains. Muslim involvement in prison chaplaincy is now relatively well established (certainly compared to other sectors). Consequently, we felt that it was important to record the voices of chaplains still struggling to win recognition for their work, often in relative isolation, and sometimes without a central organisational infrastructure or professional association to provide support. The 'mixed-sector' chaplains (where one of their roles was within the Prison Service) provided us with important comparative data about the structural development of different sectors.

Although sector was one of the main determinants of our sampling strategy (and we will be looking at the demographic composition of our sample, by sector, shortly), we had an interest in the wider Muslim chaplaincy community generally. What kind of generalisations can we make about the background, education or qualifications of Britain's approximately 400 Muslim chaplains? Mindful of the fact that our study

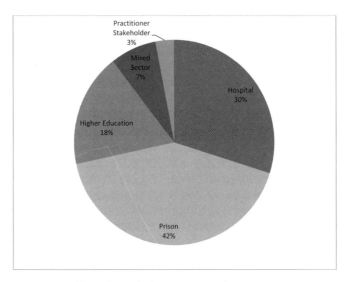

Figure 1.3   Composition of sample, by sector

was qualitative, not quantitative, nevertheless we collected basic biographical data from our participants, enabling some general observations to be made.

For example, well over half of chaplains in our sample (58 per cent) were less than 40 years of age. This is not surprising in relation to the demographics and relative 'youthfulness' of Muslim communities in Britain, but still, our research shows that the Muslim chaplaincy population in Britain is likely to be a relatively young one. Similarly, in relation to 'place of birth', the chaplains in our sample reflect statistics for 'place of birth' for Muslims in Britain overall, derived from the 2001 Census. Where the 2001 Census showed that 46 per cent of Muslims had been born in the UK, among our sample the figure was 47 per cent, and as we would expect, a large proportion who had been born overseas originated from South Asia. However, there were important differences between sectors in relation to both age and place of birth, and these are discussed further below.

Opportunities for Muslim women to enter chaplaincy roles have increased in recent years. Most, if not all, women's prisons employ a part-time or sessional female Muslim chaplain, and hospitals serving communities with a large local Muslim population have also appointed female chaplains. Given that chaplaincy seems to provide an important avenue for Muslim women to take on professional religious roles, we were particularly keen to ensure they were included in our study, to the extent that they were in fact *over-represented*. Thus, approximately one in five of the chaplains in our study (21 per cent) were women, and of this number, half of them were working in the NHS.

During interviews, we did not ask chaplains to identify themselves with a particular religious 'school of thought'. However, as they told us about their

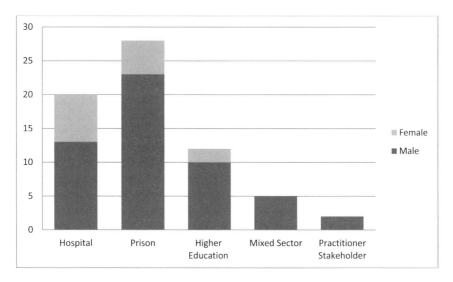

Figure 1.4   Composition of sample, by sector and gender

religious education, training or qualifications prior to taking up their chaplaincy roles, we were often able to draw some conclusions about the diversity of Islamic traditions represented in our sample. For example, among the 58 per cent of our sample who had the religious title 'alim or 'alima, nearly half were from a 'Deobandi' background, and all, with one exception, had trained in a dar ul-uloom in the UK. It would be difficult and unwise to extrapolate from these figures in order to make more general assumptions about the 'schools of thought' followed by the wider Muslim chaplaincy population. However, if our sample can be regarded as to some extent indicative of wider trends, the fact that one quarter of our sample were British-born, British-trained Deobandi Islamic scholars of South Asian background, it is clear that amid the diversity within the Muslim chaplaincy population, a relatively distinctive and homogenous group of people have been drawn into chaplaincy work.

This would square with what we know about the history and development of Islamic religious institutions in Britain more generally, and the fact that scholars from the Deobandi tradition were most proactive in the establishment of Islamic religious training institutions in Britain in the late 1970s and 1980s. Consequently, the graduates of these seminaries have been especially well-placed to take up the newly available chaplaincy positions. Among the other 'ulama in our sample, they had mostly studied overseas, including at the University of Madinah (n=3), or at Al-Azhar in Cairo (n=2). Others had followed a formal Islamic Studies curriculum with a particular teacher (informally).

We did not formally record the nationality or ethnicity of the chaplains in our study. However, regardless of country of birth, the majority were South Asian (about 83 per cent) while the remainder were a mix of Arab (Egyptian, Saudi Arabian, Lebanese), African (Libyan, Somali, Afro-Caribbean) and White/British. It is probably fair to say that there is far greater ethnic and racial diversity among Muslim chaplains than is likely to be the case among the Christian chaplaincy community. Nevertheless, the fact that South Asians appear to constitute such a significant presence within the Muslim chaplaincy population raises particularly interesting issues relative to the ethnic and religious background of Muslim prisoners in particular. For example, Black Muslims constitute 34 per cent of the prison population, but less than one per cent of the Muslim population in Britain overall (Quraishi 2008). Figures from HM Prison Service indicate that around 41 per cent of Muslim prisoners are Asian or British Asian ('HM Chief Inspector of Prisons – Muslim prisoners' experiences: a thematic review' 2010), but 2001 Census data indicate that approximately 75 per cent of British Muslims are South Asian. It is evident that there is a mismatch between the ethnicity of Muslim prisoners and the overwhelming dominance of South Asian chaplains. There are very few Black or Black British Muslim chaplains in the UK, despite the fact that Black and Black British Muslims are clearly over-represented in prisons. A Somali chaplain whom we interviewed noted the particular added value he could bring to his work (in a large Young Offender Institution) on account of the fact he could relate to the African/Afro-Caribbean heritage of the Muslim offenders in a way that his South Asian colleagues could not. An Afro-Caribbean convert working as a volunteer in a large Midlands prison also had strong views on this matter:

> … as an Afro-Caribbean Muslim, and particularly as a revert Muslim, our voice or our perspective isn't being addressed by the major Muslim communities. This caused problems at [big London prison] a couple of years ago. There was revolt when the Arabs and the Afro-Caribbean's got together and basically forced out, I think he was, a Gujarati Imam, because of the fact that he couldn't relate to anybody … I know of only two non-Asian Imams in the prison system. The rest of them are predominantly Pakistani, Gujarati, Bengali, and I thought a lot of it at the time was jobs for the boys (Usama, former MIHE student).

Clearly, this reflects the views of a single individual, and the accuracy of his statements are questionable in light of the clear ethnic diversity that we encountered among Muslim chaplains in our study. However, the predominance of South Asian Muslims is indisputable, reflecting some tensions and inequalities around the process of becoming a Muslim chaplain in Britain, explored in more depth in Chapter 3.

Demographics, by Sector: Prisons

A brief description and explanation of the diversity among prison chaplains is warranted, since it highlights where and how Muslim prison chaplains might be distinctive within the overall Muslim chaplaincy community. For example, among the 27 prison chaplains we interviewed, 5 of them were women (18 per cent). Given that the total number of female Muslim prison chaplains in England and Wales is 12 (based on figures from the PSC), this means we interviewed nearly half of all female Muslim prison chaplains. They were deliberately over-represented in our sample because of our interest in exploring the relatively new and distinctive contribution that Muslim women are making in chaplaincy roles. Our sample of prison chaplains also suggests that compared to the general Muslim chaplaincy population, Muslim chaplains working in the Prison Service are more likely to be qualified religious scholars. In our sample, 75 per cent of prison chaplains were 'alims/'alimas, and this rises to 86 per cent if we consider the male prison chaplains alone. The prison chaplains were also distinctive in relation to 'place of birth': some 55 per cent of them had been born in England or Wales, and overall, a third were British-born, British-trained, and most closely associated with the Deobandi tradition. The relative 'youthfulness' of those Muslims drawn into chaplaincy work was particularly apparent among prison chaplains; 63 per cent of our sample were under 40 years of age.

Demographics, by Sector: Hospitals

Rather like the prison chaplains, there is a distinctive group of British-born, British-trained, male Deobandi scholars within health care chaplaincy. Individuals with this background constituted 30 per cent of our sample. Clearly, the influence of a relatively homogeneous group within health care chaplaincy needs to be considered in relation to our data analysis and findings. Rather like the prison chaplains, well over half of the Muslim health care chaplains in our sample had been born in Britain, and were under 40 years of age (65 per cent). Compared to the prison sample, slightly fewer Muslim health care chaplains were 'alims/ alimas, but it is possible that this lower figure reflects the fact that Muslim women constituted well over a third of our sample (but only 18 per cent of the prison chaplaincy sample).

Demographics, by Sector: Education

We interviewed 11 educational chaplains and this group were typically much older than their prison or hospital counterparts (less than a third were under 40 years of age), and there was only one 'alim in the sample. The vast majority (73 per cent) had been born overseas. These figures suggest that the profile of those in educational chaplaincy is quite different compared to those in publicly funded chaplaincy in prisons and hospitals. As noted above, establishing the number of Muslim chaplains in education with any accuracy is difficult, and therefore a clear indication of how and to what extent women are involved in this work is equally hard to estimate. However, it would seem that women currently have far less influence in educational chaplaincy, and this is reflected in our sample. Only two of the eleven chaplains we spoke to were women.

While this 'dissection' of some of our sample may appear to be overly detailed, an appreciation of how and in what ways the Muslim chaplaincy population might be distinctive in particular sectors is important to consider, particularly in relation to the analysis of our data that follows.

Data Analysis: NVivo

Our varied qualitative data collection methods based around fieldwork with 65 chaplains generated a vast body of data for analysis. It was clear that a qualitative data analysis software programme would be the most efficient means for storing, coding and analysing data and NVivo was selected for this purpose. At the midpoint of our fieldwork, we began to read interview transcripts in detail, with a view to developing a coding frame that might help to answer our research questions. We continued to refine and revise this coding frame over a 12-month period, so that the resulting NVivo project reflected the precise particularities of our study.

As we began to look at our data via NVivo queries, it became evident that we would need to refine our analytical process. For example, it was apparent that the experiences of chaplains in different sectors were significant, as was gender. Similarly, there were some distinctive experiences and views expressed according to whether an interviewee was an 'alim/'alima, or not. Sometimes, the length of time an individual had worked in chaplaincy was an important consideration. Consequently, we analysed some of our data according to these particular 'attributes' (gender, sector, 'alim/non-'alim, length of service), enabling us to fine-tune the process of data analysis, and thereby reveal the complexity of Muslim chaplaincy experiences.

Conclusion

This chapter has mapped some of the social, economic and political drivers behind the growth of Muslim involvement in chaplaincy in Britain. We have indicated the degree to which Muslims are now an integral part of chaplaincy work in many public institutions, and justified our approach to research in this emergent field of religious activity. But underlying our project remain some broader questions about the place of Muslim religious professionals in British society, the influence and contribution that Muslims are bringing to the chaplaincy profession and the role of religion in public institutions. Chaplaincy provides a particular illuminating and distinctive lens through which to reflect on such questions. It is a field of religious activity,

> ... structured internally in terms of power relations. Positions stand in relationships
> of domination, subordination or equivalence (homology) to each other by virtue
> of the access they afford to the goods or resources (capital) which are at stake
> in the field ... a field is, by definition, 'a field of struggles' in which agents'
> strategies are concerned with the preservation or improvement of their positions

with respect to the defining capital of the field … it is the crucial mediating
context wherein external factors – changing circumstances – are brought to bear
upon individual practice and institutions (Jenkins 2002: 86).

The theoretical perspectives of Pierre Bourdieu have been influential in shaping
our understanding of Muslim chaplaincy practice, politics and education. We have
begun to appreciate the significance of Bourdieu's ideas in relation to questions
such as how Muslim chaplains deploy various kinds of religious, educational and
social capital as part of their work, and the means by which they accommodate
Islamic traditions, alongside the secular norms that govern public institutions. It
is inevitable that as a newly emergent profession, the effort to define and shape
the role 'Muslim chaplain' is fraught with tensions around status, authority and
credibility. There are many interested parties engaged in the process, each with
varying levels of power and capital.

A study of Muslim chaplaincy provides a lens through which to look at the
internal diversity within Muslim communities, and divergent understandings
about the place of Islam in public institutions. We have been interested in the
social construction of this newly emergent professional role, the religious
understandings that underpin it and the power differentials among those who
are influential in shaping it. Our study indicates the way in which chaplaincy
is having an integrative effect in relation to Muslim religious professionals as
a new category of religious actor, and the capacity of Islam to accommodate to
the structures of public institutions. We see how chaplaincy is enabling British
Muslims to participate beyond the boundaries of religious communities, and to
engage in debate about modern ethical and pastoral issues.

The new involvement of Muslims in chaplaincy work reflects a major shift
in relation to religion in British public life. It can no longer be assumed that
chaplaincy is a distinctively Christian activity. The degree to which Muslims are
now employed as chaplains has reshaped chaplaincy in Britain as a whole, and
stamped upon it the hallmark 'multi-faith' in a definitive way. Islamic religious
practice more often associated with mosques, Muslim homes and other private
spaces is now routinely undertaken in prisons, hospitals and on educational
campuses. Muslim chaplains have been vital to the gradual institutionalisation
of Islam in many public institutions. They embody the struggles that are to be
found at the intersection of Christian pastoral care traditions and structures, the
secular norms of public life and the diversity of Muslim communities in Britain.
The challenges they face on a daily basis, exemplified by the examples with
which this chapter commenced, point towards the significance of their work –
within and beyond the institutions – and the value of research which explores
their role, their impact, their education and training. The remainder of this book
considers these questions, and the distinctive educational, pastoral, advisory
and religious roles that they play in Britain today. We begin this discussion in
Chapter 2, by situating our findings within the Islamic scriptural and prophetic
tradition.

Chapter 2
Pastoral Care in Islam

Introduction

Although there is no tradition of institutionalised chaplaincy in Islam, there is an implicit theology that supports and encourages what might be called 'pastoral care'. Pastoral care and pastoral roles are central to Christian ministry and ultimately derive from Jesus' description of himself as 'the good shepherd' (John 10.11). While Islam has not followed the same trajectory of developing a professional ministry in which the pastoral role is central, it is possible to identify within Islam significant elements of belief and practice which are perhaps best characterised as broadly 'pastoral'. These are fundamentally to do with helping people individually and corporately to grow and to flourish, and to resist and overcome diminishment and debilitation as they try to love God and humanity (Pattison 2000). These theological and practical elements have allowed and encouraged Muslims to become involved in chaplaincy practice.

This chapter explores the theology and historical traditions that support the involvement of Muslims in chaplaincy today. Examining the core beliefs and practices of Muslims, it becomes evident that pastoral care and concern for those who are suffering, sick or poor forms an intrinsic part of the Islamic tradition. Likewise, stories and anecdotes from the life of the Prophet Muhammad function as templates for pastoral practice. In the second part of the chapter, we look at how pastoral care has been practised in Muslim societies over time, in hospitals, prisons and educational institutes. We end by considering briefly how pastoral support is practised today in Muslim majority countries.

At the heart of the Muslim faith is the belief in the oneness of God, and the Prophethood of Muhammad (570–632 CE). Muslims believe that God communicated His message to humankind through divine revelations given to the Prophet. Muhammad taught the people of his time through the message of the Qur'an, and through his practice (sunna). As a result, the divine message of the Qur'an, the prophetic example and the verbal sayings of the Prophet (the hadith) become the main sources for the shari'ah, which literally means 'watering hole' or the 'path to a watering hole' (Saeed 2006), a composite term for Muslim theology, law and ethics. The relationship of this technical usage of the word to its etymology suggests that shari'ah is not static and ossified in time and space. It takes into consideration culture and context, providing a dynamic framework for scholars to find solutions to new issues.

Within Islam, religious scholars ('ulama; sing. 'alim) undertake the preservation and interpretation of religious knowledge derived from Islamic sources. To qualify as an 'alim or 'alima (a female scholar) one is required to study the core Islamic subjects to an advanced level with a teacher, and to exemplify this religious knowledge in practice. The 'ulama command authority and wield a certain amount of religious power. They have served in a range of religious roles over time as leaders of prayer (imams), preachers, judges and legal scholars (muftis). Chaplaincy roles are a new addition to this range of functions, although as we shall see, chaplaincy is by no means exclusive to Islamic religious professionals.

The Five Pillars

The Islamic faith is founded on five pillars composed of conceptual beliefs and ritual practices. Core practices involve witnessing that God is one, and that Muhammad is his final messenger (shahadah); prayer (salat); fasting during the month of Ramadan (sawm); giving a portion of one's savings to the poor (zakat); and pilgrimage to Makkah (hajj) for the fit and able. The first pillar divides into seven sub-divisions, all of them related to faith in the unseen realm (ghayb). Some have major implications for Muslim chaplains in their everyday practice, such as belief in God, life after death and ideas surrounding destiny.

Belief in the unseen shapes Muslim worldviews and understanding of issues related to theodicy, such as suffering, pain, grief, evil, free-will, destiny and the balance between God's omnibenevolence and omnipotence (Jackson 2009). Throughout Islamic history, imams have assisted Muslims with questions surrounding religious punishment, sin, evil and forgiveness. The utterance 'I have committed an evil and God will never forgive me' is probably familiar to most imams. However, with little training in pastoral and counselling skills, alongside limits on resources and time, few imams have had the scope to fully engage with the more complex spiritual needs and questions of their congregations.

The second most important pillar of Islam is prayer. Prayer brings comfort to the believer and can easily be a cause of distress if suitable facilities are not available in a place of cleanliness. A Muslim has to wash prior to the prayer (wudu), with ablution providing physical and spiritual preparation for prayer. If performed correctly, minor sins are 'washed away'. The actual prayer comprises certain postures such as standing, sitting, bowing and prostration. Prayer remains valid for those unable to perform these gestures due to sickness or disability. The prayer also includes recitation from the Qur'an; for Muslims this has healing powers and soothing effects. The weekly congregational prayer on Friday (jumu'ah) is particularly important; it is compulsory for men to attend to listen to the Friday sermon (khutbah), and to meet fellow believers. Muslims spend a considerable amount of time preparing for Friday prayers, and will make particular efforts to take a shower and wear fresh clothes beforehand.

Friday prayer is spiritually important but it also has a social dimension, enabling Muslims to gather together at the mosque. Local mosques provide a context for sharing community news, and some social support. In larger towns and cities, congregational worship provides a context for meeting those from neighbouring communities, and hearing about national news. At a global level, the hajj provides a context for Muslims to meet one another from around the world.

Fasting is the third pillar of Islam, requiring Muslims to abstain from food, drink, sexual intercourse and intoxicants of any kind (for example smoking tobacco) from dawn to sunset. During the month of Ramadan (the 9th Islamic month), adult Muslims who are fit and healthy fast from dawn until dusk, believing that depriving the body of its base desires and nutrients will help the soul to grow spiritually. The month is seen as a time when one can empathise with the poor, and those who regularly lack sufficient food and water. The elderly, the sick, pregnant women, young children and those who are travelling are not required to fast, according to Islamic law. However, cultural understandings of fasting are so deeply held that chaplains or imams may have to convince people in these categories that they should *not* fast. During Ramadan, Muslims wake before dawn to eat the pre-fast meal (suhur). Fasting ends at sunset, usually by eating some dates and drinking water (iftar), prior to a hot meal. When Ramadan ends, the Eid festival is celebrated, beginning with communal morning prayers, followed by eating luxurious foods, wearing new clothes, gift-sharing and visiting relatives and friends. In remembrance of the poor, Islamic law stipulates that every person must pay a mandatory charity (sadaqat al-fitr) so that those who are less fortunate can share the happiness of Eid.

Although the remaining two pillars (hajj and zakat) rarely have a direct bearing on chaplaincy activity, they emphasise the 'social levelling' that is inherent within Islam. For example, Muslims with sufficient resources are required to pay a mandatory tax of 2.5 per cent out of their savings each lunar year. Giving in this way 'purifies' material resources, and results in the redistribution of wealth in favour of the poor. Alongside this mandatory tax, Islamic law stipulates other taxes which may be optional, or necessary. These include giving at the end of Ramadan (sadaqat al-fitr), optional charity (sadaqa), a financial substitute for those unable to fast (fidya) or a financial penalty for those who break a fast intentionally (kaffara). These different forms of tax show the importance that Islam attributes to creating a welfare system that involves the circulation of money, support for the poor and a balanced economy (Haneef 1979). Likewise, pilgrims on hajj will rid themselves of any adornments, and will wear identical, simple garments. In this way, the rich become indistinguishable from the poor, and all Muslims, regardless of their social position or material wealth, undertake the same rituals, side by side.

Rites of Passage: Birth and Death

Muslims believe that life in this earthly world (hayat al-dunya) is one of four 'abodes' demarcated by birth and death (Murata and Chittick 2000). The first three abodes are temporary, the last eternal. These four abodes are: the soul's realm (alam al-arwah), the worldly life (hayat al-dunya), the realm of the grave (alam al-barzakh) and the final abode (hayat al-akhira). The earthly material world is also known as the 'testing ground' (dar al-imtihan). One's fate in the final abode is decided on the basis of conduct during life on earth. Consequently, Islamic teaching advises Muslims to give their children a good God-conscious life so they may prosper in the hereafter (Haneef 1979). This teaching starts before the child is born. The mother is encouraged to recite from the Qur'an as much as possible (or be in company where prayers and Qur'an recitation is occurring) so that the Word of God can affect the child in her womb. At birth it is recommended to call out the adhan (call to prayer) in the right ear of the newborn and the iqamah (call to begin the prayer) in the left ear, underlining the importance of introducing God into the infant's life. This has traditionally been done by the father, or another male relative, but women can also make this 'call', and some female Muslim chaplains report doing so (Lahaj 2009).

According to Islamic sources, a 'soul' is breathed into an unborn foetus 120 days into gestation when the soul makes the transition from the 'realm of the soul' to the 'life in this world'. From this point, Islamic scripture forbids abortion without a valid medical reason as this would interrupt the natural transition of the human from one realm to another.

Death is the final barrier for the transition into the next world, the world of the grave (alam al-barzakh). The believer is not supposed to be afraid of death. It provides a release from the burdens of life and enables preparation to meet the Almighty. According to the Prophet, 'death is the gift of a believer' (Al-Tabarani, Mu'jam al-Kabir cited in al-Haythami 1994). The timing of this will occur according to God's will, as part of the unfolding process of fate. The Qur'an states: 'there is a time set for every people: they cannot hasten it, nor, when it comes, will they be able to delay it for a single moment' (surah al-Araaf, 7:34). Muslims believe that the human body is held 'in trust' from God. As a consequence, life and health are viewed as sacred, and human beings have a responsibility towards the body and its well-being. Since death is a moment of transition through which the believer must inevitably pass, close relatives regard it as their duty to support this final journey. The Qur'an is recited at the bedside (particularly surah Yasin) so that the words of God will accompany the passing soul. If possible, the dying person is encouraged to seek forgiveness from God for past sins, and to recite the shahadah (a process called talqin): 'There is no god but Allah and Muhammad is his Messenger' (Keller 1994: 222).

Death is defined in Islam as the soul leaving the body permanently. Once dead, the body must be prepared to meet the soul in the next realm. This is done through four stages: (a) washing the body, (b) shrouding, (c) the funeral prayer and (d) the burial. The body is washed with camphor water so that it is ritually clean. Perfume is rubbed on to the seven limbs used in prostration (the forehead, arms, knees and feet). The body is then wrapped with three pieces of shroud for men and five pieces for women. In some cultures, the body is taken to the house of the deceased for a few hours so that family members can say farewell. Burial occurs as soon as is reasonably possible, usually within 24 hours because, according to Islamic sources, 'the soul feels pain until the deceased is laid to rest' (Arshad et al. 2004: 484). The body is then taken to the mosque or an open space where the funeral prayer is held. The imam then prays to God to forgive all the sins of the deceased and asks that the journey of the soul is made easy. The funeral bier is carried to the cemetery by six members of the community, subsequently alternating with other members, allowing all members of the community to share in carrying the body.

At the cemetery, the body is lowered into the grave while the Qur'an is recited. Members of the family will throw the first three handfuls of soil over the body, reciting a verse of the Qur'an with each throw: 'From it (earth) We have created you', 'To it We shall return you', 'And from it We shall resurrect you once more (surah Ta Ha, 20:55). Everyone takes turns in using the spade to cover the body, and once buried, a final prayer is recited before the congregation departs.

The Role of the Family in Islam

Muslims traditionally live in extended families. When a couple marry they take on mutual responsibility for the extended family of their new spouse. The words used for 'family' in Arabic are usra and 'a'ila. Usra literally means 'to bond' whereas 'a'ila comes from a root word which means 'to have needs' (Lane 1863). While the cornerstone of society is the family, at the heart of the family is the role of the mother. The members of the family are in need ('a'ila) of each other for support and comfort. They are bound to each other through the mother or more precisely through the mother's womb, known as 'rahm' in Arabic. The word 'rahm', meaning womb, is derived directly from the name of God, al-Rahman, the most Compassionate. The Prophet said in a hadith, 'the womb is derived from the name of al-Rahman' (al-Bukhari, al-Adab al-Mufrad). For Muslim scholars, it is no coincidence that the word for womb, 'rahm', is derived from God's name. God has filled the mother's womb with His qualities of compassion and mercy, and it is because of these qualities that members of the family bond to each other.

Families extend mutual support in many ways. Children become the responsibility of the whole extended family (Hewer 2006: 128). For example, during childbirth or illness, a woman can be confident that her other children are in the care of a grandmother, sister or aunt. Uncles, brothers or a grandfather may assist by taking children to and from school. During financial difficulties, family members often pool resources to help one another. Those with disabilities, the elderly and infirm are usually cared for within the family home. The Qur'an reminds Muslims of their obligation to parents: 'Lower your wings of humility towards them in kindness and say, "Lord, have mercy on them, just as they cared for me when I was little"' (surah al-Isra 17:25).

Besides the family, a Muslim derives their sense of identity from being part of, and contributing to, a worldwide community of faith (ummah).

> In the debate between those who claim the primacy of society and those who emphasise the primal significance of the individual, Islam takes a middle course

and believes that this polarisation is in fact based on a false dichotomy. There is no society without the individual; nor can the individual survive without society (Nasr 2004: 159).

Support in Muslim communities is not confined to family members but is extended outwards to neighbours and friends. 'People are dependent on God', said the Prophet Muhammad, 'and the most beloved to God are those who are caring towards God's creation' (Abu Ya'la cited in al-Haythami 1994). In fact the word 'ummah' (community) is a derivative of the word 'umm' (mother), which conveys profound truths about unity, family and belonging in Islam.

There is a ritual dimension to this sense of belonging, so that alongside personal individual rituals ('ayn), such as the five daily prayers, there are additional rites that are necessary for the community (kifaya). Both of these categories have legal and metaphysical implications. For example, funeral prayers are a communal responsibility. If a person dies without receiving proper washing and burial rites, the immediate family and the whole community are responsible in the sight of God. However, even if only a few people assume the responsibility, they have discharged the obligations of the whole community.

Calling (da'wah), Witness (shahadah), and Pastoral Care in Islam

Like Christianity, Islam is a missionary faith. The call to Islam is directed not only towards the individual conversion of non-Muslims, but also toward the betterment of all humanity. Simple acts of kindness are forms of da'wah, so that helping a person at a time of spiritual crisis is an aspect of 'calling to the good'. But da'wah is also related to the concept of shahadah or witnessing to the truth. The Qur'an says, 'We have made you into a middle community, so that you may bear witness [to the truth] before others' (surah al-Baqarah, 2:144).

Pastoral care in Islam starts with divine love and compassion. The Qur'an opens with the verse: 'In the name of God the most Compassionate (Al-Rahman) the most Kind (Al-Rahim)' (surah al-Fatiha 1:1). Both of these names of God share the same root word 'rahma' meaning 'mercy'. They convey the meaning of compassion which is not only perfect, but is inclusive of all. A reflection of God's mercy for his creatures is the instruction to Muslims, that alongside fulfilling their duties towards God, they have a responsibility towards others (surah al-Baqarah 2:177), irrespective of their differences in creed or colour (surah al-Hujrat 49:11):

> People, We created you all from a single man and a single woman, and made you
> into races and tribes so that you should get to know one another. In God's eyes,
> the most honoured of you are the ones most mindful of Him: God is all knowing,
> all aware (surah al-Hujrat 49:13).

The example of the Prophet is pivotal in Islamic pastoral practice. Muslims believe that as the recipient of divine revelation, the Prophet Muhammad was the first to implement the message of the Qur'an. They believe that he is the perfect role model to follow, and several Quranic verses attest to this truth (surah al-Ahzab, 33:21; surah al-Anbiya, 21:107). Muhammad saw himself as a continuation of the biblical Prophets and their message. Brought up as an orphan and then raised in the healthy environment of villages, he spent part of his life working as a shepherd, thereby continuing a tradition of previous biblical Prophets. He referred to the head of the house as a shepherd, 'every one of you is a shepherd and every one of you will be asked about his flock' (al-Bukhari).

The Qur'an refers to the Prophet as 'most kind' (ra'uf) and 'most merciful' (rahim), both qualities being among the attributes of God (surah al-Tawba 9:127). It records the range and depth of his interpersonal skills, and how people were drawn to his warmth and compassion (surah aal Imran 3:159). During the early days of Islam, after he was visited by the angel Gabriel for the very first time, he feared for his life and questioned whether he had been possessed. He called his wife Khadija, and asked her to cover him with a blanket as he shivered and perspired. She comforted him, saying

> Never! By Allah, Allah will never disgrace you. You keep good relations with your kith and kin, help the poor and the destitute, serve your guests generously and assist the deserving calamity-afflicted ones (al-Bukhari).

Muhammad's extensive pastoral encounters provide a rich source of inspiration for today's Muslim chaplains. One well-known story particularly reflects the Prophet's approach to pastoral care. During his ministry in Makkah, Muhammad faced hardship and rejection from the city's non-Muslims. An elderly lady used to throw rubbish onto him from her window, every time he passed her house on his way to the mosque. One day, she did not throw any rubbish. Although happy to avoid this calamity, when a second day passed without the rubbish being thrown at him, Muhammad became concerned and enquired after the health of the woman. Being told that she had fallen ill, he sought permission to pay a pastoral visit. She was wary that he would exploit her vulnerability and take revenge for having thrown rubbish at him. Instead, he comforted her by saying that he was no longer concerned with her past actions, and was there to support her recovery and well-being (Dudhwala 2006).

Muslim chaplains can derive important principles from this story, regarding the Prophet's actions as the basis for an inclusive, non-judgemental model of chaplaincy. The well-being of their clients, and the communities and institutions in which they serve, goes beyond the particularities of race, religion, culture, theology or sexual orientation. The Prophet said

> 'help your brother, be he the oppressed or the oppressor'. The Companions asked 'we understand helping the oppressed, but what does it mean to help the oppressor'? The Prophet replied, 'help the oppressor in not reoffending again' (Al-Bukhari).

Visiting the sick and caring for the elderly are so central to Islam that carrying out these duties provides an opportunity to meet with God directly:

> 'O son of Adam! I fell ill yet you did not visit me'. To this the bewildered person will reply: 'O my Lord! You are the Master of the entire universe. How could I call on you?' Allah will tell him: 'One of my servants fell ill but you did not visit him. Had you called on him you would have found Me beside him' (hadith cited in Murad 2005: 38).

The Prophet visited the sick himself and also encouraged his followers to do so. He said, that 'as a Muslim calls on a sick Muslim brother, he gathers the fruits of Paradise during the entire course of his visit' (Ahmad and Tirmidhi)' (hadith cited in Murad 2005: 38). Islamic sources are replete with examples of this kind. Books like al-Bukhari's 'Book of Manners' (Al-Adab Al-Mufrad) reflect the range and extent of material upon which Muslim chaplains can draw. Of particular significance in multi-faith Britain, is that such hadith

> emphasise the inherent value of the charitable act to the one who acts on behalf of God, that is, the one who visits the sick. According to [these] hadith, the one who visits the sick discovers the presence of God. The doctrinal correctness of the sick person is irrelevant (Kowalski 2009).

Pastoral Use of Scripture

For Muslims, the Qur'an has healing powers. Regarded as the uncreated Word of God, reciting it on, or for, a person will have healing effects. The Qur'an calls itself 'a healer' (surah Yunus 10:57) and its opening chapter is also known as the chapter of healing (surah al-Shifa). In the hadith literature, the Prophet referred to the healing properties of particular Quranic chapters, such as the opening chapter, the throne verse (ayat al-kursi) and the last two chapters of the Qur'an. He encouraged his followers to use this healing potential by reading particular verses, and then gently exhaling in the direction of the sick person (or blowing onto a cup of water, from which the sick may drink). The use of the breath as a channel for the Divine healing power of the Qur'an is known as ruqya or damm (Keller 1994: 880).

In addition to the Qur'an, the Prophet himself used a range of prayers in times of trouble or sickness. These were originally found in the hadith literature. However, later scholars compiled the invocations found in the Qur'an and hadith into prayer manuals that could be used in pastoral care. The two most famous texts, still used by Muslim chaplains today, are al-Nawawi's (d. 1278) *Manual of Devotional Prayers* (al-Adhkar) and al-Jaziri's *Fortress of a Believer* (Hisn al-Muslim) (Padwick 1969).

Another important source related to healing practice was medicine derived from prophetic traditions. This was a reaction to the Galenic medicine which Muslim physicians were practising (Rahman 1989). Muslims believe that so-called 'Prophetic Medicine' is supported by Divine spiritual potential, even though treatment may be for mundane physical ailments. One of the foremost advocates of prophetic medicine was the theologian Ibn al-Qayyim al-Jawziyya (d. 1350). Ibn al-Qayyim wrote no less than four books on this subject: Prophetic Medicine (al-Tibb al-Nabawi), Healing of Sick with Judgement, Wisdom and Justification (Shifa al-Alil fi 'l-Qada wa al-Hukm wa 'l-Ta'lil), Sickness and Healing (al-Da' wa' 'l-Dawa') and Medicine of the Heart (Tibb al-Qulub) a book on the healing powers of the Qur'an.

In addition to these sources, the writings of well-known Sufis and mystics were often 'pastoral' in nature. For example, the 12th-century Sufi theologian al-Ghazali (d. 1111) wrote a monograph, the title of which translates as 'The Ninety-Nine Beautiful Names of God' (*al-Maqsad al-Asna fi Sharh Asma Allah al-Husna*) (al-Ghazali 1995: translation by David Burrel and Nazih Daher). al-Ghazali outlines the meaning of each of the 'Names', followed by an explanation of the implications or counsel to be derived from them. He described how Muslims could 'adorn themselves' with the qualities bound up with these names (al-ta'alluh, meaning 'imbibing divine characteristics' (see also Kowalski 2009)). For one in need of pastoral care, al-Ghazali's manual can be regarded as means to reclaim the immanence of God into the heart.

Sometimes, particular Sufi texts have acquired a reputation for their healing and spiritual powers. One such book is the *Mantle Ode* (Qasida al-Burda). There is indeed a supernatural story associated with the Ode, connected to its author, al-Busiri (d. 1297), a magistrate in the deltaic region of Egypt. The stresses of his life led to him suffering a stroke. From his hospital bed, al-Busiri contemplates his situation, praying to God for strength and forgiveness. However, because of his sins he does not dare to approach God directly, and decides to use the Prophet as an intercessor on his behalf. He writes the Mantle Ode as a tribute to the Prophet for helping his intercession. Legend recounts that after writing his Ode, al-Busiri had a dream where the Prophet took off his mantle and put it on al-Busiri. When he woke up he was cured (Murad 2009). The Mantle Ode is one of the most celebrated pieces of poetry among Muslims, and has been translated into numerous languages. Mosques and private houses are sometimes adorned with its verses, and it became a practice in some Sufi traditions to recite the Mantle Ode over the sick patient, in the hope that they might feel the same benefit as al-Busiri himself.

Pastoral Care in Medieval Islamic Hospitals (Bimaristan)

Having explored a range of texts that may be used to support Islamic pastoral practice, we now consider some of the day-to-day traditions of spiritual and religious care since the prophetic era particularly to contextualise our more recent research on Muslim healthcare chaplains. It is important to start by reiterating the importance of the family. In traditional Islamic societies, caring responsibilities lay with household members; only those in extreme situations, or with very particular needs, were admitted to medical institutions (Dols 1992). Receiving care within the family setting, patients are surrounded by Islamic worldviews that integrate the spiritual with the physical. The Islamic view of health is entirely holistic, thus traditional codes of practice for Muslim doctors stressed the need for physicians to be religious and God-conscious. Al-Majusi, a medieval Muslim doctor, writes that physicians

> ought to be God-fearing, and faithful to their teachers. Their aim should be to help and heal the sick and not only to seek financial gains. ... [They] should be chaste, intelligent, religious, kind and considerate (Anees 1984a: 317).

Within the specialist branches of modern medicine, it can no longer be assumed that Muslim medical professionals are able to provide the holistic approach of their counterparts from earlier centuries. Seen in this light, the evolving role of Muslim chaplains in healthcare today could be seen perhaps as helping to revive the spiritual dimensions of patient care, this time as part of a multi-professional medical team.

The Umayyad Caliph al-Walid (reigned 705–715) was said to be the first founder of a hospital known as 'bimaristan' or 'maristan' for the blind and for lepers. Servants and guides were employed to help the patients (Rahman 1989: 66). However, more fully operational hospitals were established during the Abbasid caliphate (750–1257). The idea and support for these hospitals came from the Bimaristan College in Gundaishpur, founded by the Sassanid ruler of Persia in 555 CE. They were notably multicultural, as Muslim physicians sought to benefit from all available medical knowledge, irrespective of religion or culture. The first hospital in Baghdad was founded by the Abbasid Caliph Harun al-Rashid (d. 808) and was managed by a Christian doctor, Jibril b. Bakhtisha. The doctor brought with him a dispenser, a Persian Christian, whose son eventually became the head of the hospital (Rahman 1989). Ali b. Isa, 'the good vizier' from Baghdad, founded a bimaristan in 914 CE. He also appointed a Christian physician, Abu Uthman al-Dimishqi, as the medical director of this hospital, as well as of those in the holy cities of Mecca and Medina. This man was succeeded by another Christian physician, Sinan b. Thabit, who himself founded another hospital. Meanwhile, several centuries later, Moses Maimonides (d. 1204), the illustrious theologian, scientist and philosopher, eventually settled in Cairo as the personal physician to Salah al-Din Ayyubi (d. 1193) and his son.

Hospitals during Mogul India were also sensitive to patient needs. Alongside Muslim hakims and practitioners of prophetic medicine, they also employed Hindu herbalists (veds) to provide dedicated care for any Hindu patients reluctant to be treated by Muslim doctors (Rahman 1989: 73). There is also evidence that special medical centres were founded near to larger mosque complexes so that people could receive medical care after the Friday congregational prayers (Rahman 1989: 67). Ali b. Isa, referred to above, also requested Sinan to arrange medical care for those in prison. In a letter to Sinan, Ali wrote:

> May God prolong your life! I have been thinking about prisoners, who because of their overpopulation and the rugged conditions of their residence must be

frequent victims of diseases. But they are unable to pursue their own benefits and see doctors from whom they can seek advice about their health-afflictions. It is therefore behoving that you set apart some doctors to visit them daily; that medicines and medical drinks be carried to them; and that the doctors visit all prisoners and treat the sick (cited in Rahman 1989: 66–7).

The largest and greatest hospital built in Cairo, Egypt, was the Mansuri hospital, founded by the Mamluk ruler Mansur Qala'un (d. 1290), in 1284. Alongside its many therapy facilities, such as a cold room, a hot room, hydro-therapy and music therapy, it also had a mosque and a chapel. Meanwhile, in some cities, particular quarters were reserved for lepers. Such people usually relied upon the care of religious institutions, the imams/directors of whom focused on both the spiritual and mundane needs of patients. For example, a hospital for lepers called 'Jami' al-Qatila' survived in Damascus up to the beginning of the 19th century (Dols 1983: 911), and as the name suggests, a mosque (jami') was part of the complex.

The al-Dimnah hospital in Qayrawan built by the Aghlabid prince Ziyadatullah I (817–838 CE) incorporated medical facilities, a mosque and ablution facilities, and employed female physicians from the Sudan (Anees 1984b: 102). It also drew upon the skills of specialist physicians known as 'fuqaha al-badan', meaning specialist legal scholars concerned primarily with the human body. These physicians, as the first part of their title suggests, were imams versed in the prophetic medical tradition, and were familiar with the practice of cupping and blood-letting (ibid.).

These historical institutions and practices reinforce the point that Islamic traditions take a holistic view of health and well-being. Physical ailments can cause spiritual disease, and vice versa. Not surprisingly then, medical texts were taught in traditional Muslim learning circles, alongside Islamic subjects. For example, in India a book on medicine (mizan al-tibb) was taught to the novice student, alongside books of Arabic grammar. Consequently, the imams of the mosques in rural villages were often trained in aspects of Islamic medicine, albeit poorly in many cases; they provided medical and spiritual advice for people as best as they could.

There is historical evidence that Muslim physicians were sensitive to the mental-moral-spiritual aspect of patients. The famous philosopher-physician Avicenna (d. 1037) relates a story that a physician close to the Samanid king was having dinner with him once when a female servant came in with a plate of food which she placed on the floor. When she tried to stand up, she could not because of an attack of lumbago. At the king's request, the physician stepped in to treat her, first asking her to remove her scarf and expose her hair. She declined on the basis that it would be immodest to do so. The physician then ordered that her trousers be pulled down. When the servants approached to carry out his command, the woman immediately stood up, fearing the immense shame that such exposure would cause. But her lumbago was cured. Avicenna quoted this anecdote as evidence that some psychological-spiritual phenomena can overcome physical disabilities.

Michael Dols, an expert on medicine in traditional Islamic societies, notes that many patients were cured through conversational therapy with Islamic scholars.

Quoting from al-Nishpuri's Book of the Wise Fool (Kitab al-Uqala al-Majanin), Dols writes of an encounter between a patient and an Islamic scholar, a renowned Arabic philologist by the name of al-Mubarrad (d. 898). Al-Mubarrad saw a young man chained to the wall of the hospital. Seeing the ink-well in al-Mubarrad's hand he asked if he was a religious scholar or philologist. Al-Mubarrad replied that he was the latter. The patient invited him to sit down and they had a deep, restorative discussion together on Arabic language and poetry.

Pastoral Care in Medieval Islamic Prisons

While it is relatively easy to find evidence of pastoral and medical care in medieval hospitals in the Muslim world, it is harder to find sources that illuminate pastoral practice in prisons. Although there are some references to prisoner care in the genre of law manuals known as adab al-qadi (etiquettes of the judge), these are not extensive. One reason for this apparent silence is that prisons in medieval Muslim societies rarely functioned as a form of punitive detention (Gorman 2007; Schneider 1995):

> Incarceration was carried out almost exclusively under the rubric of siyasa [secular governance]; only in the rarest of instances did it fall within shari'a's jurisdiction. In the words of one historian of the Islamic prison, the 'absence of imprisonment as a prescribed penalty in Islamic law (shari'a) meant that its application, as a punishment and a disciplinary practice, was associated with offences against political authority, to punish those who broke man-made law'(Gould 2012: 181, citing Gorman 2007: 96).

Prisoners avoided the social stigma of imprisonment because they were not regarded as having committed any criminal offense, in the legal sense. The prison 'had not yet been criminalised' (Gould 2012: 182), because it was fundamentally associated with the self-interest of the rulers. It was not about community safety, the social good, or the betterment of the individual (ibid.).

The shari'a dealt with crime largely through the imposition of financial penalties or corporal punishment, and these often functioned as effective deterrents. The prophetic statement (later turned into a legal maxim), 'prevent the application of capital and corporal punishment in the case of doubt' (Doi 1997: 224), reduced the use of capital punishment. Looking at the practices of the Prophet, nearly all the people punished for illicit sexual relationships (around ten) were punished on the basis of confession, not on the basis of trial and evidence, and even the confession was disliked (Lucas 2011). Ali notes that that the 'jurists' writings demonstrate a real aversion to both accusation [of fornication] and confession' (Ali 2006: 63).

Meanwhile, in traditional Islamic societies the treasury (bait al-mal) had some responsibility for providing welfare to those who were destitute or unable to work. Thus, if an individual was caught stealing food, through poverty or starvation, there would be no punishment because the state was regarded as at fault for failing to meet his needs. When a famine broke out in Medina during the time of the second Caliph Umar (d. 644), he suspended capital punishment for stealing, since it would constitute an injustice to the people (Doi 1997: 224).

Although medieval Muslim prisons were not regarded as having a punitive function, there is evidence of some regard for prisoners' pastoral needs. During the reign of the Abbasid Caliph al-Ma'mun (d. 833), the Great Imam Ibn Hanbal (d. 855) was imprisoned. Ibn Hanbal's incarceration was not due to a crime that he committed or to political motives. Rather he was incarcerated because of his theological position on the nature of the Qur'an (Watt 1968: 87–8). As a result of his views he was tortured and imprisoned for over two years. But during his time at the Dar al-Mawsaliyya prison, records indicate that he regularly led the Friday prayer (al- Isfihani n.d.). Also there is evidence that the State hired religious scholars (Ahmad b. Rabah and Abu Shu'ayb al-Hajjaj) to visit Ibn Hanbal daily, to try to convince him that his theological position was wrong (Ibid.).

Pastoral Care in Medieval Islamic Educational Institutions

Relatively little information is available on pastoral and religious care in medieval educational institutions. However, there is evidence that professors of Islamic sciences connected spiritual care with their teaching. Abd al-Latif al-Baghdadi (d. 1231), a scholar from Baghdad who later took up a professorial position at the al-Madrasa al-Aziziya in Damascus, is said to have constantly advised his students regarding spirituality alongside their studies: he advised them to reflect on their deeds before sleeping, and urged them to seek forgiveness from their sins. He writes:

> … when you have finished your study and reflection, occupy your tongue with the mention of God's name, and sing his praises, especially at bedtime, so that your very essence becomes soaked up and your imagination permeated with Him, and you talk of him in your sleep (Makdisi 1981: 88–9).

Some Islamic colleges created staff positions dedicated to students' spiritual and pastoral needs. These posts included the college head or the master of a Sufi lodge (Shaykh al-Ribat, shaykh al-khanqa) and the 'student monitor' (arif). Such individuals were responsible for protecting young students and novices from harm, caring for their souls, and giving spiritual advice (Makdisi 1981: 216).

Students experiencing financial hardship were supported from endowment funds (waqf) by individual professors, and also by fellow students who pooled their money for needy classmates (Makdisi 1981: 182). Abu Hanifa (d. 767) was said to have given his student Abu Yusuf (d. 798) 100 dirhams so that he could concentrate on his studies relieved of the worry of earning a livelihood. Al-Qasim b. Asakir (d. 1204), the chair of Nuriya Hadith college in Damascus, donated his entire salary for impoverished students. Abu Mansur al-Khayyat (d. 1106), a scholar of the Qur'an and imam of the mosque of Jarda in Baghdad, dedicated his time to teaching the Qur'an to blind students. He did not charge for his teaching services, and proactively raised funds for them within the market. On his death, it is said that he had taught 70,000 blind students (Makdisi 1981: 180). Just as contemporary higher education chaplains deal with problems that arise in student relationships, medieval scholars and teachers faced similar issues. Makdisi recalls the story of a student who fell in love with a slave girl. He became distracted from his studies, not only because of his love for the girl, but also because he lacked sufficient resources to buy her out of slavery and to marry her. The professor took the love struck student to the market, bought the slave girl for him and from that time on the student was able to resume his studies effectively (Makdisi 1981: 183).

These legendary and sometimes light-hearted accounts point to some profound truths about personal development, the acquisition of Islamic knowledge and the role of teachers in Islamic educational institutions, both historically and in the contemporary period. Muslim scholars have agreed upon three Arabic words that outline the meaning and purpose of education (Halstead 2004), and these illuminate the implicit 'pastoral' role of teachers. The first word 'tarbiya' derives from the Arabic root 'raba' (which means to grow, or to increase) and it refers to the development of individual potential, and to the process of nurturing and guiding young people to maturity. The second term, ta'lim, comes from an Arabic root word which means 'to know, or to be informed', and refers to the imparting and receiving of knowledge, usually through training, instruction or another form of teaching. The third word is ta'dib and this derives from the root 'aduba' (which conveys the sense of being refined, disciplined or cultured) and from this word we also have the term 'adab', meaning good manners and personal conduct. Ta'dib refers to the process of character development, and learning the principles of social and moral behaviour within the community. Islamic education thus covers individual development and God-consciousness, the transmission of knowledge and the development of an understanding of society and its social and moral rules. This comprehensive approach to education means that 'no aspect of a Muslim's life can remain untouched by religion' (Halstead 2004: 522). Because of this, teachers in Islamic colleges and schools, both past and present, are 'expected to exemplify ... the content of that which is taught' (Hewer 2001: 521). Teachers within the Islamic tradition, therefore, are not simply transmitting knowledge and information; they have always been expected to act as guides and exemplars in all aspects of personal conduct, thus making their role profoundly 'pastoral'.

Chaplaincy in Modern Muslim Societies

Given the history and origins of institutional chaplaincy, it is not surprising to find that documentary evidence for its practice by salaried 'chaplains' in contemporary Muslim societies is virtually non-existent. For example, while there are now a range of websites and professional associations for Muslim chaplains in the West, we could not establish the existence of equivalent bodies or resources in Muslim societies to the same degree. However, through our interviews with Muslim chaplains in England and Wales, it is clear that institutionalised forms of religious care are well established. For example, a prison chaplain from London was part of a delegation to Syria. Whilst visiting Syrian prisons, it was evident that religious teachers were engaged in religious and educational activities, such as Qur'an study programmes and corporate worship. Prisoners were especially encouraged and supported in memorisation of the Qur'an, perhaps due to the perceived rehabilitative potential of this practice.

Another interviewee for our project noted that religious teachers have considerable involvement in the administration of prisons in Malaysia, while there is evidence that imams make regular visits to prisons in Saudi Arabia. Precisely what their religious and pastoral care involves requires further research. Web searches suggest that Muslim chaplains are functioning in Indonesia and Malaysia. For example, the Royal Malaysian Police force includes the Bahagian Agama dan Kaunseling (Religious and Counselling Division) or BAKA, while all three armed forces have chaplaincy support through 'Kor Agama Angkatan Tentera' (KAGAT), or the 'Military Religious Corps'. Their role appears to include the same combination of educational, pastoral and advisory work that is common in most military chaplaincy.

Compared to the relative lack of information regarding prison and military chaplaincy in Malaysia, we uncovered rich insights into healthcare chaplaincy. Imam Hasrizal is a Muslim chaplain at Malaysia's National Heart Institute.[1] Imam Hasrizal was trained in classical Islamic law and theology from his native Malaysia, and later in Jordan. He has previously served as Imam at Belfast Islamic Centre, Northern Ireland. In his blog he discusses many issues related to chaplaincy practice. For example, in a seminar on worship for patients in hospitals delivered for the Penang Medical College Islamic Society, he discusses issues related to worship and ablution for patients. He tries to give a balanced view of the challenges created by religious prescriptions and practical reality. One such challenge relates to following a school of thought (Shafi, in the case of Malaysia) and the patient's level of Islamic knowledge. He writes:

> It is common to my own experience that when you guide them on how to perform the Salat, they will ask, is this Syafie [shafi]? Well, mumbling about differences between mazhabs [schools of thought] would be the last thing you want to do while patients are connected to all those wires and machines. With the intention to help them, you might be the most effective cause of death![2]

---

[1]   http://abusaif.wordpress.com/about/, last accessed December 2011.

[2]   http://abusaif.wordpress.com/2007/11/16/seminar-on-ibadah-for-patients-in-hospital/#more-12, last accessed December 2011.

Imam Hasrizal calls for a patient-oriented approach to care, which he calls 'practicleness' [sic], while other posts note the personal impact of his pastoral work. For example, he recalls an 18-year-old patient receiving a successful lung and heart transplant. Although he couldn't be with her at the time, he says that she remained in his prayers. The success of the operation inspired him to campaign for organ donors. He writes: 'let the examples motivate us to take the same action and register as organ donors. I start with myself ... come and join me on board'.[3] Below these words, he scanned a photo of the organ donation consent form that included his signature. In another blog post he writes in detail about the benefits of organ donation from an Islamic point of view.[4] However, it is worth noting that this is a disputed area of medical practice among Islamic scholars. Some have advised against organ donation due to ideas about the sanctity of the human body and the requirement for the deceased to be buried intact. Regardless of different interpretations, Imam Hasrizal's blog nevertheless points to the complexity of the issues faced by Muslim chaplains today, irrespective of their location or context, as they seek to resolve the between religious prescriptions, practical solutions and medical ethics.

Conclusion

We began this chapter by demonstrating that the Islamic tradition places a strong emphasis on pastoral care, visiting of the sick and mutual support in times of trouble and distress. Textual sources and prophetic traditions stress the obligations that Muslims have towards one another. We are now in a better position to discuss why, despite the rich pastoral care tradition, chaplaincy was never an integral part of Islam. We offer three possible explanations, beginning with the idea that in traditional Muslim society no single institution or individual could claim absolute authority in terms of interpreting the word of God. The Qur'an encourages all believers to know and understand their faith, and although scholars may assist with that process, there are no special ordination processes or powers attributed to scholars that give them privileged access to God. The decentralised structures of religious authority and leadership in Islam, combined with the lack of rituals that require the essential input of an imam or religious scholar, have mitigated the evolution of priestly roles from which institutional chaplaincy might evolve.

Secondly, we have seen in this chapter that Islamic traditions and laws outline the mutual rights and responsibilities that family members have for one another. Where families have played an integral role in the provision of support and pastoral care, there has been little need to delegate caring obligations and duties to

---

³ http://abusaif.wordpress.com/2007/11/07/my-prayer-for-siti-salmah/, last accessed December 2011.

⁴ http://abusaif.wordpress.com/2007/05/23/live-to-give-donate-your-organs/#more-5, last accessed December 2011.

others. But the developing role of Muslim chaplains in the West is indicative of the increasing fragility of extended family support structures. The limited availability of large affordable housing means that family members may be physically separated from one another, and thus unable to provide care. The availability of state benefits can reduce the sense of mutual financial interdependence, and some British Muslim elders fear the long-term impact and consequences of the social and geographic mobility of their children (Howe 2007). Chaplaincy roles for Muslims suggest that families are now less able to provide the economic, social, pastoral and spiritual care they once did, and that they have become increasingly reliant on external agencies and religious specialists. Institutionalised chaplaincy has not existed in historic Muslim societies because kinships ties and support structures were generally sufficient.

Changing social conditions provide a third explanation for why institutionalised pastoral care now has new significance in Islamic law. Muslim jurists have divided all religious practices into five categories: obligatory (wajib), recommended (mandub), permissible (mubah), disliked (makruh) and prohibited (haram). And as we have seen, the obligations on Muslims are further divided in to two categories: personal obligation (fard 'ayn) and communal obligation (fard kifaya). Where the five daily prayers are an individual responsibility, the Muslim theologian Al-Ghazali (d. 1111) wrote that it is a communal obligation for at least some people from the community to excel in those professions and disciplines necessary for the smooth running of the society, such as nursing, teaching, law and so on. He noted that all of these fall within the jurisdiction of religious obligation, and a society which does not fulfil these will be held accountable by God. Seen through the lens of Islamic law, the work that is involved in Muslim chaplaincy today falls under the jurisdiction of communal obligation. We make this claim based on a number of observations.

Although Islamic sources stress mutual caring rights and responsibilities, the fulfilment of these duties is now more problematic in some contexts. For example, the nature of modern public institutions, with their concerns about security, health and safety and confidentiality, can make general access difficult. Salaried Muslim chaplains can therefore assume communal obligations on behalf of Muslim communities, individuals and families who are now less able to access public institutions. As insiders to these institutions, they are better placed to facilitate the religious requirements of Muslim clients, prisoners or patients, such as negotiating the provision of halal food, or establishing spaces where prayers may be offered. Furthermore, Muslims experiencing the pressures of extended family decline in Western societies, perhaps due to social and geographic mobility, may be unable to care for those who are sick, impoverished or suffering from a disability (certainly without support). These conditions thus shift the onus of caring from the legal status of recommended for individuals (mandub) to that of communal obligation (wajib kifaya), best fulfilled by specific individuals trained and employed for the role, that is, chaplains. Furthermore, there are precedents for such salaried religious roles in Muslim history, especially the profession of Qur'an teacher and leader of prayer. Although early Muslim scholars disliked taking payment for religious teaching roles, later jurists agreed that it would be difficult for religious scholars to provide good quality instruction if they were distracted by financial concerns.

A further principle of Islamic law pertains here. The law states that any action which helps the realisation of an obligatory duty is in itself obligatory (ma la yatimm al-wajib illa bihi fa huwa wajib). For example, ritual ablution in and of itself is not obligatory (fard li dhatihi); it is only obligatory because prayer is not valid without it. Washing thus falls within the obligatory category. By the same token, where most Muslim chaplains spend a good deal of their time enabling the obligatory religious duties of Muslim clients, so their work takes on particular legal and religious significance.

We have now situated the development of Muslim chaplaincy within the context of modern Britain, the Islamic tradition and the history of Muslim societies. Clearly our treatment has been brief, but is nevertheless a vital background to the discussion in the following chapters which explore our empirical research findings in depth.

Chapter 3
Chaplaincy People

Introduction

As we saw in Chapter 2, many of the religious tasks performed by Muslim chaplains in Britain today are integral to Islamic traditions. There is nothing novel about religious specialists supporting fellow Muslims during rites of passage, or in times of hardship: delivery of religious teaching, praying for the sick and leading congregational worship have been routine for most imams over time, irrespective of location or context. However, the performance of these kinds of tasks, alongside the development of new roles and expectations arising from the context of large multi-faith public institutions in 21st-century Britain, presents some new and significant challenges, personally, professionally and theologically.

For example, Muslims in Britain are a religious minority. Muslim chaplains must function in relation to religious personnel and spaces shaped by centuries of Christian tradition (Legood 1999a; Noblett 2002; Threlfall-Holmes and Newitt 2011). They must work within the secular norms of multi-faith public institutions, where assumptions about public service, security (prisons) or infection control (hospitals) usually override any religious claims. With no established pattern of institutionalised Islamic pastoral care to guide their work, performance of the role 'Muslim chaplain' is in some ways a novel and challenging undertaking that brings unfamiliar challenges and risks.

But Muslims drawn into chaplaincy work also encounter significant opportunities, personally, professionally and theologically. They are able to raise, and in some respects to answer, the questions that religion and faith pose for an institution. Opportunities arise in their work to make Islamic traditions relevant in new spheres of modern British society. They articulate a challenge to the contemporary Muslim community about the place of Islam in Britain, and can provide role models for how to meet that challenge.

So, how are Muslims drawn into chaplaincy work? What kind of educational, religious or social capital do chaplains bring to their role, and what is the influence of more recent professionalising trends in chaplaincy (Swift 2009)? These and other questions will be explored in this chapter, which is the first to discuss the empirical findings of our research in full. We look at the routes by which chaplains acquire their roles, and reflect on their career development and progression. The key themes that underpin these discussions revolve around the social, educational and political efforts to define and shape a new role: 'Muslim chaplain'.

Religious Authority and Qualifications

The relative novelty of Muslim involvement in chaplaincy poses significant questions with regard to the educational background, religious training and 'authorisation' of chaplains. In the absence of a 'sending church' or authorising religious figure, who guarantees the credentials and suitability of Muslim chaplains in Britain? To set this discussion in context, a brief consideration of the training of imams and other Muslim religious professionals is warranted.

It is often said that there are no 'clergy' in Islam (Haneef 1979; Murata and Chittick 2000). Up to a point this is true. Religious professionals in Islam do not perform any sacramental functions, and there is no formal hierarchy of religious specialists, such as may be found in the Christian churches. Assuming that there should be no form of human intercession between God and humanity, Islam encourages all believers to know and to understand their faith, and to exercise their own interpretive judgement. However, Muslims are also exhorted to learn from scholars with specialist knowledge of the Qur'an, Hadith and other Islamic sources, and to emulate the moral conduct of pious individuals. Thus those who have committed themselves to supervised and intensive study of Islamic texts and sources, and who have learnt basic principles for the application of Islamic law, acquire a reputation as scholars. This is particularly the case if they are regarded as individuals who clearly embody and exemplify this knowledge in their daily lives through their wisdom, moral conduct and piety.

In traditional Islamic societies there is a prevalent ideological conviction, remarkably consistent across different Islamic societies and cultures, that the most important religious knowledge in Islam is transmitted intact from one generation to another without alteration by persons and events (Robinson 2009). The emphasis upon conservation of a fixed body of text and knowledge, and the ability to recall it accurately and appropriately from memory, explains the value of memorisation of the Qur'an and other key texts (Boyle 2004; Eickelman 1978). The 'scholars' are the carriers of that knowledge, and the people who embody and interpret it in new circumstances (Brown 1996). They are deemed the most suitably qualified to show how new scenarios or new knowledge are consistent with established religious knowledge. As they receive social recognition for their knowledge in scholarly religious networks, they acquire a reputation as legitimate religious authorities (Eickelman 1985). The importance of the law in Islamic traditions means that there is often a spectrum of opinion about the legality or 'correctness' of a particular action, and so ascertaining the extent of consensus of opinion among other trusted religious scholars is sometimes regarded as important. But, at the same time, Islamic sources also encourage Muslims to interrogate religious sources for themselves, to learn and discern what God is telling them and to take responsibility for their knowledge, religious education and action.

The acquisition of religious knowledge and authority rests upon a variety of scholarly traditions. For example, the Islamic Studies curriculum offered by a number of universities in the Middle East (such as Al-Azhar University in Cairo, or the Islamic University in Madinah) is widely recognised as providing a thorough basis in Islamic Studies; graduates are recognised as 'ulama (Lindholm 2002). Similarly, Islamic 'seminaries' in South Asia have developed their own traditions of learning (Metcalf 1982; Zaman 2002). Graduates who complete discrete learning components are issued with a 'licence' (ijaza) certifying their competence to teach others. Over the last 30 years, and as a consequence of the migration of substantial numbers of Muslims to Britain in the post-Second World War years, a number of Islamic colleges and seminaries (dar ul-uloom) have been established in Britain (Birt 2005; Geaves 2008; Gilliat-Ray 2006). These reflect various 'schools of thought', but currently, the majority of these institutions reflect the South Asian Deobandi tradition. Most of these institutions have been established for boys, but there are also a number of schools for girls, some of whom go on to more advanced Islamic Studies that enable them to graduate as 'alima.

At present, the advanced religious curriculum currently offered in many Islamic colleges and dar ul-uloom in Britain has little or no currency in the world of mainstream higher education (Mukadam and Scott-Baumann 2010). Although a number of projects are currently underway to try to bridge the gap between the teaching and learning offered in dar ul-uloom and that provided in universities, this is likely to be a long-term, complex endeavour.[1] The consequence of the current educational scenario is that the religious training and education of many Muslim chaplains in Britain is meaningful within Muslim communities, but has little formal recognition beyond them (Beckford et al. 2005).

This raises issues for public institutions in Britain that have become familiar with the idea that chaplains have usually undertaken a professional bachelor's degree in theology as part of ordination training.[2] This degree qualification, validated by a British university and subject to formal quality control processes, guarantees minimum educational standards (Gilliat-Ray 2001a). Furthermore, many degree programmes that lead to Christian ordination and ministry include a pastoral placement of some kind (for example working in a prison chaplaincy, or within a parish). Currently, the curriculum within dar ul-uloom carries no external validation, and provides little opportunity for the acquisition of pastoral skills and experience in public ministry. This means that institutions seeking to employ Muslim chaplains are faced with difficult questions about what kind of Islamic religious training might equate to a university degree or provide competence in chaplaincy. Meanwhile, many Muslims contemplating chaplaincy work have to consider whether they have the requisite personal skills to enter this field of work.

---

[1] For example, Ron Geaves is currently undertaking research entitled 'An exploration of the viability of partnership between *dar al-ulum* and Higher Education Institutions in North West England focusing upon pedagogy and relevance', funded by the Islamic Studies Network of the Higher Education Academy.

[2] The Pew Foundation report on religion in prisons also noted the high educational standards of most prison chaplains in the USA: 62 per cent held a Masters degree or doctorate, 21 per cent a BA degree.

Their ambivalence becomes clear in our study; many interviewees looked back on their early days in chaplaincy, and noted their initial sense of hesitation and uncertainty.

Education and Training

Among our sample of chaplains, 58 per cent were recognised religious professionals, meaning that they had followed a formal programme of confessional Islamic Studies, and had acquired the title or recognised position of 'alim or 'alima. However, there were considerable differences between men and women. Nearly all of these religious professionals were men. The two 'alimas in our study (one in the Prison Service, one in the NHS) both noted that they were to some extent 'pioneers': this is largely explained by the fact that the religious curriculum that many 'alimas follow in the UK tends to reinforce particular ideas about the role of women as mothers and educators of children. Girls who have engaged most fully with the ethos and education provided by dar ul-uloom for girls in the UK (most of which are Deobandi) will tend to observe strict gender segregation, are likely to wear the niqab (face-covering) in public and will often see their role as centred upon the religious education of children and other women. A more public, outward-facing engagement with society and public life is probably not encouraged, this being a likely reflection of educational and social patterns derived from 'parent' institutions in South Asia (Winkelmann 2005). A much fuller discussion of gender issues will follow in due course, but for the time being, it is worth noting that a significant number of Muslims working as chaplains in Britain today have not followed a formal Islamic Studies curriculum, such as a degree course from an Islamic University in the Middle East (for example Madinah University, Saudi Arabia), or the classical South Asian seminary curriculum (the dars-i-nizami).

However, we discovered that male chaplains who had been in their post for less than three years were much more likely to be recognised Islamic scholars compared to their male counterparts with much longer experience as chaplains. Some of our interviewees even noted that were they required to reapply for their current positions, they would probably fail to be appointed. This reflects the ongoing transition from 'visiting minister' to 'Muslim chaplain', the growing 'professionalisation' of Muslim chaplaincy and perhaps a growing recognition of other systems of teaching and learning in Islamic Studies by employers. But the clear gender difference reveals that Muslim women are rarely gaining entry to the chaplaincy profession via the acquisition of a religious qualification.

What about the levels of mainstream education that Muslim chaplains in Britain bring to their role? We were particularly interested in knowing the highest educational qualification that chaplains had attained. This was in order to evaluate the extent to which expectations about secular educational attainment might be changing, and perhaps increasing, as a consequence of the state regulation and professionalization that is now shaping chaplaincy work. Our findings were surprising, in that less than half of the chaplains in our sample (46 per cent) had received a higher education (three with doctorates, seven with MAs, four with PGCEs and 16 with degrees). The educational experiences of the remainder of our sample were varied, and included a range of certificate and diploma-level qualifications, and A-Levels. Not surprisingly, the most 'educated' chaplains tended to be over-represented in educational chaplaincy where their roles were often an extension of a teaching position.

Levels of mainstream higher education appear to be relatively low, but it is likely that at least some of our interviewees regarded their traditional (but unaccredited) Islamic Studies in dar ul-uloom or Islamic universities as 'equating' to a degree. If this is accepted, then the overall educational capital among Muslim chaplains in the UK rises considerably. What our data does show, however, is that the vast majority of chaplains *either* have a traditional religious qualification, *or* a more advanced mainstream educational qualification. Very few chaplains are now performing their role with nothing more than relevant experience to offer. But fewer still are bringing to their work both advanced religious training *and* a university-validated higher education qualification. This gap is only likely to be bridged when British universities can form the kind of educational alliances with dar ul-uloom and other Islamic colleges that many Christian theological colleges and ministerial training courses have historically forged and maintained (Coxon and Towler 1979; Russell 1980).

Many of the chaplains in our sample had some similar background experiences, prior to beginning their chaplaincy work. The most overwhelming and striking common experience, regardless of sector, gender or level of religious qualification, related to education and teaching in one form or another. About three-quarters of the chaplains in our sample had been (some still were) engaged in the delivery of education, from nursery level to degree level, both within the state sector, and in private madrasahs and study circles. Others were connected to educational institutions in other ways, either as support workers (for example, librarian) or as students (usually at postgraduate level). Many of the male chaplains who referred to education and teaching qualified this by noting that it was an extension of a mosque-based imamate position; they were responsible for the teaching of supplementary classes after school. But even those who were not 'alims were often involved in Islamic education for children. The frequency with which chaplains referred to previous (or current) roles as educators was striking, but equally not especially surprising in relation to the demographics of Muslim communities in Britain. Labour Force Survey data in 2009 established that out of the estimated 2.4 million Muslims in Britain, nearly one million were under the age of 19 (Kerbaj 2009). This fact, considered in light of the priority that many Muslim parents attach to Islamic education, means that there is an almost infinite need for teachers within many Muslim communities (Mogra 2004, 2011). Unfortunately however, much of this work is poorly paid (or voluntary) and rarely amounts to a full-time role. For our chaplains, however, it is likely to have been an important avenue for developing contacts and accessing networks that have subsequently led them into their chaplaincy roles.

Among those chaplains in our sample who had not been engaged in delivery of some form of education prior to their chaplaincy work, there were also commonalities. These clustered around voluntary community-based roles such as helping to run an Islamic charity, and undertaking informal counselling within Islamic organisations. Chaplains who are employed in part-time roles often continue their community-based roles, often alongside part-time employment or caring responsibilities.

Becoming a Chaplain

Over the last two decades, the job titles ascribed to Muslim chaplains have been highly variable. Muslims have been recruited to positions described as 'Imam', 'Muslim Advisor', 'Muslim Chaplain', 'Visiting Minister', 'Muslim Lay Visitor', 'Religious Advisor', 'Spiritual Advisor' and sometimes a combination of these titles (Beckford and Gilliat 1998). These variations seem to reflect uncertainties within public institutions, and within Muslim communities, about exactly what kind of nomenclature is appropriate for the work of a new group of religious specialists in the public sphere. However, the lack of consensus around job titles rests upon different questions and concerns, according to the constituency.

For example, some public institutions, particularly NHS hospital Trusts (such as the Nottingham University Hospitals NHS Trust), have renamed the 'Chaplaincy' department, calling it instead a 'Department of Spiritual and Pastoral Care'. This seems to reflect an effort to take account of wider social changes, bound up with an apparent shift away from corporate 'religion', to rather more individualised and apparently inclusive notions of 'spirituality' (Heelas et al. 2005). The title 'chaplain' has in some institutions morphed into an alternative designation as 'spiritual care giver', or 'multi-faith co-ordinator' ('A Man For All Religions', *Forest Health Newsletter*, November 1993, issue 18) thereby reflecting institutional uncertainties about the category 'religion', and the role of religious professionals employed in these spaces. However, some of the assumptions that have driven these changes do not necessarily reflect the religious dynamics of Muslim communities in Britain. Normative religious practice tends to revolve around observance of the traditional 'Five Pillars' of Islam, adherence to a religious lifestyle and a concerted effort to raise children according to Islamic principles (Scourfield et al. 2013). Consequently, some Muslim chaplains have resisted designations such as 'spiritual care giver'. It is only within the Prison Service that job titles have been relatively consistent, with 2003 being an important year when 'Visiting Ministers' were retitled 'Muslim Chaplains'.

Within Muslim communities adoption of the title 'chaplain' has raised a different set of questions. Should Muslims accept a title – 'chaplain' – even qualified by the addition 'Muslim', given that it resonates so distinctively with Christian traditions? While it brings some merits as a recognisable religious position within public institutions, both the title and the role remain unfamiliar for some Muslims in Britain, especially those who have had little or no contact with major public institutions, or international students coming from countries with no tradition of chaplaincy.[3] However, alternative titles from within the Islamic tradition are equally problematic, since the title 'imam' conventionally excludes women and those who, technically speaking, are not qualified religious scholars ('alim). Yet, both groups make significant contributions in the sphere of Muslim chaplaincy work in Britain today.

Terminology is also problematic in relation to the notion 'Muslim chaplaincy' itself. One of our interviewees was clear:

> I have always resisted the sense of 'Muslim chaplaincy' or 'Roman Catholic chaplaincy', or 'Sikh chaplaincy', and I just thought of 'chaplaincy' without making those distinctions. The starting point has got to be about chaplaincy and what chaplaincy has to offer rather than individual sections within that, because we don't tend to work in that isolated way. So it's always slightly difficult for me when I hear people talking about 'Muslim chaplaincy' (chaplaincy administrator).

Some of these confusions around job title and role were reflected among the Muslim chaplains we talked to. One told us that 'it was something which I wasn't really aware of, of what a chaplain's role involved' (part-time male hospital chaplain).

This unfamiliarity, especially in some Muslim communities, means that eventually acquiring a chaplaincy role and identity often seems to depend upon proximity to key individuals or religious networks associated with chaplaincy work. Tracing the growth of Muslim involvement in chaplaincy in the last decade, a relatively small number of Muslim chaplains, and their immediate circle of contacts, have performed a critical role as informants, gatekeepers and sponsors for new appointments, particularly in the healthcare and prison sectors. Many younger chaplains new to the profession spoke about the encouragement and advice they had received from more experienced Muslim chaplains. The same names seemed to recur during these conversations.

Despite this, the recruitment process for Muslim chaplains in the public sector has mirrored the shift from 'visiting minister' to 'Muslim chaplain' in important ways. In the 1980s and 1990s, prisons and hospitals often tended to approach local mosques or Islamic centres to find volunteer 'visiting ministers', sometimes for ad hoc, temporary or more permanent religious input (Beckford and Gilliat 1998). Some newly qualified, British-trained Islamic scholars also took proactive steps to become involved in chaplaincy, and sought volunteering opportunities by telephoning chaplaincy departments, or sending job applications on a speculative

---

[3]   Some Muslim chaplains have added the title 'Imam' to their identity badges, alongside 'Muslim Chaplain', in order to make their role clearer for those Muslims who may be unfamiliar with the meaning of the title 'Muslim Chaplain'.

basis. But over time, as the role Muslim chaplain has formalised and become salaried, so, too, recruitment has become increasingly standardized. Although the chaplains in our sample often tended to hear about new vacancies and opportunities through family and friendship networks, they also referred to awareness of open advertising via the Muslim press, via chaplaincy and Islamic websites and via professional Muslim chaplaincy associations. There is now a diversity of routes by which prospective chaplains might come to know of new opportunities.

There are, however, important variations according to sector. For example, many of the higher education chaplains in our sample acquired chaplaincy roles as an extension of an existing teaching, student or academic support role, and were often approached informally about taking on the role. There is less of a sense that they were 'recruited' to a newly available and publicly advertised position. This contrasts with HM Prison Service, where becoming a full- or part-time chaplain now depends on a rigorous selection and recruitment process. Adding to the complexity of recruitment processes, students of the 'Certificate in Muslim Chaplaincy' at Markfield Institute of Higher Education have sometimes managed to convert their 60-hour course placement into more enduring chaplaincy work which, in some cases, has become salaried. Across most sectors, initially voluntary, sessional or part-time work has sometimes provided sufficient institutional capital to enable more enduring appointments to evolve.

Networking remains a key means by which opportunities become known, but Muslim chaplains increasingly have to go through a more formal selection process, often involving an interview, in order to become appointed. HM Prison Service has become especially adept at testing whether applicants have an aptitude for chaplaincy work. For example, shortlisted applicants are asked to deliver a short sermon to the selection panel. They are keen to find out whether prospective chaplains can make their sermons relevant to the prison context:

> Sermons they are brilliant at, they are trained to deliver sermons, no problem. Although commonly, two things are missing, one is closeness. You don't find an imam in a sermon saying ... 'You know, it's interesting the other night I was walking down the road'. No. It'll be 'the Prophet, salla allah alayh wa sallam, said ...' ... [t]hey don't break down into story mode very much. You don't say, 'today we'll talk about neighbours'. This is prison! Talk about 'cell mates' (chaplaincy administrator).

But it is the role-play scenario that provides the most decisive indication to the Prison Service Chaplaincy recruitment panel: applicants are asked to imagine themselves breaking the news of a death in the family to a prisoner, with an actor taking the prisoner role:

> You would be shocked how many have formal desk, chair, and say 'come in' and they won't go up, meet ... empathy, you know care and attention on your face. So it's quite fascinating to see the ... I don't know how to put it, skills of,

pastoral care skills … of empathy and that kind of thing. And that sieves them out … (chaplaincy administrator).

In the health context, chaplains reported similar kinds of experiences as part of selection procedures. One explained that he had been asked during interview how he might counsel a young teenage Muslim girl wishing to terminate a pregnancy arising from a relationship with an unmarried partner.

This use of challenging hypothetical scenarios as part of selection procedures (and later training programmes) seems to reflect the accumulation and sharing of experiences among Muslim chaplains, and the gradual identification of the pastoral issues that can pose distinctive challenges in relation to the work of Muslim chaplains in public institutions. Recruiters appear keen to appoint chaplains who can think and act contextually. However, it is worth reiterating what a significant shift this involves for most qualified religious scholars ('ulama). Their training will have largely involved the acquisition of religious knowledge and etiquette. If they have gone on to take up imamate positions, the relationship they have with a congregation will often be formal, distant and hierarchical:

> The imam-congregation relationship in our communities is one that you don't … you're not intimate with them. You don't befriend an imam. You ask [the] imam for [a] fatwa [religious opinion] he gives you a fatwa and then he leaves. In the prisons when you've got a Lifer Unit, you build relationships (chaplaincy administrator).

Despite the use of more formal and apparently transparent processes to recruit and appoint chaplains (especially in some sectors), the actual outcome of selection processes can perpetuate significant inequalities of opportunity reflecting varied educational and social capital within Muslim communities. For example, not all Muslim communities in Britain have been able to establish the kind of religious training institutions that can produce suitably qualified individuals to serve as chaplains. Among those that have, chaplaincy networks have naturally evolved around the charisma and experience of particular individuals. As these networks gain strength and prominence, they inadvertently exclude those who are disconnected from them:

> I know that if you are Deobandi or a Barelwi you will have mates that you know who are in Prison Service who'll say 'well first there's this, and then there's this …' [so] sharing their notes (chaplaincy administrator).

The outcome of these informal networking processes means that Muslims from smaller ethnic groups (for example Kurds, Afro-Caribbeans, or Somalis), or from particular social or religious groups (for example Salafis, or converts) are far less likely to become Muslim chaplains in Britain. They often lack sufficient access to networks of social and religious capital that might enable their successful recruitment.

This is compounded in some cases by the sheer unfamiliarity of chaplaincy work. Some chaplains in our study were initially hesitant about entering this field of religious activity. The ambivalence and uncertainty sometimes had a spiritual dimension. For example, although like many professional chaplains, some felt 'called' by God (Hicks 2008), and retrospectively attribute their chaplaincy role to divine intervention, others approached more cautiously, with much self-critical uncertainty as to their suitability. Assurance might then come not only from divine signs (in one case, a dream) but also through encouragement by family and friends. Even then, some embarked on the recruitment process almost experimentally, and with little real intention of staying in post long term. One prison chaplain was initially concerned about the spiritual pollution he might suffer through exposure to the 'evil' environment of prisons. Despite these voices of caution and uncertainty, some of the chaplains in our study offered clear reasons for wanting to become a chaplain. These reflected a range of personal, financial, professional, structural and explicitly religious motivations, with important distinctions evident according to gender and sector.

Explicitly religious motivations for becoming a chaplain tended to revolve around the idea that chaplaincy work is a natural way to fulfil Islamic obligations incumbent on all Muslims. For example, health care chaplains referred to religious texts about the rewards of visiting the sick (see Chapter 2); prison chaplains justified their work by referring to prisoners as spiritually 'sick', and in need of religious 'medicine'; educational chaplains viewed their work as a means of fulfilling Islamic duties around mission (da'wah), making particular effort to distinguish this from proselytism, and stressing the emphasis on improving institutional understanding of Islam. Chaplains derived a sense of satisfaction from the idea that they were engaged in valuable religious work which might bring them spiritual rewards in this world, and the next, most especially through being granted forgiveness of sins, and frequent opportunities to remember God. Some expressed the idea that they were blessed to have the chance to serve the cause of Islam via chaplaincy work, and stressed the importance of retaining pure religious intentions. More experienced chaplains were able to look back at their work, and feel a sense of personal satisfaction having helped to alleviate the burdens of others, having made a difference to individuals and families.

Sometimes, a more collective religious awareness of the spiritual fate of Muslim prisoners or hospital patients has been an important catalyst for the take-up of chaplaincy positions. For example, knowing that stillborn babies born to Muslim parents were being buried by Christian chaplains was sufficient motivation for a group of 'ulama in one British city to support a colleague into chaplaincy work:

> I was still teaching, and I thought 'which is my way?' The school is calling me
> to do full time, the hospital is calling me to do full time. I did salatul istikhara
> [a prayer for seeking guidance] and I did mashura [consultation] again and
> I realised that, no, I think there is more work to be done in chaplaincy. So I

decided to come here. One of the things that really pushed me to becoming full-time was the baby death rate that we have in [Wellbridge] is quite high. Before the Muslim chaplain post was created, unfortunately, and this is the truth, the Christian chaplain buried the Muslim babies. So that was one thing that I felt I owed to my Muslim community. I have a photograph, which is filed away, of a coffin being lowered by the Christian chaplain as the Muslim family watch over. So I was quite taken aback, because we have a large Muslim community here. Where are we going wrong? Something is not right. Something needs to be addressed here (full-time male hospital chaplain).

Some chaplains saw their chaplaincy role as providing a formal framework for undertaking religious activities that they were doing anyway, accompanied by the opportunities to develop themselves through professional training opportunities. For Muslim women in particular, chaplaincy positions provide an opportunity for professional recognition that would be more difficult for them to acquire via informal community-based work. They were emphatic, however, that their motivations were not economic, and noted that with the financial support of a father or husband, they did not need to be working in chaplaincy in order to supplement a family income.

Likewise, education chaplains who rarely receive payment anyway also noted that economics did not figure in their motivations. However, for all the talk of religious duty and spiritual reward, full-time salaried chaplains found ways of justifying their receipt of an income. For example, effective prison chaplaincy might help to reduce rates of reimprisonment (thereby saving taxpayer's money). Many spoke of rewards as both financial and spiritual:

I can see myself staying here because … it's a golden opportunity, it's everything that a person can ask for because it's doing the religious duty and getting paid for it. So what more can you ask for? Two in one, you're getting din [religion] and dunya [worldly reward] (part-time male hospital chaplain).

Some of the chaplains in our study expressed considerable dissatisfaction with the terms and conditions of many mosque-based jobs in Britain (and the overall lack of posts available to newly qualified 'alims). For them, the attractions of chaplaincy work outweighed the merits of remaining in mosque positions. Their views provide an interesting commentary on the structures and expectations that govern some mosques in England and Wales, certainly in comparison with the kind of assumptions that shape institutional chaplaincy. For example, chaplaincy positions often carry a job description, are undertaken in a context of transparent employment policies and rights and often bring comparatively generous remuneration:

There were some colleagues that were being paid £50–60 working in the mosque, and I didn't see it much as a career really, in the sense that … not financially.

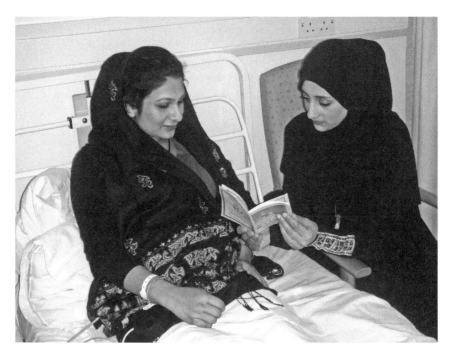

Figure 3.1   Shaheen Kauser, Muslim Chaplain, Bradford Teaching Hospitals NHS
                Foundation Trust (by kind permission of Shaheen Kauser)

> So, caring for people was part of my nature and then learning more about the
> chaplaincy field, I was quite intrigued by this, and I really wanted to become
> a chaplain. For two reasons, financial as well as spiritual, let's be honest. The
> financial because I've still got to support my family, and it's something different
> (full-time male prison chaplain).

> There were a couple of things which led to my decision. One was the mosque
> that I was in, I mean I feel bad saying it but there was a huge compatibility
> problem with myself and the committee of the mosque. I was in my sort of mid-
> twenties. All the committee were obviously in their sixties and seventies, and it
> was difficult for me to get them to change their mentality and their thinking. So
> I used to, for example, insist on doing the prayers and the khutbah [sermon] in
> English, because I thought actually that's the purpose of the khutbah, to get the
> message across, but it was a really uphill battle (full-time male prison chaplain).

The prospect of being regarded as a 'professional', and having the opportunity to
undertake training and study to develop new skills was attractive for many.

This contrasts with mosque-based roles, which often depend upon the patronage
of the mosque committee, are usually poorly-paid, offer little scope for autonomy

and where professional recognition is likely to be limited. One chaplain enjoyed the sense of freedom in chaplaincy; he was not tied to being in a particular place at a particular time, unlike colleagues working in mosques. Interestingly, when the Archbishop of Canterbury wrote in 1948 that chaplains in the new NHS should not receive Consultant grade salaries, this was because he feared 'highly paid career chaplaincies might draw clergy away from parish ministry' (Swift 2009: 42):

> ... [having] got this exposure to how secular professional organisations work, what I realised was the mosque wasn't allowing me to be who I was ... there was a set model that was there for Imamate, and that is the model you had to work in. If you worked beyond that model, you were doing something innovative and therefore you were challenging the established norm. Sometimes you were pressured by the management committee, sometimes you were pressured by your other peer Imams. And ... you were meeting the same static community all the time ... you were always speaking to the converted, if you know what I mean. You were always speaking to people who are already confident to come to the mosque. What about the people who aren't comfortable and confident to come to the mosque? Who is reaching out to them? And I thought chaplaincy was one way you could go out (mixed-sector full-time male chaplain).

Our data clearly suggests that some Muslim religious professionals are being drawn away from community-based work. Chaplaincy is providing an attractive career path for some of the most able and energetic Muslim religious leaders in Britain, particularly those who have had the chance to develop their skills via employment and training opportunities in HM Prison Service and in the NHS. This is an observation that is now increasingly well known in the public domain. A series of articles and letters in *The Times* newspaper in January 2012 included an interview with the Muslim Advisor to the Prison Service Chaplaincy. He commented:

> I believe I have got the cream of Muslim Imams in Britain, which is a shame in one sense. I have had prisoners say to me, 'Tell me, why do I have to go to prison to get a good Imam?' That is the sad state of affairs we have (Ford 2012).

Qualities of a 'Good' Chaplain

Having established some of the motivations and routes by which Muslims in Britain enter chaplaincy work, what are their reflections about the kind of professional skills, Islamic knowledge or personal character required to be effective in the role? If one sought to establish what Muslims regard as the qualities of a good imam, it is likely that they would stress depth of religious knowledge and piety. We asked the chaplains in our study what they regarded as the qualities of a 'good' chaplain. It was clear that religious knowledge and piety provided the essential foundation; knowledge of Islam was regarded as vitally important. But this knowledge was expected to be delivered via highly effective 'people skills'. There was a clear consensus, irrespective of sector, gender, length of service, full/part-time or 'alim/non-'alim, that chaplains are expected to be good Muslims and exemplars of Islam. Their motivations should be deeply religious, springing from immersion in faith, and evident in their daily lives. But at the same time, they need to be equipped with a range of interpersonal, listening and communication skills, and to have the knowledge and confidence to work within a multi-faith context. Beneath this consensus, however, there were significant tensions in our study around 'what counts' as appropriate religious knowledge for chaplaincy work. The necessity of being an 'alim (or not) was debated extensively. And beneath the obviously contested perspectives on this matter were broader economic, social and professional struggles. Likewise, the silences around necessary 'people skills' were indicative of some of the structural constraints and professional inequalities that some Muslim chaplains in Britain currently encounter.

Before considering the more contentious issues around qualifications and religious training, a brief look at the kind of relational/interactional skills that chaplains rated highly is indicative of their absorption of a broadly liberal social worldview that is espoused by public organisations seeking formal equality and diversity. Many of the 'people skills' stressed by chaplains can be found in most standard counselling textbooks. Thus, ideas about being non-judgemental, non-directive and respectful of people, and treating them as individuals, maintaining confidentiality and being good at listening were regarded as key professional skills for chaplains. One chaplain recognised this approach as essentially humanistic, but most, if not all chaplains were able to route this kind of approach back into basic Islamic virtues and attitudes. For example, 'sincerity' could be translated as being about good intentions or 'niyyah' (al-Bukhari); 'humility' has the equivalent Islamic virtue of 'tawadu'' (al-Bayhaqi); and 'good character' would be recognisable to Muslims as 'husn al-khuluq' (Muslim). Patience, or 'sabr', is a well-known disposition that Muslims try to cultivate in daily life (surah al-Baqarah 2:155). Christian chaplains can no doubt do the same in relation to biblical texts, and would almost certainly centrally subscribe to such a list of characteristics. However, there was an interesting convergence between 'secular' counselling skills and the role of Muslim chaplains as people from whom authoritative religious advice can be sought. A number of chaplains thought that taking a person-centred, non-judgemental, listening approach was the necessary prelude to the delivery of more sensitive and appropriate religious advice. This would be completely counter-indicated in the counselling world, intrusive or even abusive.

Beneath these discrete professionally orientated and delivered skills, chaplains identified more innate or intangible qualities of character for effective chaplaincy. Many talked about having an aptitude or disposition towards the work that was important (along with having the right motivation). Compassion and caring are arguably not skills that can be taught, and being flexible, open-minded, accessible,

Figure 3.2   Imam Abdul Mumin Choudhury (left), Chaplain at Guy's and St Thomas's
NHS Foundation Trust, in conversation with Imam Faisal Ahmed (right),
Muslim chaplain at HMP/YOI Isis & HMP/YOI Rochester

pragmatic, patient, kind, friendly and confident are qualities that are more or less
developed in most people. Chaplains talked about the importance of being able to
get on with people of different kinds (clients and staff), and having the common
sense, approachability, personal and religious maturity and judgement to know
how to do this effectively. Some chaplains working in the Prison Service noted
the value of having wisdom (one called it 'wit'). This might be translated as being
'streetwise' or 'jail-wise', meaning that attempts by prisoners to deceive or mislead
chaplains would be recognised and managed effectively. In this respect, Muslim
chaplains in Britain echo their American counterparts:

> Corrections is tough, you know? I tell people that corrections is a bit
> counterintuitive, because as a society, we're based on trust. Well in corrections
> we're dealing with people who have a track record of not being trustworthy,
> so where is the balance between suspicion and treating people with respect?
> (interviewee in Hicks 2008: 411).

The silences within our data about the qualities of a 'good' chaplain were
particularly revealing of some historical/structural constraints and inequalities
that are currently impacting upon Muslim chaplains. For example, there was little
mention of team-working skills, leadership, organisational and management skills

(for example chairing meetings, managing others) or teaching skills. This seems to indicate that most chaplains are still basically focused on providing advice and care to individuals or groups of clients, rather than being extensively involved in managing or leading teams. This reflects the relatively recent involvement of Muslims in chaplaincy, and the struggles they are experiencing as they try to acquire positions of leadership. However, all this is beginning to change as more Muslim chaplains acquire full-time positions, and begin to gain seniority within their institutions. Some have used the social capital they have acquired to win financial support to undertake professionally accredited management training (for example an MBA, in one case). When this occurs to a greater extent, more chaplains are likely to recognise that being a 'good' chaplain now requires competence in managerial skills, and as well as religious and pastoral functions.

Some chaplains in particular contexts thought that some kinds of expert knowledge were important for effective chaplaincy. Prison chaplains familiar with legal and sentencing processes could use this as part of relationship-building with prisoners. Education chaplains with an understanding of academic regulations could advise students about how to manage difficult situations (for example complaints) in relation to their studies. Health care chaplains almost made a virtue of their ignorance of medical procedures and diseases. They saw their distinctive religious knowledge as contributing to a professionally driven, team-based approach to patient care. However, an appreciation of legal and procedural matters around death and burial is vital requisite knowledge for a Muslim chaplain in health care (particularly when they wish to expedite funeral arrangements). The ability to deploy institutional know-how via a range of languages was also mentioned as an important skill for enabling pastoral conversations and for supporting clients as they navigate bureaucracy, though we discuss issues of language and translation in more depth in Chapter 4. One prison chaplain commented that in contrast to mosque-based work, 'imams need to realise that they are not the most important person in the prison … they are the cog in the whole machine [and] that cog needs to work as a part of the machine to make an impact' (part-time male prison chaplain). This suggests an appreciation of where and how chaplains can be effective within a wider institutional context, and a direct recognition that 'we can't forget we're on institutional turf – you can't just do whatever you want' (Hicks 2008: 411).

Do Muslim Chaplains have to Be 'Scholars'?

One of the most distinctive tensions to arise in our study revolved around the question of religious knowledge and authority, and, in particular, whether it was necessary to be a qualified 'alim (or not) in order to work as a chaplain. It was evident that non-'alims were more likely to have come into chaplaincy as an extension of other work or community-based roles, for example higher education teaching, nursing/allied health professions or counselling. They did not accept that they were in any way inferior, and some laid claim to being especially client-focused, and more in tune with the needs of the institution. They grounded their authority in their life experience and personal piety, rather than in specific forms of Islamic training, and when religious advice was required, perhaps on a point of Islamic law or ethics, they recognised the limits of their knowledge. In such circumstances, they did not feel their position was in any way diminished if the opinion of a religious scholar was sought; many non-'alims knew precisely how to access scholarly networks for advice.

By contrast, most 'alims were adamant about the necessity of having advanced religious knowledge in order to be a 'good' chaplain; they indirectly criticised those without advanced religious training. This view was particularly apparent among prison chaplains, where the proportion of 'alims is highest. However, their criticisms of non-'alims appeared to be not only about issues of religious authority and effectiveness, but also about wider economic, social and professional struggles to consolidate Muslim involvement in chaplaincy. In particular, there seemed to be some 'resentment' that existing positions were being occupied by individuals they regarded as unqualified for the job, thereby restricting opportunities for a growing number of Muslim scholars deemed more worthy. Before exploring this tension further, there are some more general observations that can be made about the arguments for being a religious scholar, which reflect both general and sector-specific perspectives.

Generally speaking, the advantages of being an 'alim or 'alima in chaplaincy revolved around an ability to manifest authority both to the institution, and to clients via speech, demeanour and dress. A command of Quranic Arabic, an in-depth knowledge of the hadith and an ability to recite key texts in the right contexts and situations gave religious scholars a particular perceived advantage. Furthermore, an appreciation of Islamic law and usul al-fiqh (Islamic legal theory) was deemed by some to be essential for working effectively across the diversity within Muslim communities in Britain. Those with scholarly credentials are more able, it was argued, to recognise how and why different schools of thought might have varying approaches to religious matters. Some recognition of these differences enables chaplains to offer advice appropriate to the client's own school of thought. Regardless of sector, 'alims felt uniquely placed to offer authoritative religious advice with confidence. They believe, and, more importantly, *they believe that others recognise*, that they have a particularly close relationship with God on account of their knowledge of the Qur'an, and the embodiment of Islamic tradition derived from 'alim training:

> The charismatic quality of an individual as perceived by others, or himself, lies in what is thought to be his connection with (including possession by or embedment of) some *very central* feature of man's existence and the cosmos in which he lives (Shils 1965: 201).

Without a 'sending church', or an authorising religious figure (for example an individual equating to a Bishop), those who are trained as 'alims appear to derive a sense of confidence and authorisation from their status that non-'alims sometimes seem to lack.

However, it is very likely that the strength of the argument around religious authority has increased with the shift from 'visiting minister' to 'Muslim chaplain' since the early 2000s. There was a time when the requirement for in-depth knowledge of Islam was probably not essential, particularly when chaplains were visiting institutions sessionally, perhaps only to lead Friday prayer. As the scope and complexity of the job has expanded, so the opportunity to deploy more extensive Islamic knowledge has grown, with obvious consequences for the evolving professionalisation of Muslim chaplaincy.

Sector-specific knowledge is also regarded as important by some. For example, being an 'alim in HM Prison Service was deemed by some to be essential in delivering Islamic education classes, or the weekly Friday sermon. Competence in Arabic and an ability to communicate the fundamentals of Islam via reference to Quranic or Hadith texts was thought vital for bringing about the rehabilitative transformation of prisoners:

> The power of words to *do* things is a function of the authority and appropriateness of their speaker, not to mention the appropriateness of audience and context. The power of words is, if you like, socially constructed in the conditions of their reception and authorisation. But the essential point is that words *do* have power (Jenkins 2002: 155).

It is also possible that in a social world characterised by a clear division between prisoners and officers, the religious capital of an 'alim is more likely to lead to them being accorded respect and religious authority by prisoners (though this is not always the case). Working in a uniformed environment, 'alims who choose to wear religious dress make a further visual claim to distinctiveness.

Being an 'alim in the National Health Service brings a different set of challenges and advantages. Muslim health care chaplains are often required to give advice on ethical issues. These frequently revolve around difficult questions about life and death, such as the circumstances in which a life-support machine can legitimately (from an Islamic perspective) be switched off. Chaplains reported the reassurance that families derive from their scholarly credentials. However, our data showed that there was a good deal of anxiety, even among those qualified as 'alims, about giving the wrong advice. For some, there is an underlying fear that they may be punished on the Day of Judgement for having misguided people. Consequently, 'alims not only fear that non-'alims might give the wrong advice (out of ignorance), but they often also seek reassurance about their own judgements. The degree to which 'alims feel responsible for their decision-making in 'life and death' situations is evident from the fact that many of our respondents said they would ring a fellow scholar (or, better still, a legal authority, such as a mufti) in order to get a 'second opinion'. This is for a number of reasons.

Firstly, they seemed keen to be able to offer patients (or their families) a range of 'options', for example regarding the legitimacy of turning off a life-support machine. To some extent, this empowers the family (the final decision rests with them), but both chaplains and families are simultaneously 'covering their backs', Islamically, knowing that other religious scholar/s deemed to have more knowledge, were consulted. This thereby limits the extent to which they are personally responsible (perhaps on the Day of Judgement!) for the ultimate outcome of the decision.

Secondly, some 'alims working in the NHS have clearly absorbed some prevalent ideas in medical health care regarding team-work. They noted that doctors would not decide to turn off a life-support machine without the input of the wider medical team. The justification that chaplains provided for 'ringing round the scholars' seemed to mirror prevalent working practices and assumptions in the NHS. Muslim chaplains have learned to appreciate a style of professional practice (teamwork) which, as well as being consultative, in fact simultaneously reinforces their own sense of professional belonging and expertise. Only they have sufficient knowledge to debate complex legal and ethical matters among one another, using shared technical vocabulary (Fournier 2000). Thus, some important aspects of their professional activity become hidden behind a screen of 'mysteriousness', and the exclusionary boundary between 'alim and non-'alim is once again subtly reinforced.

A notable finding in our research is the degree to which Muslim chaplains were consulting and networking amongst themselves, and turning to UK-based religious authority figures for ethical advice. Their points of reference were not overseas or 'back home'. There is now a sufficient critical mass of 'alims/muftis in the UK who are able to deal with the issues chaplains are confronting. This might indicate an important geographical shift in the location of Islamic religious authority in the West. Finally, although it was clear that chaplains were often well-networked (whether they were 'scholars' or not), none explicitly stated that being a 'good chaplain' depended upon extensive religious networks. This is a dimension of 'being a good chaplain' that we have therefore inferred from the evidence in our data.

Defining the Chaplaincy Role

The transition from 'visiting minister' to 'Muslim chaplain' has involved the evolution of a new field of religious practice. It has become a field of 'struggles' in which chaplains are concerned both to consolidate this new sphere of activity, collectively, but also to improve their own positions within it through training, education and professionalising activity. Amid these struggles, the value and significance of being a religious scholar ('alim or 'alima) has increased, not only because of the growing complexity and demands of the role (which increasingly depend upon an ability to manipulate esoteric abstract knowledge) but also because there is collective strategic advantage to be derived from raising the educational, religious and social capital required to be a chaplain. A classic process of professionalisation is well underway (Freidson 1986; Macdonald 1995).

But just as there are significant inequalities of opportunity surrounding entry to the chaplaincy profession, there are also some individuals and organisations that have had far greater capacity than others to exercise a defining influence on the emergent shape of the profession. Because there is now a sufficient critical mass of Muslim chaplains, there is now a struggle to define, and to educate for, an increasingly professionalised role. Significant debates and tensions are beginning to arise around questions of authority, seniority, qualifications, standardisation and certification. This is amplified by a lack of consensus, both within and outside public institutions and Muslim communities, about precisely 'what counts' as a valid religious qualification for Muslims entering the chaplaincy profession.

The economy of power relations in chaplaincy is marked by the unequal distribution of particular forms of social, religious and educational capital. Despite the overall religious, ethnic, social and educational diversity among Muslim chaplains, British-born, British-trained Islamic scholars who reflect the Deobandi school of thought are having a disproportionate influence on the development of Muslim chaplaincy in Britain. Due to the history of British Muslim institution-building outlined earlier, they have generally been among the first to occupy new full-time chaplaincy positions. On the strength of their experience and acquired reputations, they have become an invaluable resource within the administration of chaplaincy, for example taking up secondments to the PSC Headquarters. Here they perform important functions in helping to manage, document, organise, codify and thus regulate the practice of Islam in the Prison Service. In the process, they inevitably create a distinctive body of specialist disciplinary knowledge and influence about the conduct and role of Muslim chaplains in prisons (Fournier 2000: 71), and consequently acquire an enhanced level of personal expertise, seniority and power over others (Foucault 1982). Amid the diversity of tutors who contribute to the Certificate in Muslim Chaplaincy at Markfield Institute of Higher Education, it is hard to escape the fact that many (but certainly not all) of the religious scholars who contribute to the programme have trained within Deobandi seminaries in Britain, and are connected to the associated scholarly networks. Participation in the MIHE programme, along with the informal networking that surrounds it, gives these chaplains a certain degree of influence to shape those who might eventually enter chaplaincy work.

Meanwhile, the formal establishment of new professional associations and networks for Muslim chaplains (especially in relation to the key sectors of prisons and health care) has been mostly strongly influenced by Deobandis, thereby consolidating another sphere of networking and information-sharing. 'Regimes of power are sustained by the regular patrolling (or pushing forward) of boundaries' (Swift 2009: 119). By virtue of their boundary-pushing initiatives, chaplains from this school of thought are having a decisive influence in the process of negotiating and sustaining 'what counts' as Muslim chaplaincy practice and discourse in a number of ways:

> Those who profess specialist knowledge and esoteric skills have come to acquire a crucial role in helping to shape the problems that must be governed, in giving techniques for the conduct of their authority in relation to those who are their subjects, and in making up the relays that link programmes of government to the multitude of dispersed sites where conduct is to be judged, assessed, evaluated, understood and acted upon (Rose 1996: 3).

The influence of Muslim chaplains who have been trained within Deobandi institutions has not gone unnoticed in certain quarters, especially in relation to HM Prison Service (Brandon 2009). In most cases, and often on the back of unsupported claims and lack of evidence, this is often (and uncritically) assumed to be negative. While the 'politics' of Muslim chaplaincy will be discussed more fully in Chapter 5, it is worth noting here some of the distinct advantages that arise from the fact that Muslim chaplaincy in Britain is emerging and professionalising via the influence of a relatively homogenous group who often have shared experiences of religious training and formation.

Firstly, there arises a certain consistency in relation to religious norms and interpretations. These chaplains will most likely refer to a similar body of religious and legal texts in order to arrive at decisions about the practice of Islam within their institutions. Although many of them have been profoundly shaped by their experiences as chaplains, perhaps becoming more 'liberal' or more willing to exercise interpretive judgement, they will have nevertheless started their careers on the basis of a more or less shared experience of religious training and socialisation as 'alims. Raising and upholding professional standards is made easier if there is a shared starting point, if key decisions around policy and training are shaped by individuals who inhabit similar worldviews, and who are engaged in the same kind of cultural 'work' (Abbott 1988).

Secondly, for senior public sector officials charged with the management of religion in public institutions, the relative lack of religious diversity among some of the most influential and experienced Muslim chaplains is also convenient. As Dinham notes, 'policy … has a tendency to homogenise faiths' (Dinham 2009: 16). If numerous different schools of Islamic thought began to contest 'what counts' as Muslim chaplaincy practice, or challenged prevalent ideas about the practice of Islam in British public institutions, this sphere of religious work would then become disruptive and more difficult to manage. If the utility and value of chaplaincy (for example in promoting health and well-being, or reducing reoffending) became overshadowed by rivalries and dissonance, questions would undoubtedly arise as to the wisdom of publicly funded religion in the first place. Chaplains thus have to maintain the difficult balance between being visibly and demonstrably valuable, while also being almost entirely invisible. This can be seen as a hangover from a time when 'New Labour wanted the popular outcomes of religion (cohesion, education, identity) without recognising its complexity' (Swift 2009: 77).

Thirdly, the coherence that derives from the relative homogeneity of the early pioneers in chaplaincy has arguably been essential for establishing the social, educational and religious foundations for 'Muslim chaplaincy' in the first place, particularly within a relatively short time-frame. The social capital bound up in networks of relationship and trust among a particular group of religious scholars, largely derived from their shared experiences of religious training and education, has been marshalled in ways that have helped Muslim chaplains, individually and collectively, to move from simply 'getting by' to 'getting ahead' (Saegert et al. 2001: 105, cited in Dinham 2009), especially in the prison and hospital sectors.

If there is reliance upon particularly influential and experienced chaplains in the effort to shape and define the Muslim chaplaincy field, this is in part a reflection of the lack of books and material resources about the conduct and nature of the work, certainly when compared to the extensive literature that surrounds Christian chaplaincy and pastoral theology. At this critical moment in the evolution of 'Muslim chaplaincy', the requisite know-how is most easily found within the experience and knowledge of individuals, not in books or journal articles. It is perhaps not surprising then, that an entry-level certificate course for Muslim chaplains places particular emphasis on experiential learning, as opposed to intensive academic study. A number of the chaplains in our sample had taken the 'Certificate in Muslim Chaplaincy' provided by Markfield Institute of Higher Education in Leicester. The last part of this chapter considers the significance of this course, the reflections of former students and the wider educational and training needs of Muslim chaplains in Britain today.

Training to be a Chaplain: The MIHE Course

Following several years of consultations with Christian chaplains and theological educators, the MIHE course was first launched in 2003. It offers participants a basic understanding of the range of contexts in which chaplaincy work is undertaken via eight days of training and a short residential programme, spread over seven months. At the time of writing, it remains unaccredited, but nevertheless it is often recognised as valuable in the public sector, especially in view of the lack of accredited alternatives. The emergence of the course marked an important stage in the transition from 'Visiting Minister' to 'Muslim Chaplain'. It signalled a point when a leading British Muslim educational institution began to take some control over the emerging field of 'Muslim chaplaincy' and recognised the educational potential of this sphere. It has also provided a social and professional space where Muslim chaplains of different backgrounds (or those aspiring to become chaplains) could build a sense of professional solidarity and community across different sectors. Not surprisingly, students of the MIHE course formed an association to try to sustain this sociability – the 'Association of Muslim Chaplains'. However, this body was remarkably short-lived, and lost momentum within a few years.

In the early parts of the course, students meet a range of experienced Christian chaplains from a range of sectors who offer an overview of the history, context and pastoral aspects of the work. Their input provides a platform for the subsequent input of Muslim chaplains who expose students to some of the challenges of the role, based on their own experiences. Students are often confronted with hypothetical scenarios, with the trainers in question probing and testing student responses. These were some of the situations they were asked to consider during our observation of the course in 2009:

-A Muslim prisoner has been continuously disrupting the Friday prayer and
has not heeded your warnings;
-You find out that your line-manager is living in a homosexual relationship;
-A senior member of a local Muslim community is sick in hospital. Members
of the congregation ask you, as the hospital chaplain, how he is.

Discussion of these scenarios present students with some of the realities and dilemmas they might encounter as chaplains, and an opportunity to explore their own reactions. Perhaps more importantly, they appreciate that there may be no single right or wrong answer to some challenges.

Integral to the course is a compulsory 60-hour placement. Early in the programme, students must find a host institution and a co-ordinating supervisor. Exposure to the lived realities of chaplaincy practice pushes students' religious, educational, personal and social boundaries, and gives them a sense of the frustrations and rewards of chaplaincy. For some MIHE students, a successful placement has sometimes led to eventual long-term employment in the host institution.

Students are attracted to the MIHE course for a range of reasons. Some are considering becoming chaplains, and want to test their vocation via a structured training programme. A number of quite experienced chaplains have felt the need to have 'certification', even via an unaccredited course, sometimes to satisfy their employing institution, or to bolster their own self-confidence. One chaplain joined the course to 'check' she was performing her role appropriately. Generally speaking, students often fall into one of three categories. They are either 'ulama who have Islamic knowledge but perhaps little pastoral skill, or they are committed Muslim community workers who feel they have pastoral skill, but often lack in-depth religious knowledge. A third group are simply 'exploring' chaplaincy as a possible career path.

The gender balance of students is variable, from being over 50 per cent female, to less than 10 per cent female, in some cohorts. But the mixed-gender teaching environment has been an important part of the educational experience:

[That year] more than 50 per cent were women. The dynamics changed in
the classroom because there were imams and there were women in the same

classroom. I remember the first day when they entered one of the imams was saying, 'where will the women sit?', you see, and I said 'you sit wherever you like, but I can't put a curtain between you, you have to sit in a classroom situation'. This was a shock for him. And the women were there, facing 'ulama for the first time as equals and the dynamic was that, OK, if this is the issue, let me quiz these imams. The dynamics changed ... so the imams were at the receiving end of that, but within 2 sessions, 2 months, 3rd month they've become very good friends. The imams ... they've become much more open (MIHE course teacher).

Although the course has developed, and remains valuable for those wishing to explore chaplaincy careers, there is now a critical mass of experienced chaplains whose educational needs are unmet. A number of our interviewees lamented the opportunity for more in-depth training that might enable them to reflect on their accumulated experience. Furthermore, as chaplains begin to gain sector-specific expertise, the value of more advanced sector-specific and inter-sector training is evident. For example, Muslim health care chaplains have acquired particular expertise around grief, sudden death and suicide, but these are issues that prison or higher education chaplains may also have to manage. The scope for sharing of expertise across sectors is now quite evident.

The value and significance of the MIHE course goes beyond the formal teaching and learning that it provides. It offers a marked-out route into chaplaincy. Its ethos as an Islamic college that welcomes visitors and students from very different backgrounds and faith traditions makes it an educational 'half-way house' between dar ul-uloom and wider society. As an outward-facing Islamic college, it provides the ideal setting for learning about chaplaincy. However, by virtue of what is taught and the choice of trainers, MIHE is an important part of the wider process of defining the Muslim chaplaincy profession. By giving legitimacy to particular voices it reinforces distinctive perspectives and approaches, thereby becoming part of the more general 'professionalising' of Muslim chaplaincy. However, there are now other training providers besides MIHE. The emergence of these initiatives points to the competition that is now shaping the effort to educate 'professional' Muslim chaplains.

The Inequalities of Training

Muslim chaplains have differential access to entry-level and continuous professional development training. These differences, and the inevitable inequalities that arise from them, are most apparent in relation to sector, contractual status and gender. However, against a background of very limited (if non-existent) opportunities in the early 2000s, there has been very rapid progress. For example, HM Prison Service has provided regular conferences and workshops, although the PVE funding stream that has supported this might be regarded as suspect by some (see Chapter 5). We were invited to contribute to one of these programmes and it was clear that in addition to the sharing of good practice and the opportunity to debate new issues, chaplains were benefitting from networking and mutual professional support. Most striking was the degree to which intra-faith debate was taking place, with chaplains from different schools of thought offering different Islamic perspectives on common (and sometimes very controversial) issues. The Prison Service has designed training programmes for Muslim chaplains that introduce complex religious challenges, with the deliberate aim of being disruptive of interpretive assumptions and established patterns of thought:

> So for example we have the whole issue of dog searching. Now it's a big thing in the Prison Services. Certain prisons are investing in disposable aprons that they put on visitors so that the dog does not touch their clothing. In the prison cell, for example, if a dog comes into search for drugs and so on, they remove the bedding from the prisoner and they get a fresh load of clothes, and all this is there because the Hanafis believe that the saliva of dog is najis [impure], whereas the Malikis believe that they're ok, all animals are clean ... we have nice little juicy discussions. We have maybe, about five or six very staunch Maliki scholars, so they'll debate on this issue, then you have the Shafi mix and the Hanafi mix, so it's quite good ... when we meet up in the evening we sit and we can discuss until early hours in the morning. And that I think I find very exhilarating (chaplaincy administrator).

New health care chaplains in the NHS attend a generic 'Induction' programme at the 'Cardiff Centre for Chaplaincy Studies' at St Michael's College in Wales. Courses increasingly accommodate Muslim participants. A similar introductory programme, but one more specifically tied to Muslim health care chaplaincy, is offered by 'Muslim Spiritual Care in the NHS' under the auspices of the Muslim Council of Britain (MCB). At the time of writing, discussions are underway between the MCB and St Michael's College regarding the possible accreditation of this programme.

Efforts to establish training resources for Muslim higher and further education chaplains have been proposed since the late 2000s by the 'Association of Muslim Chaplains in Education' (AMCed). However, new initiatives seem to founder for want of resources, and an insufficient critical mass of possible contributors. Meanwhile, those Muslim chaplains who are currently the only employees or volunteers in a particular sector (for example the military, HM Courts, retail shopping centres, airports, and police) have no faith-specific training available. Their training usually requires ability to 'Islamise' Christian chaplaincy training.

These inequalities around training point to differential opportunities to acquire the skills and the identity 'chaplain'. They also explain the variations that are now becoming apparent in the professionalization of Muslim chaplains, according to sector. Those working for HM Prison Service and the National Health Service enjoy far greater advantages, compared to those working in other spheres. These two public sector bodies can be credited with having stimulated the professional advancement of numerous Islamic scholars in Britain. However, our research demonstrated that alongside sector, contractual status and gender were also very significant factors that can make professional identity and advancement problematic. For example, several part-time chaplains noted that they had wanted to do the MIHE course (or indeed, other institutionally provided training programmes) but this created tensions with line-managers unwilling to fund their participation, or felt that continuing professional development should be done in 'their own time'. Part-time chaplains resented having to choose between the delivery of pastoral care, and the acquisition of new skills or knowledge within the limited time available to them.

Given that very few full-time chaplaincy positions are currently occupied by Muslim women, they are especially vulnerable to the inequalities that can derive from taking part-time or voluntary roles (Davies 1996). However, many of the Muslim women in our study noted that current training opportunities, including those offered by Islamic organisations, were often insensitive to the realities of their lives and their religious perspectives. Some women were juggling part-time chaplaincy work alongside caring responsibilities. Training programmes that required full-time attendance – perhaps a long way from home – made it difficult, if not impossible, for women to attend. Furthermore, some of the women we spoke to noted that their husbands/fathers were sometimes reluctant (on religious grounds) to allow their wives/daughters to travel unaccompanied, and to stay away from home overnight in order to attend mixed-gender training courses. Consequently, some Muslim women are indirectly excluded from the kind of training opportunities that might enable their professional advancement.

While most training programmes continue to be shaped by masculine visions of professional work (Davies 1996), the prospects for change remain limited. Indirect exclusion not only deprives women of opportunities to acquire new skills and knowledge, but also limits their scope for networking, and identification with role models and mentors. The structural position of Muslim women in chaplaincy today in many ways seems to mirror that of male 'visiting ministers' 20 years ago; their work is often part-time (or voluntary), confined to a particular locality and often undertaken in considerable isolation from peers. They might also be confined to particular dimensions of work, particularly those that are 'left over' at the point where male colleagues have drawn a boundary (for example women's ward/prison wing, mother and baby unit). Unless they happen to work within a particularly supportive chaplaincy team (and some do) most Muslim women in chaplaincy are deprived of the opportunity to take up broader institutional roles. At present, the number of Muslim women in chaplaincy in Britain who are exceptions to this general rule is probably less than five.

Conclusion

Despite the rapidity and the extent to which Muslim chaplains have been drawn into professional public sector chaplaincy, they are largely isolated from mainstream chaplaincy discourses, particularly those that are expressed in the written form. While it is now commonplace for experienced Muslim chaplains to contribute to conferences, training programmes or consultation exercises, they are rarely authoring books or journal articles about their work. For example, electronic chaplaincy discussion groups, such 'Chaplaincy-Spirituality-Health – a network for chaplains, educationalists and researchers' – has become a significant forum for sharing of experience, know-how and policy among health care chaplains in Britain. Muslim chaplains in the NHS might be receiving these communications but they are not publicly engaging with or contributing to them. Similarly, a search of key academic journals devoted to chaplaincy (for example *Journal of Health Care Chaplaincy*, *Scottish Journal of Health Care Chaplaincy*) has rarely (if ever) carried an article authored by a British Muslim chaplain. A number of Muslim higher education chaplains have authored religious books and articles, but these have not been directed towards chaplaincy, and the intended readership is predominantly Muslim (Siddiqui 2001). Recent professional publications about chaplaincy in Britain, some of which rest upon the contributions of practitioners and are directly concerned with multi-faith issues, do not include Muslim perspectives (see for example Threlfall-Holmes and Newitt 2011).

The lack of Muslim engagement in mainstream chaplaincy discourse is a reflection of the ongoing transition from 'visiting minister' to 'Muslim Chaplain'. But it is also a direct consequence of the educational profile of Muslim chaplains discussed earlier in this chapter. Experienced Muslim chaplains with in-depth religious knowledge who have trained as 'alims (currently an 'elite' group within the profession) do not currently have the *educational* capital – in terms of formal writing skills – to shape mainstream chaplaincy discourse, except at the level of policy. Meanwhile, Muslim chaplains with undergraduate and postgraduate degrees rarely have the requisite *religious* capital to shape Muslim chaplaincy practice or policy, and their predominance in part-time or voluntary roles limits them further still. This gap between educational and religious capital, which tends to fall along the fault line that divides the 'alims from the non-'alims has resulted in the creation of a professional 'space' that few Muslim chaplains in Britain are currently capable of filling. The lack of advanced chaplaincy training programmes for Muslim chaplaincy which carry greater academic content is perpetuating the impasse. Unless and until these are developed, the ongoing professionalization of Muslim chaplaincy will be hampered.

The apparent absence of Muslims within formal academic and professional chaplaincy discourse contrasts very significantly with their increasing presence, seniority, agency and practical influence within public institutions on a day-to-day basis. Furthermore, it is questionable as to how influential chaplaincy discourse actually is, at a day-to-day level, among those who actually deliver routine pastoral care? 'Chaplaincy Studies' is a nascent academic field that still lacks a professional journal, and the production of serious intellectual work remains sporadic. So in the next chapter, we map the practice of British Muslims working in chaplaincy in detail, and point to the ways in which they are using their social and religious capital to make distinctive contributions to the work of many chaplaincy departments.

Chapter 4
Chaplaincy Practice

Introduction

Thus far, we have established the background to Muslim chaplaincy in the UK and discussed the formation and identity of those who take up chaplaincy posts. In this chapter, we investigate what chaplains actually do in practice, and consider the extent to which their day-to-day work is shaped by gender, contractual status and whether they are religious scholars (or not). At its core, this chapter describes the ways in which Muslim chaplains undertake and facilitate Islamic practice within secular institutions, and the resources upon which they draw.

We did not undertake quantitative research for this book, so we make no attempt here to evaluate precisely how chaplains allocate their time to different activities. If all the time that is available is one four-hour session per week, there is little scope to engage in a wide variety of tasks. Meanwhile, a full-time chaplain may be able to do many different things. We simply try to present a picture of the sorts of things that chaplains typically might do on a regular basis, bearing in mind that some chaplains might never do, or contemplate doing them.

One of the objectives of our research was to explore the motivations and action guiding ideologies of chaplains, and the extent to which they are imitating, learning from or reacting against non-Muslim chaplaincy practices and models, explicitly and implicitly. These provide an opportunity for a more reflective and evaluative appreciation of Muslim chaplaincy practice, and we address these more theoretical issues in our concluding chapter (Chapter 8). For the time being, we are simply concerned to 'map' the work that Muslim chaplains carry out in their routine work. We focus on activities commonly and routinely undertaken by all chaplains, irrespective of their institutional setting, and we begin by describing those activities that are distinctive to Muslim chaplains as an important part of their own religious tradition for which they are bound to take primary responsibility. Thereafter, we look at broader activities, such as pastoral visiting or administration, which are common practice for chaplains of different religious traditions.

Chaplaincy Practices Distinctive to Islam

Friday Prayer

Due to the theological, social and spiritual significance of Friday prayer (explored in Chapter 2), it is not surprising to find that chaplains invest a good deal of time in ensuring that Friday prayers can be performed in their institutions. But it is here that gender differences become immediately apparent. We found that female chaplains are not particularly involved in the organisation of Friday prayer because, according to most interpretations of Islamic law, it is optional for them, as opposed to obligatory for men where possible. However, perhaps in an effort to mirror the practices of their male counterparts, some female prison chaplains have organised and led congregations for women on Fridays. When they are unable to do so (for practical or personal reasons) some female prisoners have contested their authority or judgement, as the following interview extract (derived from the experience of the only female Islamic scholar ('alima) currently working in HM Prison Service) makes clear:

Interviewer: Do you ever come in on Fridays?

Chaplain: No I don't. I don't come in on Fridays a) because as far as we were taught women don't have to partake in congregational prayers so I don't think there's a point in making things difficult for yourself! We've got the same [spiritual] reward for praying in our own rooms or cells, you know, there's no point in putting staff and the establishment under pressure. We had an inspector soon after I started and he was asking me … I think his main experience was with male establishments, and he said, 'there's no ablution facilities here, is that something that you're concerned about, and there is no prayer hall?'. I said 'it's not really an issue'. I think [the chaplaincy team here] were quite pleased with that because that's what they'd had with [the previous chaplain, Hiba], and there's always a fear when you have a new Muslim chaplain that she'll bring in a whole new set of rules and want everything changed.

Some of the [other] female chaplains [are] doing Friday prayers and a lot of the time it's because they don't know any better or they haven't been taught otherwise, but then the problem is when I have women transferring from other establishments they say 'well the last Muslim chaplain used to do Friday prayers with us, you're hopeless'! And I was like 'no I'm not'! Once I explain it to them, they're fine (part-time female prison chaplain).

Most male chaplains working in prisons invest a good deal of time in ensuring that Friday prayers are conducted in their establishment. One chaplain estimated that organising the event beforehand, preparing the sermon and attending might take up to 15 per cent of his time each week. The hourly investment increases considerably in establishments holding very large numbers of Muslim prisoners or in young offender institutions where congregational gatherings can pose a distinctive security risk. To mitigate these, some Muslim chaplains will spend time engaging in conflict resolution between prisoners beforehand (to minimise the risk of fighting) or carefully checking the names of those who have applied to attend. In this way, particularly troublesome prisoners can, if necessary, be excluded from the Friday prayer, only resuming attendance on the basis of good behaviour.

In large prisons, holding two separate Friday congregations can help to avoid disturbances, but this brings its own logistical and practical challenges. The movements of two large groups of prisoners, to and from Friday prayers, means that chaplains must make careful preparations to ensure the process happens smoothly, that wing staff are properly informed and that there are sufficient officers available to escort prisoners. However these tasks are managed, the administrative or pastoral workload can be significant, and this only increases if Friday prayers become a site of dispute or bad behaviour.

In one prison we visited, there had been a disturbance at Friday prayer during the previous week. One of the tasks of the chaplain in preparing for the upcoming prayers was to view CCTV footage of the fight with security staff, recorded via cameras installed in the prison mosque. Their task was to identify trouble-makers, evaluate the staff response and to ensure that the Friday congregation would be more peaceful the following week. Chaplains are therefore directly involved in managing religion in prisons in ways that go well beyond straightforward administration.

Friday prayers provide Muslim prison chaplains with unique opportunities to manifest and perform their religious authority, both to prisoners and to staff. By their body language, their dress, their demeanour and their speech, they often exercise a powerful influence on the behaviour of prisoners, and upon the perceptions officers may have about them.

For example, one prison chaplain noted that during a sermon, a prisoner new to Islam started to ask provocative questions. Other prisoners became angry at his interruptions, and asked the chaplain to remove the disruptive prisoner from the prayer hall. The officers present sensed the escalating tension, and were poised to call for security backup. The chaplain continues the story …

> So I stood up straight away and I told the staff 'actually, you need to back down because I'll take care of it … just you being in this alerted sense is agitating the prisoners even more'. So I sat the officers down, and I went forward and rather than telling the prisoner off, I said [to the others] actually 'where's the love, where's the mercy, the compassion that we should have for each other?'. This prisoner had a genuine question [and] although he should not have done it in this way, this Muslim brother is very new to Islam … probably doesn't understand the etiquettes of jumu'ah. So afterwards the officers came up to me and they go 'we don't know why we ever doubted that you'd control it'. And you know, rather than telling the prisoner off, which everyone expected, I actually told the others [prisoners] off. They went away with a different image of what Islam was. I could have easily told them off and said [to the officers] 'actually, please take him back', and it would have solved the problem … and it would have made all the prisoners happy. But it was the wrong thing to do. I just felt, no, why do I want to deprive this one guy from his jumu'ah, and actually I want to train the staff as well (full-time male prison chaplain).

Figure 4.1   Imam Farid Khan, Muslim Chaplain at HMP and YOI Parc, South Wales

Chaplains use Friday prayers as an opportunity to educate staff and prisoners about a range of religious and practical matters. Contested issues, such as jihad, substance abuse, gender and sexuality are all among the subjects that might form the basis for the Friday sermon. Meanwhile, in the weeks leading up to Ramadan, chaplains might use Friday prayers to advise prisoners on more mundane matters, such as how to clean their food flasks (used to keep their evening meal hot until sunset). It is more time efficient to do this during a collective gathering, rather than speaking with each prisoner individually. But when a prisoner is unexpectedly absent from Friday prayer, this can be the catalyst for chaplains to make a personal visit to his cell, to enquire after his well-being. This ability to extend the chaplaincy role to encompass pastoral follow-up work with individuals known personally to chaplains is a significant marker of the shift that has occurred since the early 2000s, from 'visiting minister' to 'Muslim Chaplain'.

The extent to which we have focused our discussion on Friday prayer in prisons is indicative of its institution-wide significance, and the amount of time that it can involve for chaplains, certainly in comparison to other sectors. Muslim prison chaplains facilitating two Friday congregations for up to 150–200 prisoners may be very fully occupied for at least two hours, not to mention the hours involved in preparation. In contrast, Muslim chaplains in the health service are often leading Friday prayers for busy medical staff, and the entire ritual may last no more than

30–40 minutes, with minimal preparation. It is no less significant, spiritually or socially of course, but their performance has few, if any implications for the overriding purpose of the institution. By contrast, Friday prayers in prisons can pose a significant security risk for an institution primarily concerned with the incarceration of criminals. Meanwhile, for Muslim chaplains in higher education, it is not so much a matter of organising or leading the Friday prayer, but more a question of trying to negotiate with the institution to enable students to attend, without missing lectures or examinations held on Friday lunchtimes, or supporting students to identify suitable preachers of the sermon.

Halal Food

In some ways, the rise and success of Muslim chaplaincy in British public services can be calibrated against the process of ensuring that sources and methods of preparation of food accord with religious needs for purity. To be acceptable to Muslims, meat and poultry must meet the Islamic requirements of slaughtering, as well as being free from coming into contact with non-halal products throughout production, delivery, storage, preparation, cooking and serving. The food must be prepared using utensils that are kept apart and cleaned under running water. If either of these conditions are unmet, food is ritually unclean and unacceptable. So the task of ensuring that Muslims, whether staff or service users, have access to halal food is central to allowing the full practice of Islam in public institutions. Many institutions have been slow to take this on board, and chaplains have struggled to ensure that halal precepts are observed.

Alongside the religious importance of halal food, the presence or absence of halal food in their institution functions as a personal barometer for chaplains to measure their effectiveness and success, or their inefficiency and failure. When we asked chaplains to tell us how they knew that they had been successful in their role, amongst other things, most of them mentioned their success in introducing or guaranteeing halal food for their clients. Where chaplains were unable to do this they expressed considerable frustration, and attributed their failure to institutional racism and discrimination. Some of the chaplains who have been successful in introducing halal food for clients are now working to ensure its provision in public canteens and visitor centres. But in addition to facilitating halal food locally, more senior chaplains are sometimes engaged in delivering national level cultural-awareness training programmes and lectures on the subject, as well as writing policies and conducting meetings with in-house catering departments. For the time being, the question of halal food is likely to remain a live issue.

The question of halal food in prisons, in particular, has been and remains of particular significance. In an environment where prisoners

> … are denied rights and opportunities enjoyed by the rest of the population …
> symbols of belonging and of commitment to revered sources of collective identity

tend to be highly prized and vigorously defended, especially if prisoners believe that disrespect is deliberately shown to them (Beckford and Gilliat 1998: 8).

The Prison Service Orders (PSO) offer strict guidelines related to halal food. These include policies related to delivery and reception, storage, production, serving, cooking and handling. For example, the PSO relating to the serving of food states that 'distinctly separate utensils must be identified and used for the serving of Muslim meals ... utensils must not travel across from Halal to Haram trays and vice-versa. It is desirable that Muslim prisoners are employed to serve the Halal meat dishes'.[1] With regard to holding it reads, 'when using hot cupboards and hot trolleys Halal dishes should be placed in a separate compartment wherever possible, and in any event must be covered and marked halal at all times. Separate utensils are to be used in the decanting process (Ibid.)'.

In their research with Muslims in British and French prisons, Beckford et al. found that the provision of halal food was a contested issue 'partly because of the wide discrepancy between prison officers' and inmates' perceptions' (Beckford et al. 2005: 107). These discrepant views were concentrated around issues of cross-contamination between halal and non-halal food during storage, handling or serving. Our research established that Muslim chaplains in prisons still invest considerable amounts of time in monitoring these boundaries, particularly once food has arrived in their institution.

This tends to involve ensuring that halal/non-halal utensils are colour-coded, using laser temperature monitors, and ensuring that halal food is shielded on both sides with metal sheets during serving. Flowing water must be used to wash the halal food utensils and dishes, and perhaps of more significance is the introduction of monitoring processes to ensure these standards are maintained.

> We monitor every unit randomly. We advise the staff on what is right and what is wrong. We have an Excel spreadsheet which we produce at the end of a few months, clocking up what has happened, where the cross contamination happened, and how to address it (full-time male prison chaplain).

During our fieldwork, we saw a 'halal food checklist' which required chaplains to tick the relevant 'yes' or 'no' box to indicate whether measures to prevent cross-contamination were being observed. But despite these efforts, cross-contamination still occurs due to staff ignorance, deliberate but subtle subversion of the policies and straightforward human error. Indeed, during research in one prison, we accompanied the chaplain to the canteen while he carried out a random check. He found that halal and non-halal utensils were being washed together, without the use of running water. He was obviously disappointed and took immediate action to notify kitchen staff. Meanwhile, one female prison

---

[1]   PSO 5000, p.30, www.justice.gov.uk/.../psipso/pso/PSO_5000_prison_catering_service, [accessed 28/05/2012].

chaplain we spoke to said that the constant misuse of utensils reserved for the preparation of halal food was becoming an equality and diversity issue in her establishment.

Arising out of the tensions and disputes about the cross-contamination of halal food, another issue that has occupied Muslim chaplains is more centrally to do with the religious/legal question of 'what counts' as halal. As the number of Muslim prison chaplains increased after the early 2000s, along with the growing inclusion of chaplains from different schools of Islamic thought, discrepant interpretations regarding the authenticity of different methods of slaughter became highly contested. Although these issues are now largely resolved, it is worth hearing what some of the Muslim chaplains in our study had to say on this issue, because their views point to much larger questions about the 'authenticity' of Islamic rituals and practices in a non-Muslim society, and the role of Muslim chaplains in deliberating these.

The problem first arose when chaplains found that the so-called 'halal' meat and poultry did not conform to what they regarded as the exact conditions for halal slaughter. Islamic law dictates that animals should be individually slaughtered and the name of God (the bismillah) must be invoked by the slaughterer on each animal, at the time of slaughter. Since this inhibits mass production, some halal abattoirs have used mechanical slaughtering and have tried to conform to Islamic law either by blessing the knife with the name of God, or using a voice recording of the 'bismillah' played on a loop, whilst the animals were slaughtered on a conveyor belt using a mechanical blade. For some Muslim chaplains this process of slaughter rendered meat haram (forbidden).

In March 2009, a full-time prison chaplain in London noted that,

> … we're having *huge, huge* problems with it because there's so many differences of opinion as to what you would class as halal and what you wouldn't. And the meat that we have in the Prison Service, it is mechanically slaughtered and the tasmiya [reading the name of Allah] is probably a 'blessed blade' or has a tape recorder or something like that. Is that halal or not? Prisoners come and ask you all the time, 'imam is it halal'? Some imams will just stand up and say, 'the food here is haram' and they've done that, a lot of imams have done that.

Not surprisingly, this scenario raised serious concerns for Muslim prisoners, for Governors and for catering managers. Governors were understandably confused as to why their Muslim chaplains might regard meat as unacceptable, despite it being labelled with certification describing it as authentically halal.

This issue became so contested (among Muslim chaplains themselves) that the PSC Headquarters and the Muslim Advisor had to establish a process of consultation with Islamic scholars to resolve the question as to what might count as a 'halal' method of slaughter. After much negotiation and deliberation a workable solution to the problem was achieved, and one that, not surprisingly, conformed to more conservative strands of Islamic thought. The Prison Service in

England and Wales has now found a provider in Ireland for poultry, and there are ongoing efforts to find a halal provider for beef and lamb. The poultry provided by the Irish company is checked by an individual, and certification paperwork carries the logo of the Ministry of Justice and the Prison Service. The wording reads: 'Certificate of authentication: HALAL'. Underneath, it states,

> I certify that the meat is halal and has in all of its stages met the requirements contained in the HMPS Halal standard as set out by Islamic Law. I certify that: i) the slaughterer was a Muslim; ii) every animal was manually slaughtered; iii) the tasmiya was said verbally on every animal; iv) that tagging/packaging was appropriately monitored.

It carries the name of the slaughterhouse, the plant number, the date of slaughter, the name and signature of certifier, the product and number of boxes, a traceability code and a best before date.

Despite these efforts, the problem of cross-contamination is found across all sectors, even in prisons. But well-networked Muslim prison chaplains working for a single employer (HM Prison Service) with centrally determined regulations have been especially effective in lobbying for more stringent regulation of these issues, and are better placed to challenge bad practice. By contrast, Muslim chaplains in the health service told us that they sometimes advise patients that so-called 'halal' food may not be reliably so.

The question of 'what counts' as halal remains unresolved, both within NHS Trusts, and in higher education institutions. This is a reflection of discrepant views held by Muslims in Britain more widely, and the existence of rival certification bodies that reflect different schools of thought (Gilliat-Ray 2010b).

Observance of Ramadan and Celebration of Eid Festivals

Adult Muslims who are fit and healthy are required to maintain a dawn-to-dusk fast during the Islamic month of Ramadan. Muslims who may have neglected daily prayers for much of the year will often make particular effort to observe the requirements of the Ramadan fast. Alongside its spiritual importance, it is a time of increased sociability and thus poses particular challenges for Muslims who are incarcerated, hospitalised or otherwise separated from their families.

Ramadan impinges on the work of chaplains in most institutions, but in very different ways. For example, higher education chaplains may try to negotiate alternative examination periods for students observing long fasts during the summer months. Although hospital patients are likely to be exempt from fasting on medical grounds, some individuals chose to fast anyway, and it may be important for chaplains either to support them in this, or to use religious arguments to deter them. This can become very important if, for example, patients are refusing to take life-saving medication. Here the religious authority of an 'alim can be especially important.

Not surprisingly, Ramadan poses particular issues in prisons. Like halal food, it is of symbolic importance to prisoners; the degree to which institutions support their observance of the fast is another of the markers by which Muslims feel they are being treated fairly and with dignity by the institution (Marranci 2009). During Ramadan, Muslim prisoners will require food at different times from all other inmates, and this involves a very significant adjustment in the normal routines of an institution structured by highly regulated regimes. Because of the disruption involved, many Muslim prison chaplains will begin preparations for Ramadan several months beforehand, talking to catering services, prison officers, Governors and so on. Having these conversations seems to be far easier for chaplains who are employed full-time in the same institution, and likewise becomes harder for part-time or sessional chaplains.

Ramadan interrupts the normal flow of time and activity in prison regimes, and it is precisely this disruption that creates opportunities for chaplains to draw upon the social and religious capital of the wider Muslim community. The daily fast in Ramadan is broken at sunset each day with 'iftar', which traditionally involves eating dates and drinking water or milk (thereby emulating the example of the Prophet Muhammad). These provide rapid sustenance prior to offering the maghrib prayer (sunset) and then eating a full meal. In Muslim communities, iftar is a highly social event to which all are welcome. Some prison chaplains endeavour to replicate this sociability within their establishments, deliberately inviting senior managers. One chaplain commended a local mosque for their proactive support of Muslim offenders:

> The mosque is very active, they'll come during Ramadan, they'll send imams to do the qira'at [recitation of Qur'an] and lead sermons, they will sponsor iftars. Fantastic thing they do which the Governors love … so all the Governors and staff … we've had twenty-thirty before, they go over and the hospitality is *brilliant*, it really is. The Governors just love it! And I think actually, that's the Islam I want them to see, you know what I mean [laughs] (full-time male prison chaplain).

Preparing for the Eid celebrations at the end of Ramadan also involves considerable amounts of time for most chaplains, especially those working in prisons. Many prison chaplains will do their utmost to support prisoners suffering isolation from their families and communities. Some chaplains mitigate this by arranging for visitors from a local mosque to come into the establishment to join the Eid festivities, or make provision for curry and other dishes to be donated from local Muslim charities. They will endeavour to make the event as sociable and as celebratory as possible. In many prisons, Eid is now an inter-religious, institution-wide event attended by senior staff. The communications and networking that now shape the celebration of Eid in many prisons reflects the cumulative investment of time by chaplains, over many years. But it is also indicative of the fact that Muslim prisoner experiences can be highly variable, depending upon the networks of social and religious capital upon which chaplains are able to draw, or not.

Apologetics and Teaching: Explaining Islam to Others

All Muslim chaplains in any context would see it as an important part of their role to personally exemplify and to commend Islam by their demeanour and behaviour, as well as by speech and preaching. This stops short of direct proselytisation, but there is much rejoicing if people convert or renew their commitment to faith, matched by unhappiness and concern if they fall away from it.

In the context of public institutions, where a main part of their role is to make the practice of Islam possible, an important role then for Muslim chaplains is explaining aspects of Muslim faith and practice to outsiders such as staff members and fellow clients. Chaplains believe that the onus is on them to correct any misunderstandings of Islam that staff have.

One hospital chaplain developed a 'frequently-asked-questions' sheet on Islam to distribute in the wards. In hospitals chaplains may find themselves explaining to clinicians why pregnant women will not attend maternity scans in Ramadan (they cannot drink water during the day, and therefore will not have the required full bladder necessary for an accurate scan result), or why certain customs must be observed at death. This quotation below illustrates this point:

> One day the Chronic Pain Consultant rang me and she said, 'we have a patient in the hospital, and we think this patient has got mental health issues, because he's fastened his leg and won't walk and he doesn't want to talk to us and he's saying his pain is too much … we are referring him to the Mental Health Institute'. I said, 'I don't think it's probably that. How old is the patient, around 60? Maybe he hasn't got that … it could be a form of him managing his pain'. I explained, 'In India and Pakistan, when people are working in the fields, when they are in pain they will fasten something tight around the legs or arms or wherever they have pain. That is the way they look at it because they can't afford to get treatment'. That was very very eye-opening for them … the cultural aspect of how people manage their pain (full-time male hospital chaplain).

As a consequence of this interaction, the chaplain became centrally involved in working with clinicians to help Muslim patients manage chronic pain. It is unlikely that he could have done this work effectively without being both an Islamic scholar ('alim), full-time, and able to translate between different linguistic, cultural, religious and institutional worldviews.

In prisons, female chaplains might have to explain why they wear headscarves, why male Muslim prisoners wish to turn up their trousers so they fall above their ankles (in imitation of the Prophet) or why they want to carry small tooth-cleaning sticks (again, imitating the Prophet). Many chaplains are treated as experts not only on Islam but also on all Asian religions, so they may be asked to explain why Sikhs or Hindus adopt the practices that they do. Understandably, they do not always welcome this.

One of the main roles that 'alims, imams and Muslims steeped in faith have towards others is that of exemplifying and teaching the religious tradition both by example and word. While there is little scope for a formal, extended teaching role about Islam in health care it can nevertheless occur informally. For example, hospitalised patients with the prospect of only a few weeks of life may nevertheless ask chaplains to help them learn Quranic Arabic, so that they can recite the Qur'an correctly. Sickness and death can be occasions for chaplains to remind Muslim clients about God's mercy.

Educational activity is much more significant in the prison and education sectors. In higher education, chaplains may work closely with the Islamic Society, teaching students about basic issues in Islam, including responding to textual readings, sermons and other things that might promote 'extremism'. In prisons, the teaching role is an elaborated one, partly because prisoners may be very ignorant about the basics of their faith (some of them convert or recommit to their faith in prison). In a number of prisons we visited, prisoners could choose to take a range of Islamic classes, from basic to advanced. They might learn how to pray, how to read the Qur'an in Arabic, and acquire an understanding of Islamic teaching on issues pertinent to their offending behaviour, such as substance abuse. The production and delivery of this kind of teaching can be far easier for trained Islamic scholars. This is especially the case in those prisons holding individuals for terrorism-related offences; these prisoners might have a particularly in-depth knowledge of Islamic texts, even if their interpretations are misguided.

Prayer and Recitation of the Qur'an

Alongside formal daily prayers, Muslims also engage in informal supplication to God. They may pray in much the same way as people from other traditions, by asking for God's help in relation to themselves, or others, in their own form of words. Not surprisingly, this kind of supplicatory prayer is especially important in the work of health care chaplains, but features very little in the work of higher education chaplains. In prisons, chaplains are occasionally asked to pray for, or with, inmates. These prayers usually relate to requests for God's mercy and forgiveness for the crime committed, or a good outcome to a court appearance. Prisoners may also request the prayers of chaplains when they lose a loved-one, and have been refused an application to attend the funeral prayer (usually this will be on the grounds of security).

This is exactly the scenario that one of the chaplains in our study encountered. He deemed that the best pastoral response for the grieving prisoner would be to allow him to offer the funeral (janazah) prayer in his cell, as far as possible at the same time as the funeral prayers were being read at the graveside outside the prison. This decision was directly contrary to the school of law in which this chaplain had trained:

> Now the fiqh [legal tradition] that I follow … I don't read gha'ib salat al-janazah [absent funeral prayer], you know if [the body of the deceased] is not there you don't read the janazah salah [funeral prayer] but in the hadith [teachings of the Prophet] and there are certain other 'ulama [scholars] that follow that if the person's not there, you still read. And I said [to the prisoner], 'look fine, if you want to read it, this is the way you read it'. Now normally outside I would never have done that. But here I know I have to do that, I have to give him something and because it's based in shar'iah. 'That's up to you' I said, 'at the end of the day it's up to you, if you're going to do it that's fine, if you don't want to do it, that's fine as well, but I'm giving you an option' (full-time male prison chaplain).

This illustration of the way in which a Muslim chaplain may have to facilitate prayer is interesting for a number of reasons. In particular, it shows how chaplains may be willing to adjust their own personal theological position for the benefit of others and a good pastoral outcome. In this particular case, the prisoner's grief, and the restrictions of the prison setting, provided the justification for the chaplain's actions. Ironically, the confines of a prison, both physically and bureaucratically, enabled the development of imaginative religious practice and thought. Alongside this, however, we must note the fact that the chaplain states explicitly that he would not have exercised such 'free-thinking' outside the prison. Our research shows that this recognition of exceptionality is not unusual.

A female prison chaplain explained how she had dealt with a similar scenario:

> I have had to deal with a bereavement that a prisoner had … in Africa, somewhere far away, so they couldn't even get there. I just asked … whether she wanted to pray together … so we offered some nafal salat [supererogatory prayer] and then just made du'a [supplication] for the person … that Allah forgives their sins and carves them a place in jannah [paradise] and then I have asked, 'cos she wasn't able to read the Qur'an in Arabic, whether she wanted me to read like, Surah Yasin, and then she repeated it after me, so I have done that … and I think the prisoner felt she was doing something (part-time female prison chaplain).

Supplication can form a major element of visits to hospital patients and their families as a response to pain, illness, anxiety (about self or others), imminent death or guilt (Padela et al. 2012). Most health care chaplains, irrespective of their gender, religious qualification or contractual status, reckon to spend at least

Figure 4.2   Maulana Mohammed Arshad, Head of Chaplaincy, Bradford Teaching
Hospitals NHS Foundation Trust, praying with a patient

some time in prayer or recitation of the Qur'an in the context of bedside visits
to patients.

Learning perhaps from Christian counterparts, many chaplains ensure they
have prayer cards or prayer leaflets with them (sometimes in more than one
language, for example, Urdu) to leave with patients, thereby overcoming any
potential problems of infection control. They may also use prayer beads, to recite
the 99 Names of God. In the hospital setting, however, chaplains of both genders
must exercise particular caution in either carrying or giving to patients copies of
the Qur'an or selected portions of it. This is because patients may be unable to
perform the ritual ablutions that are required before handling the holy text.

During our fieldwork, we saw patients request prayer in different ways.
Sometimes they asked chaplains to pray with them at the bedside, and sometimes
they simply requested 'remember me in your prayers'. Chaplains also took the
initiative by offering to pray in this way. Not surprisingly, when chaplains recite
portions of the Qur'an from memory, they often used those verses deemed to
have particular healing power (see Chapter 2), and it was notable that qualified
religious scholars (of both genders) tended to make much more use of prayers in
Arabic, compared to non-'alims.

For the most part, there is clear understanding of the main principles and
practices that must be facilitated if Muslims are to be able fully to practice their

religion in secular institutional contexts. However, there is some evidence that some Muslim chaplains, in some institutions, try to expand the desirable into the absolutely essential. For example, some chaplains have tried to argue that a feast at Eid (immediately after Eid prayers) or the wearing of particular styles of Islamic dress is essential to being a Muslim in the prison context. While these things might certainly be desirable and would be expected of pious Muslims outwith institutional life, they are not essential to the practice of the faith. Most Muslim chaplains recognise that this is the case.

Thus far, we have identified some of the principal ways in which the role of Muslim chaplains is distinctive on account of specialist religious knowledge and skills. An appreciation of what constitutes ritual purity, how particular rituals are to be performed (or adapted according to the context), critically depends upon an ability to appreciate and deploy a particular body of religious knowledge. In the following pages, we go on to explore how Muslim chaplains undertake activities that are likely to be routine for chaplains of most religious traditions. We are especially alert to the way in which Muslims carry out these tasks, but from a distinctive Islamic perspective.

Pastoral Care for Individuals

An experienced hospital chaplain described himself as being rather like a spiritual 'satellite navigation' system for patients in the midst of illness:

> It's about restoring that faith that they have and for a slight moment they are not lost, but there's a shadow, it's cloudy. It's like you're on the motorway and you think, 'am I on the right route or not'? You're still travelling until your satnav says, take the next left in 200 yards or something and you think, yes, I am on the right route ... and I see that I am that satnav (full-time male hospital chaplain).

A main component of all chaplaincy work, irrespective of religious tradition, is formed by encounters with individuals, both clients and staff. Often these are brief, casual encounters which may lack depth and substance but may not lack significance and meaning. However, pastoral encounters can be more conscious and intentional, taking the form of visits. The nature of such visits and care encounters varies very significantly across sectors, but, irrespective of context, our data shows that the more senior and responsible chaplains become, the less time they spend visiting clients, especially on a 'cold-calling' basis. It is also evident that Muslim chaplains have learnt skills of client-led pastoral care:

> I've had an old man burst into tears ... even though many men won't cry in front of women, but it does happen. So when that happens then the doors are completely open for a whole different dialogue after that. [I am] just to be there and to give whatever they need or they *want* should I say, not even

in my perspective of what they need but what *they want,* so then things will happen like, 'Can you tell me what you believe … do you think that it's possible that I'm coming back to hospital all the time because I'm being punished for something or because I'm not praying or …' you know some people start asking those questions (part-time female hospital chaplain).

In higher education, personal encounters tend to take place in public spaces where chaplains put themselves consciously in the way of meeting people. So thcy might hang around the prayer hall at lunch time to meet students, or join them for coffee in student cafés. Chaplains report that some of the issues they discuss in one-to-one encounters include marital problems, inter-cultural marital issues, drinking problems, examinations and academic success and help.

In hospitals, visits to specific patients are at the core of practice. These visits are sometimes at the request of patients or their families, or staff, and sometimes they are an outcome of pastoral 'hanging around'. A phrase long associated with Christian chaplaincy work is that of 'loitering with intent' (Johnston and McFarland 2010; Pattison 1994), a phrase which describes a policy of having deliberately 'unstructured time' (Pattison 1994: 180) to wander about the institution to see what might unfold along the way. Relatively few Muslim chaplains appear to have adopted this kind of policy, and even part-time chaplains, less implicated in the time-structuring round of training programmes, administration or meetings, still tended to organise their 'rounds' according to deliberate routines and specific referrals. A personal encounter can take place in a ward, corridor, quiet room or bedside, and might involve a whole range of activities, such as listening, advising, comforting, praying, reciting scripture, patient advocacy and so on.

Most chaplains aim to meet the needs of the patient by addressing their agenda, listening and being non-judgemental. Inevitably, other conversations with staff and visitors are born from these encounters. So secondary outcomes of pastoral visiting are the discussions that happen on corridors and in staff bays, and these can turn into opportunities to dispel misunderstandings about Islam. Most chaplains reckon to talk to, and to help non-Muslim patients if the opportunity presents itself, and most were emphatic that they were available to all patients and staff, not just Muslims.

For chaplains working in prisons, some kinds of pastoral visiting are obligatory. Prisoners held in the segregation unit, in the hospital wing, or those who have just arrived in the establishment are visited daily. Chaplains also take significant responsibility for undertaking tasks that other staff might find difficult, such as breaking bad news to prisoners about illness or bereavement in the family. Other occasions for pastoral visiting include responding to requests by prisoners to convert to Islam, explaining religious texts and helping prisoners to learn classical Arabic, to simply helping prisoners manage the prison regime.

Insofar as pastoral encounters with individuals who are strangers has become a mainstay of Muslim chaplaincy practice, and insofar as these encounters are taken to be non-judgemental and client-led, it would seem that this is a direct import from Christian and secular professional practice. As we have seen in Chapter 2, pastoral care in Muslim communities tends to revolve around families, not paid professionals, so the apparent development of a pastoral role that rests on counselling skills, such as non-judgemental listening, is a significant innovation. We consider the implications of this in more depth in Chapter 8.

Family and Community Liaison

A very distinctive emphasis of Muslim over most Christian chaplaincy practice is to be found in the amount of time that must be given over to family and community liaison. As we have noted, care and concern for individuals within Islam is largely mediated through families and communities, so chaplains cannot either replace these wider relationships or ignore them. Indeed, a major part of their work is to link with families, certainly within health care and particularly when problems arise.

Chaplains become conspicuously engaged in family liaison work in hospitals when large crowds of visitors arrive to visit the dying or recently deceased. This can be difficult both for other patients and clinical staff, especially if there are anxieties or tensions. Some chaplains have developed a repertoire of skills to enable compassionate 'crowd control' (see Chapter 6, p. 126). As death approaches, chaplains often have an important role in informing both families and staff of what is going on, and the rituals that must be performed after the patient has passed away. This is especially the case in families where not all members are Muslim. Britain's religious diversity is mirrored in microcosm in family structures, and the occasion of death might require chaplains to explain the requirements for an Islamic burial, and undertake significant liaison between families and religious organisations:

> Sometimes I do go to funeral arrangements, particularly when it's a mixed family. For example the brother that died whose family were all Christian … I made sure I went to the mosque and I was there, that the family would feel that they were part of the funeral because they feel, this is our loved one and we don't know what's happening. All this Muslim community do the prayers and everything and we're just standing here and they feel so left out and some terrible things can happen and do happen I'm afraid to say, so I'm very protective about that and I will try to ensure that I am there and I will speak to whoever I can beforehand, I will talk to the imam of the mosque and I will say, 'please, if you brother will speak and say some English words for the family to feel that they are part of this funeral process', or if now, get somebody else in to say something or I will find somebody to come in or I'll do it myself if you want, but could we please make them feel that they were part of it as well. I'll do that kind of thing (part-time female hospital chaplain).

Institutional chaplaincy in many ways cuts across the sense of 'community' and 'brotherhood' that is an intrinsic part of Islam. For many chaplains the issue is not whether or not to be involved in the communities and families of clients, but how far to be involved. To some extent this is governed by temperament and opportunity, but pastoral responsibility clearly extends far beyond the individual in their institutional context and it really seems to be a case of seeing how far they wish to go. A number of chaplains own to keeping in contact with patients and their families long after they have left the institution.

Administration

Chaplains were not particularly interested in talking explicitly or at length about their administrative work, but nearly all of them, at whatever level and however few hours they work, are involved in a variety of administrative activities. One part-time chaplain reported that most of the two hours he was paid for each week was spent on answering e-mails and basic office work. One chaplain joked ironically that he spent all day in his office, while another quipped that he turned on his computer at the beginning of the day and that was that.

In addition to attending meetings of the chaplaincy team, chaplains often get involved in other meetings in their institutions and beyond, for example about racial equality, care of the dying and so on. Generally, the higher up the organisation and more paid hours a chaplain has, the more they are likely to be involved in administration and organisational meetings and the less they are involved in day-to-day visiting and work with clients. This would be generally true for non-Muslim chaplains too. Senior, co-ordinating chaplains often depend on junior colleagues and volunteers to get the routine work of pastoral visiting and organisation of worship done.

Training and Staff Education

Like most chaplains of all religious traditions, many Muslim chaplains, whether full or part-time, are involved in staff training and education, both formally and informally. Typically, they take part in generic courses informing staff about chaplaincy as well as specifically Islamic awareness courses where people are taught about cultural awareness, Ramadan awareness and issues related to Muslim women and gender equality. In the health sector, chaplains can be involved in giving Islamic perspectives on mental health, death and bereavement and equality and diversity. Some chaplains in this sector also train chaplaincy volunteers and undertake Islamic medical ethics training at universities. In prisons, training of staff might also focus on equality and diversity or race relations. But a new dimension of Muslim chaplaincy training work now also includes security and counter-radicalisation.

Staff training is often delivered via formal courses, but Muslim chaplains also educate staff members in other, less formal ways. They answer the questions of staff as they go about their work, even using humour as a way of challenging ignorance. One female chaplain for instance told us that when people ask her about why she wears the hijab, she says, 'I've had a bad hair day. I haven't got ten minutes to explain this to you but catch me at lunchtime and we'll talk' (part-time female prison chaplain). Some other prison chaplains admit to using the sermon at Friday prayers as an opportunity to teach people about Islam, thereby educating non-Muslim officers (as well as prisoners) about the truths of Islam beyond stereotyped misunderstandings. Sadly, however, we did not find out nearly as much about the content and methods used by chaplains in their training activities as would have been desirable to provide a more complete picture of this aspect of their work.

Interpreting, Translating and Use of Language

Due to the wide range of ethnic groups whose members are Muslims, many of whom are immigrants, interpreting is often a vital and time-consuming, if unofficial, activity undertaken by Muslim chaplains. Some chaplains know a number of different languages, and in some situations, they may be the only people on the staff of an institution who can speak to particular clients. This can be very important, as in the case of one health care chaplain who was able to explain to ward staff that a patient was consistently missing his evening meal because it coincided with a daily medical procedure outside the ward. Normally such a person would be able to make this known, but language difficulties can obviate normal channels of communication. Service users are often relieved to be able to speak in a language other than English, even if it is not their own first language. For some service users, being able to speak to someone who understands their language is vital to their sense of well-being. They can express their grievances and complaints with ease and in ways that would have been difficult, if not impossible, had the chaplain not been able to speak their language. For prison chaplains, the capacity to be able to understand and speak the language used by street gangs is an added bonus in winning the trust and confidence of prisoners. It is a skill developed out of many hours of listening to prisoners.

Chaplains also use language as means to self-empowerment. When prisoners are waiting to be escorted back to their wings after Friday prayers – a particularly difficult period of time to manage – chaplains who use religious vocabulary can use this to assert their authority and control on prisoners. Language is also sometimes used by chaplains as a means of communicating with one another. In prisons holding large numbers of Muslim prisoners, it may be routine for there to be more than one Muslim chaplain present at particular times in the week. Depending on their background, they may prefer to speak to one another in a shared community language, rather than relying on the use of English. Some chaplains told us there were double standards around this matter. On the one hand, some prison staff were suspicious and resentful about this language use (or the use of Arabic with Muslim prisoners) but the same officers would not think twice about asking a chaplain to interpret for them.

The capacity to be able to speak in languages other than English and to be able to translate can be seen as part of chaplains' care and advocacy for their co-religionists (and indeed for other non-English speakers). However, chaplains themselves are a bit wary of being taken for granted as translators, or as one chaplain says 'clinical interpreters'. They tend to see translating as a vehicle for their work, and are cautious about letting it become one of the central reasons for their value in the institution.

Miscellaneous Activities and Troubleshooting

Depending on their contexts, Muslim chaplains, like chaplains of other religious traditions, can become involved in all manner of miscellaneous activities that all build up their relationships with their clients and colleagues. In the health sector, many of the important miscellaneous activities revolve around life and death. So chaplains may make the call to prayer (the adhan) in the ears of newborn babies, help to name children, arrange for families to see their deceased relatives, take part in funerals and expedite death certificates. Court chaplains can find themselves referring clients to services such as housing support, alcohol detoxification centres, food and shelter providers, as well as filling in forms for them. Community chaplains concerned with prisoners leaving jail may meet them at the gates and from there help them to get involved in the community. Many requests can be quite pragmatic, such as arranging gym sessions for women that are supervised by female warders in prisons, making phone calls for prisoners, or helping students to access hardship funds. All of these small services can take time, but can make a good deal of difference to the lives of service users.

During our research, it became evident that some chaplains have a vital part to play in 'troubleshooting'. One of our interviewees told us about a pastoral incident where he had been able to broker the resolution of an especially sad and difficult incident, requiring of him an ability to bridge a range of linguistic and cultural divides involving grieving families, senior hospital managers and a community-based health care team. His account indicated the depth and quality of the relationships that he had evidently established with the most senior clinical and managerial staff of the hospital, and the critical troubleshooting role that he had played in managing what could have been a public relations disaster for the hospital. Meanwhile, a prison chaplain was able to persuade a suicidal prisoner not to take his own life, which in this case he was threatening to do by swallowing broken glass from the television set in his cell. Some of the most important work done by Muslim chaplains is therefore 'off the record', virtually impossible to document and far from the public gaze.

Ethical Issues

Islam, like other Abrahamic religions, is extensively concerned with right behaviour and action and so it might be expected that ethical issues and problems would be a main, overt concern of Muslim chaplains in all sectors. However, our research does not directly reflect this. In prisons, for example, the only overtly ethical issue that was identified as such was the question of whether or not it is legitimate to accept funding raised from gambling in the National Lottery for a community chaplaincy project (it is, it was concluded, in certain qualified circumstances). In higher education and in prisons there is much concern about preventing extremist religiously inspired action, which might be construed as an ethical issue broadly understood. But it is only really in health care that ethical issues form a major area of chaplaincy concern and effort. Here, ethical issues can be divided into those concerned with being a chaplain, particularly a female chaplain, and ethical issues arising in chaplaincy practice.

With regard to chaplaincy practice, many chaplains were concerned that the advice they might give on ethical issues should be accurate and authoritative. Examples include decisions as to when a life-support machine can be switched off, whether a pregnancy can be terminated or whether a particular form of medication containing bovine products can be used if there are no alternatives. Many ethical problems arise once people are dead: are still-born babies permitted to have the prayers and rituals associated with the dead if they have not had life beyond the womb (as would now be common in hospitals for non-Muslims)? How can the cremation of aborted foetuses be prevented? How can chaplains ensure the proper treatment of corpses so that modesty is maintained as much in death as in life? This means making sure that bodies are covered properly and not seen naked by non-related persons. Beyond this, patients often seek advice on treatment issues: what practices should be followed when male doctors, such as obstetricians, have to look after Muslim women in labour, or when male coroners may need to inspect the bodies of dead Muslim women? Can alcohol be legitimately used as a routine sterilising agent by Muslims?

Chaplains seeking to mediate authoritative teaching and guidance in these kinds of situations are under a great deal of pressure from patients to find the 'right' answer. Patients want to be assured that they are obeying the will of God. This reflects the importance in Islam of legal exactitude as the eternal destinies of both the chaplain and the patient may be at stake if the wrong judgement is given. It is not surprising, then, that many chaplains believe that it is necessary to be an 'alim in order to be able to do their jobs effectively. But at the same time, they want to share this onerous responsibility by 'ringing round the scholars', individuals whose judgement they value, and whose authority they can rely on. This authoritative advice-giving style of dealing with patients involves giving them information, but in a non-judgemental way. It does not extend to telling them what to do. Some Muslim chaplains are very clear about the distinctiveness of the institutional chaplaincy role in comparison with community-based leadership roles:

> As a chaplain what I would do is present the information ... and it's up to them
> to decide. When I am sitting on the minbar (pulpit) [in the community], I will
> tell the person what to do (part-time male hospital chaplain).

This belief in being non-judgemental, certainly within chaplaincy, is perhaps
influenced by institutional expectations and the example of non-Muslim chaplains
whose practice has been shaped by liberal, individualistic counselling paradigms
of care and communication. The point of particular interest here, however, is the
ability of chaplains, especially those retaining community-based leadership roles,
to alter their style of religious authority according to institutional context.

Alongside particular ethical issues that chaplains might face in their work, there
are a number of everyday situations that can make them uncomfortable, irrespective
of sector. As chaplains become exposed to new people and communities, as well as
the bureaucratic workings of public institutions, they are confronted by situations
which often require an ability to think and act in new ways.

A simple example of what this might mean in practice can be seen in relation
to the differing norms surrounding gender relations within and outside Islamic
communities. Most schools of Islamic law regard any physical contact between
unrelated men and women (even a simple handshake) as sinful, and contrary
to the teachings of Islam (Haneef 1979; Khuri 2001). Aisha, the Prophet
Muhammad's wife said, 'No, by God, the Prophet never touched the hand of a
woman' (al-Bukhari). But the requirements of modesty and assumptions about
the separation of unrelated men and women can pose particular challenges in the
mixed-gender context of a British prison or hospital where conventional norms
of formal greeting are likely to include shaking hands.

This issue became a challenge for one newly appointed hospital chaplain.
He admitted to being reserved toward female non-Muslim colleagues, refusing
to 'look them in the eye' or shake their hand. His behaviour was interpreted
as discriminatory and misogynist, and formal disciplinary action was taken
against him. Subsequent mentoring by a more experienced Muslim chaplain,
however, offered him a new perspective on traditional assumptions about gender
relations. Although he explained to the senior chaplain that his understanding of
Islamic law did not permit contact with members of the opposite gender, even
for professional reasons, his more experienced colleague rejected this narrow
legal interpretation. He explained that in a public workplace, a theology of
pluralism should prevail. This is because chaplains have to encounter people
with many different religious, philosophical and ideological beliefs which may
be at odds with their personal worldviews, at times. The more experienced
chaplain explained how his own approach, developed over some years, involved
a consideration of the different weight and significance of individual sin, as
against collective sin. He argued that if the newly appointed chaplain deemed
shaking hands with the opposite gender as sinful, it would, nevertheless, only
constitute an individual sin. In contrast, if the outcome of not shaking hands was
the portrayal of a negative and bigoted picture of Islam, this would become a far

more serious collective sin. He suggested that in such circumstances preference must always be given to maintaining a positive impression of Islam and the avoidance of collective sin, even at the expense of worries about compromising personal piety. Clearly, those who feel unable to make such compromises rarely stay in chaplaincy.

Some Muslim women who work as chaplains have interpreted Islamic teachings about dress and modesty in ways which lead them to prefer wearing a face covering beyond the privacy of their home. Few are able to carry this practice into their chaplaincy work, and they recognise that it would be difficult to do so. It is a decision they feel able to justify, on the grounds that it is for the greater benefit of Islam and the people they will encounter in their work. However, questions then arise as to whether they should allow their faces to be seen in photographs of staff in the hospital, for example on posters or websites? This violates Muslim ideals, not only around gender, but also around the disputed question of photography. Some schools of Islamic thought deem that it is unacceptable to 'create' visual representations of living beings (for example sculpture or photography) because it threatens the ultimate reality of God as the one and only creator of life (Arshad et al. 2004). And if these two religious challenges were not enough, for some chaplains (of both genders) photographic images of themselves test cultural assumptions about modesty and humility. Fundamental customs are threatened in these cases and most chaplains, and here we are often talking about female chaplains, have to come to some kind of working understanding and compromise in facing these situations. It is simply not possible in a British public health care institution to exercise a ministry to all people who need their services if Muslim chaplains cannot deal flexibly with the norms which would prevail outside in the Muslim community.

Our discussion so far has explored some of the distinctive practices and issues that pertain to the work of Muslim chaplains. Although we have nuanced this discussion by considering some of the ways these practices are shaped by gender, or religious qualifications, we conclude this chapter with a more sustained evaluation of how chaplaincy practice might be shaped by the personal characteristics or contractual status of chaplains. We begin with consideration of how trained Islamic scholars carry out their work in ways which might differ from those who have not earned the title 'alim or 'alima.

Islamic scholars employed as chaplains are more likely to feel confident in their interpretation of legal judgements and in giving advice. They can conduct Islamic teaching classes and can pray with clients with a particular sense of authority, derived from a sense of confidence in their religious training. They are more likely to quote the Qur'an in the original Arabic, and they may be regarded as having more authority by service users. They believe, and they believe that others believe, that they have a particularly close relationship with God on account of their knowledge of the Qur'an and their embodiment of it. By contrast, as we saw in Chapter 3, non-'alims are more likely to have come into chaplaincy as an extension of other work, such as teaching, counselling or work in the voluntary sector. They do not accept that they are in any way inferior and may lay claim to being more focused on the needs of clients and the institution, perhaps being more empathic. But they are less confident in making judgements about the tradition and advising on ethical matters. Consequently, they may consult other religious authorities more, and may feel less able to quote Islamic sources and texts as part of their practice. They repose their authority in their experience rather than in specific Islamic training though they would claim to be good Muslims immersed in, and exemplary of the tradition. One non-'alim chaplain talked about the deficiency of 'alims thus:

> ... they may have done seven years of 'imam-ship' training, [but] what they often lack is an understanding of the concept of pastoral care, with chaplaincy, the bulk part of it is about pastoral care. The advice giving, religious advice giving is only one aspect of it really, so if you want to be a chaplain really, in my humble understanding, you've got to understand pastoral care (part-time female hospital chaplain).

However this is not to say that 'alim chaplains do not know their limitations. Our data shows that religious scholars working as chaplains do understand the importance of client-centred chaplaincy and they often gain these skills as they progress in their role. One senior hospital chaplain is now aware that his knowledge in relation to complex ethical questions now needs to be matched by a greater understanding of the sociological and psychological aspects of patient care.

Women/Men

As mentioned in Chapter 3, there is a notable difference in the educational background and subsequent practice of male and female chaplains. Most female chaplains we spoke to are over the age of 30, and have some form of prior experience relevant to chaplaincy work, such as counselling, community work or a health care profession. Many, but not all, men come into chaplaincy from a scholarly religious background that does not prepare them for the challenges of complex multi-faith institutions that are shaped by entirely different principles to those with which they are familiar. These gendered differences in education and background can give female chaplains a particular advantage as they begin their work as chaplains, since they are often already familiar with the mechanics of public institutions and the realities of multi-faith team work. Indeed, chaplaincy roles are often empowering for women; they grant them religious authority and recognition that would be otherwise hard to achieve.

Most female chaplains found their gender to be enabling, certainly in contrast to their male colleagues. This is because male clients are probably content to receive support, information or pastoral care from a female chaplain, but the reverse is not always the case. One female prison chaplain, also working as a part-time community chaplain, noted that her gender put her in a unique position to manoeuvre in and out of the prison as well as liaise and talk directly with family member in their homes. In her view, her unrestricted access to the wives and mothers of offenders was critical for their eventual rehabilitation:

> In my role, I jump everywhere. I'm not constrained as the 'alims are. I freely talk to the [women in the visitor family centre]. I've gone into their homes, sat with their mums, their fathers, their wives (part-time female prison chaplain, working in a male establishment).

For this individual, the performance of her role as a woman was also an integral part of her broader educative role in the prison:

> I think the first time I went on the wings, the lads were like, 'what's she doing here? Are you the probation?' The usual, and then you say, 'Actually no, I'm a community chaplain'. 'So you are a Christian?' 'No, I'm not'. [laugh] And as a woman, as well, it's a reality check to these lads ... 'You know what, today, it's me; tomorrow it could be somebody else, you know?' And I think for the brothers here, and I think even for the establishment, I'm educating them about Islam in a kind of roundabout way. I think what it does, it makes them realise that actually there is equality in this, because look, there's a white officer and a white female officer, a black officer [and a] black female officer, an Asian guy officer and, my God, there's an Asian female officer now in our establishment. And there are two Imams. And there's a male and a female. I think it helps educate.

Very few female Muslim prison chaplains are working in male establishments. Notwithstanding the potential value of this, most of our female interviewees recognised the value of focusing their knowledge and skills on chaplaincy work directed at the needs of women in particular:

> I think generally dealing with females, you have to take a different approach to when dealing with men. And you've got issues surrounding like periods and the menstrual cycle and child birth, or we've got like the mother and baby unit, and things like fasting. And there are a lot more questions about fasting and whether it's allowed, and what's not allowed. And also we have like domestic violence, sexual abuse, a lot more sensitive with women, and they do disclose violence and you have to try and tackle that sensitively and the men probably wouldn't understand it as well. And also ... with females there's a lot of cultural influences like shame, there's a lot more shame when a female comes to prison than there is with a man and that can be really difficult for the women (part-time female prison chaplain).

Female chaplains in health care are often employed with a specific remit for particular wards associated with female patients, such as maternity, gynaecology and obstetrics. Although they can and do visit male wards if necessary, and may need to interact with male visitors and clinicians, much of their work centres on those parts of the hospital where women predominate. For some female hospital chaplains, concentrating their work around the needs of female service users might be the outcome of negotiations with fathers or husbands concerned about the implications for honour of contact with unrelated men. In many ways, this mirrors the findings of Robina Mohammad's research with Pakistani Muslim women in Britain. She noted that the

> ... spaces and times in which jobs take place are gendered, in that the place and
> time in which paid work is performed is significant in dictating the form of work
> Pakistani women are able to consider (Mohammad 2005: 193).

Although no female chaplains were working in entirely gender-segregated institutions, focusing their time on female clients is an important consideration in deciding whether they can assume chaplaincy roles in the first place.

Part-time/Full-time

To a certain extent, part-time Muslim chaplains are still doing the job of the 'visiting ministers' with whom Beckford and Gilliat conducted research in the 1990s (Beckford and Gilliat 1998). They are mainly involved in pastoral care and the facilitation of rituals and festivals. They have relatively little time to engage in the broader life of the institution, and opportunities for training and continuing professional development may be limited.

Although some part-time chaplains who have worked in the same institution over a long period of time have been able to shape policy and attend key meetings incrementally, not surprisingly one of the major grievances of part-time chaplains (in all sectors) is that they do not have proper recognition as part of the institutional staff, especially in the eyes of their colleagues. Alongside this sense of having inferior status, some part-timers feel frustrated that their full potential, personally and institutionally, is unrealised. More particularly, they feel upset and disappointed when they have not been able to attend to emergency situations that occur beyond their contracted hours. However, part-time chaplains play a vital supporting role for full-time Muslim chaplains, especially in institutions with very large numbers of Muslim clients. In these contexts, part-time chaplains are part of a broader Muslim chaplaincy 'team'. They generally feel less isolated in their work, especially compared to those part-timers who must work without the benefit of other Muslim colleagues.

Although the career path and salary potential of full-time chaplaincy positions are much sought after (quite often by part-timers wishing to extend their hours), this comes at a price. When full-time chaplains move into institutional policy-making, more substantial engagement in staff training and other more strategic work, they often lose contact with service users, except in cases of emergency or when distinctive 'troubleshooting' skills are required. Consequently, their scope to deploy specialist religious knowledge, that some will have spent eight or more years acquiring, becomes a rarer occurrence. Some experienced full-time chaplains know that they have now reached a career ceiling in terms of their chaplaincy work. In these cases, they are grappling with a sense of tension, between their religious vocations on the one hand, and the prospect of shaping their institutions more profoundly via managerial roles on the other.

Conclusion

This lengthy discussion of Muslim chaplaincy practice has mapped some of the ways in which the work of Muslim chaplains is variegated by virtue of sector, and in relation to the personal attributes of chaplains themselves. We shall engage in more theoretical consideration of the implications and significance of this work in Chapter 8. But as a conclusion to the present discussion, we offer some brief reflections based in part on the self-evaluations of chaplains themselves. What are the satisfactions and frustrations of their work? What gives them a sense of job satisfaction? Chaplaincy is necessarily a complex, multifaceted and diffuse activity, so it is not easy for chaplains of any religious tradition to evaluate their activities and role with any degree of certainty or objectivity: nevertheless, Muslim chaplains have found ways to calibrate the value of their practice through the use of a range of self-generated 'benchmarks'.

Firstly, they evaluate their work against Islamic teachings and principles. Islam requires people to engage in compassionate acts for the benefit of others. Therefore, if a chaplain helps the sick, or engages in other Islamically inspired acts based on good intentions (niyah), they hope to gain spiritual rewards in this life, and the next. If a chaplain helps a person to accept the truths of Islam, or to restore a faith, this is clearly seen as valuable and virtuous work that is intrinsic to being a good Muslim. Doing good for others brings blessing upon the self.

Secondly, chaplains use their own subjective experience to evaluate their work. One higher education chaplain reported having a sense of inner peace when he felt his work was acceptable in the sight of God; conversely, feelings of guilt and unhappiness would arise if he felt dissatisfied with his performance. A prison chaplain used Islamic sources as a means of spiritual self-assessment:

> The hadith of the prophet … where he says that when you do something good and you feel good … this is a sign of iman [faith]. So … when people around you will say, and when your heart tells you that was a good job, that was a good job (full-time male prison chaplain).

But it is not necessary for there to be a happy outcome for chaplains to feel that they have been useful. Helping to arrange a funeral, or listening to marital problems, can all be ways in which chaplains sense that they have done a good job. If intense or intimate contact can be established, this in itself can be rewarding. And if beyond this it is possible to reconcile people to their faith or to their families, this is a particular satisfaction, as is relating positively to non-Muslims and helping alienated people to be reconciled to self and others.

Thirdly, feedback from other people can be a useful way of evaluating performance. One prison chaplain felt that if his team was happy with him, then he was doing a good job. Other chaplains use indicators like the smiles and words of appreciation from clients. Health care chaplains mentioned things like the cards they receive, or people spontaneously greeting them in the street, to say 'thank you' for their help. These are all indicators of success that can help to carry chaplains through the inevitable frustrations of their work.

While it is difficult in any job focused on human relationships to be absolutely clear about its value and effectiveness, there is no doubt that chaplains themselves evaluated their work as effective and rewarding, religiously and personally. At least to external researchers, chaplains put the intrinsic personal and religious rewards of the job above any financial benefits. However, this does not necessarily stop them from feeling frustrated when demand for their services outstrips supply, and this frustration is shared by chaplains irrespective of sector, religious background, gender and contractual status. So at this poignant moment in the discussion, we cease consideration of practice and move on to examine the 'politics' that shapes the performance of the chaplaincy role, whether this involves the micro-level politics of contested institutional debates about budgets, or the rather broader politics that reflect the socio-political realities of Muslims more broadly.

Chapter 5
Chaplaincy Politics

Introduction

In a single decade, Muslim chaplains in Britain managed successfully to establish effective professional associations and networks. A small number of them have acquired positions of leadership and management of religious services within their institutions or geographical areas. In 2012, the Ministry of Justice confirmed that it was 'considering arrangements' for the appointment of the next Chaplain General to the Prison Service, recognising that there are now several sufficiently experienced Muslim chaplains who could take up the role (Pigott 2012). There was no longer an assumption that the position will be occupied by an Anglican, or even a Christian. Meanwhile, some Muslim chaplains have contributed to national level chaplaincy consultations and professional educational programmes. Policymakers, public service managers and chaplaincy teams now recognise the inclusion of Muslims as a taken-for-granted, generally welcome reality. The overall picture is one of growth, increasing professionalism and the development of contextual Islamic leadership and pastoral care.

However, beneath this success story tensions and challenges are apparent for chaplains and for the institutions that employ them. For example, chaplains in some sectors sometimes have to wrestle with conflicting perceptions of their role. Muslim prisoners might see Muslim chaplains as 'government agents' or 'spies' who are compromising their message and their religious integrity. Prison staff might regard them with suspicion as 'agents of radicalisation'. Other chaplaincy team members might resent the 'special' attention that Muslim chaplains receive, whether positive or negative. Within chaplaincy teams, disputes arise around budgets and staffing, the use of spaces and resources and the communication and sharing of information. For some Muslim chaplains, increasing seniority has sometimes been personally and professionally challenging; other colleagues may resent their authority and enhanced profile.

Meanwhile, the impact of external world events has had a disproportionate impact on the work of Muslims in chaplaincy relative to their colleagues of other faiths, particularly in higher education institutions and prisons. The events of 9/11 and 7/7 sparked a range of policy measures intended to counter violent extremism in Britain, and some of these have been directed at the recruitment and employment of Muslim chaplains, in particular. It is not always clear what kind of perceptions drive these policies, and to what extent Muslim chaplains are regarded as part of the problem, part of the solution, or both. While the rhetoric surrounding 'PVE' initiatives often attempts to avoid identifying Muslims as the particular focus of policy interventions, they are nevertheless often directly or indirectly singled out (Dinham 2009: 94). Under the guise of 'PVE', significant government resources have been invested in reports and projects intended to control and counter violent extremism, many of which are implicitly directed towards public institutions regarded as problematic sites in relation to radicalisation.

The work of Muslims in chaplaincy also provides a lens through which some of the internal debates within Muslim communities can be seen in microcosm. For example, the inclusion or exclusion of Muslim women in chaplaincy mirrors broader questions about the position of women in Islam, and the degree to which their opinions and experiences have a recognised voice in the public sphere (especially in relation to Muslim men). The extent to which they can adapt their usual norms of modesty or dress while working in mixed-gender environments is debated, even among female chaplains themselves. The tensions between different national-level 'representative' bodies for Muslims in Britain, often reflecting different schools of religious thought, are equally evident within the Muslim chaplaincy population. These are sometimes made even more complex as they become entangled with long-standing contests between various well-established professional chaplaincy bodies originally founded by Christian chaplains. The question of 'what counts' as halal remains disputed in some sectors (and who decides!) but such questions ultimately signal wider debates about the practice of Islam in a minority context.

This chapter explores the 'politics' of Muslim involvement in chaplaincy from a number of different angles. In the first instance, we revisit some of the issues that Muslim 'visiting ministers' regarded as problematic in the mid-1990s, and consider how and to what extent these remain contested, or have been replaced by a different set of challenges. Here the focus is upon the day-to-day interactions that Muslim chaplains have with their chaplaincy colleagues and other institutional staff. In the second part of the chapter, we consider the impact of external 'politics' and challenges, particularly those associated with Preventing Violent Extremism. How and to what extent have these affected the self-identity of Muslim chaplains, and in what sense have they both realised the opportunities as well as managed the threats posed by 'PVE'? In the third part of the chapter, we consider the 'internal' politics of Muslim chaplaincy and explore the meaning and implications of the contests that Muslim chaplains now have with one another, especially where these point to larger debates about the practice of Islam in European societies.

The Shifting Boundaries of Inclusion and Exclusion

Research in the mid-1990s documented some of the ways by which 'visiting ministers' of faiths other than the Christian were often routinely marginalised within publicly funded chaplaincy in England (Beckford and Gilliat 1998; Gilliat-Ray 2001b). Many 'visiting ministers' suffered the consequences of direct and indirect exclusion because of the financial, structural and procedural life of their institutions. Unfamiliar bureaucratic frameworks were obstacles to effective working. Most of their concerns were bound up with the practical conditions affecting their ability to work efficiently, such as limited access to relevant information, lack of consultation on the issues facing patients or prisoners of their tradition and lack of time in the institution. Some Muslim prison chaplains interviewed for our study recalled the effect of the struggles they had once faced as 'visiting ministers':

> [T]here were occasions that I would go to the car park and cry. Eight years ago, occasionally I'd go to the car park on the way home or here, and mainly on the way here, and I'd cry, my God, why here? Because it was such a challenge (full-time male prison chaplain).

Religion in Prison: Equal Rites in a Multi-faith Society documented the degree to which visiting ministers were almost entirely dependent upon on Church of England/Anglican co-ordinating chaplains for the conduct of their work (ibid. 115) within the Prison Service. The disadvantages deriving from this kind of 'brokerage' were felt by some Muslim visiting ministers more than others, but the general picture that emerged signalled the urgent need for a more 'multi-faith' approach to chaplaincy if steps towards greater religious equality were to be made.

Some of the implications of *Religion in Prison* were noted within the most senior ranks of the Home Office and Prison Service, leading to wholesale systematic change:

> following Beckford and Gilliat (1998) and an increased awareness of and commitment to British multiculturalism, prison chaplaincy in England and Wales pluralised and the current prison chaplaincy service is the result of a decade of relatively unprecedented growth and diversification. This commitment fashioned a multi-faith model of chaplaincy that reflected the needs of a multicultural nation, and has forged a distinct change in the landscape of prison chaplaincy (Todd and Tipton 2011: 7).

In light of the implicit recommendations arising from *Religion in Prison*, it was not surprising that the Venerable William Noblett was appointed Chaplain General to the Prison Service in 2001. From his position as co-ordinating prison chaplain at HMP Full Sutton near York in the late 1990s – a chaplaincy modelled on multi-faith principles – he too was also publicly articulating the need for a more multi-faith approach to chaplaincy (Noblett 2002), and echoing some of the same concerns as Beckford and Gilliat. His subsequent appointment as Chaplain General enabled some 'unprecedented' changes.

Breaking the Christian/Anglican monopoly in the Prison Service Chaplaincy Headquarters was further stimulated by the appointment of Maqsood Ahmed as the first 'Muslim Advisor' to the Prison Service Chaplaincy Headquarters in summer 1999, although such a position had been advocated in 1992 (Beckford et al. 2005: 74). This new position was clear evidence that the Prison Service intended to 'give more voice to Muslim opinion' (Beckford et al. 2005: 73), and was committed to more equitable and transparent recruitment and training arrangements for the then Muslim 'visiting ministers'. Later research in the early 2000s documented in detail some of the tensions, successes and internal chaplaincy politics driving the subsequent transition from 'visiting minister' to 'Muslim chaplain' in the Prison Service, many of which were pioneered by Maqsood Ahmed (Beckford et al. 2005). It showed that considerable effort was invested in improving and standardising the recruitment and selection of Muslim chaplains, and increasing the number of full-time posts available to them.

The change in title from 'visiting minister' to 'Muslim chaplain' that occurred in 2003 has been important for the self-identity of chaplains, and for wider perceptions of their role:

> It was hard work to change the attitude of some of the Governors when I first started here ... it was very different. An imam wasn't seen as a chaplain really. An imam was an imam, and a chaplain was a chaplain sort of thing. Every other faith was a chaplain, except for the imam [laughs] (full-time male prison chaplain).

Without comparable research in health care, and in light of the autonomy of different NHS Trusts, it is more difficult to chart the precise developments taking place in health chaplaincy. But as noted in Chapter 1, even prior to the appointment of 'Muslim chaplains' in the Prison Service, some NHS hospital trusts were advertising newly created posts for 'Muslim Chaplains' as early as 2000 (Gilliat-Ray 2001b), and funding was being provided by the NHS for training organised by the Muslim Council of Britain (*The Muslim News*, 27 October 2000, p. 11). Individual hospitals and trusts are responsible for appointing chaplains. There is no statutory duty to make these appointments, but there is an obligation to provide spiritual care which can often be most clearly demonstrated by appointing chaplains to act as an organisational focus. Chaplains from Christian denominations are appointed in consultation with those denominations and they are usually ordained members of them, requiring ongoing approval from their denomination of origin to continue in chaplaincy work. It should be noted that many chaplains are actively assisted by lay volunteers. They receive some training and may undertake the majority of pastoral visiting within a health care organisation, while paid chaplains engage in more specialised and organisational duties. In other sectors beyond health care and prisons, chaplaincy positions for Muslims have gradually become available (many on a voluntary basis) especially in higher education institutions, shopping centres and airports. The Ministry of Defence appointed the first full-time Muslim chaplain in 2005.

Internal Chaplaincy Politics: Day-to-day Experiences

This brief recollection of developments since the late 1990s is an important reminder that changes surrounding the work of Muslim chaplains have been contextually variable. The boundaries of inclusion and exclusion have not moved evenly across different kinds of public institution. Furthermore, as Chapter 3 demonstrated, chaplains of different gender and employment status are also vulnerable to variable experiences and opportunities. With an estimated Muslim chaplaincy population today of about 400–450, comparisons can now begin to be made about the experiences and issues faced by Muslim chaplains across different sectors, genders and according to employment status. With at least a decade or more of experience, we can now draw some conclusions about how and in what way their challenges have changed over time.

Perhaps one of the most significant observations to be made is that where the work of 'visiting ministers' was often hampered by a lack of knowledge about the machinery of public institutions, the Muslim chaplains in our study were able to make critical observations about institutional procedures from the vantage point of far better 'inside information' based on their cumulative length of service. They have become familiar with the structures and organising principles of their working environment. This, coupled with their often highly effective networks of communication (especially among those working in prisons and hospitals), enables rapid sharing of mutually empowering information.

Many Muslim chaplains demonstrated critical awareness of matters such as the practice for allocating chaplaincy staff hours or 'sessions', according to different faith traditions. This currently relies upon the gathering and analysis of statistical information about the religion of prisoners or patients at the time of hospital admission or reception into a prison (recording of religion is less common in other sectors). Muslim chaplains are now more aware of the consequences that flow from the limitations of blunt recording processes. Consequently, an experienced hospital chaplain observed that the religions of some categories of patient were often inaccurately recorded, or not recorded at all. The religious affiliation of patients with limited literacy or communication skills, or those who were cautious about the way information about their religion might be used, was unlikely to be recorded via patient information systems. These omissions were distorting the figures for the Muslim patient population in her hospital with consequent implications for the chaplaincy staffing budget. To make matters worse,

> … even when we do have a percentage to work with, and we allocate certain hours to Christian chaplaincy, to Muslim chaplaincy, to Hindu chaplaincy etc., what's not really being taken into account is actually how much is the need of chaplaincy resources for those individual patients of the different faiths. [There is] a cultural expectation as well, they [Muslims] expect that you'll be there for some time, they need you for more than five or ten minutes. Now, my Catholic colleague, he has more call-outs than any one of us, but when he's called out, what he has to do by the bedside is done like that [clicks fingers]. I'm saying the needs are different. So unless we can really start to measure up what are the needs, I don't feel that the allocation is a realistic and true one (part-time female hospital chaplain).

Staffing and chaplaincy hours were recurrent themes for chaplains working in different sectors. Voluntary or part-time chaplains believed that they were often excluded from institutional decision-making and strategic planning because their allocated hours were insufficient for their pastoral/religious work, let alone anything more.

In the context of multi-faith chaplaincy teams, where some duties are shared among all members, regardless of faith tradition, there is a difficult balancing act for part-time chaplains to negotiate, between caring for members of their own faith tradition, and working for the well-being of the broader institution. But the reverse of this conundrum also presents challenges for full-time chaplains who, because of their more expansive, institution-wide role, have sometimes been expected to support the work of staff in other departments, well beyond the strategic level. For example, Muslim chaplains have sometimes been co-opted as unofficial members of interpreting/translation services, or to lead on equality and diversity projects that should be carried by others.

Full-timers are also more likely to be regarded as available and 'on-call' 24/7, including at weekends, making work-life balance complex. A story from one hospital chaplain crystallises the issues around recording of patients' religion and patient numbers, the potential for exploitation of full-time chaplains and differing religious and cultural expectations of chaplaincy services by patients of different faiths. It also highlights the need for boundaries around professional pastoral practice:

> [Wellbridge] Hospital is surrounded by a sizeable mixed-faith population. Muslims form the largest 'minority' faith in the locality. Nevertheless, based on the religious registration of patients, it has been routine for a Christian chaplain to be 'on-call' at weekends to deal with emergencies. Over a period of four years, [Tahir] had been available at weekends also, not as part of official 'on-call' duty, but simply on the basis of clear patient need, and his own feeling of personal responsibility. Many of the weekend emergencies he was dealing with were life/death situations requiring a rapid response, such as facilitating funeral arrangements. Eventually, the interruption of his personal life at weekends reached a crisis point; he resolved to cease working at weekends. Thereafter, Muslim patients who needed a chaplain at a weekend were told 'none are available'. For him, this situation had multiple implications. He felt that the message of 'unavailability' impacted upon his reputation in the close-knit Muslim community the hospital served. Simultaneously, he recognised that allocation of the chaplaincy staffing budget, on the basis of patients' religious registrations, was an inappropriate way of ascertaining actual patient need. Meanwhile, despite his reputation in the institution, he recognised that it was unlikely he could generate the kind of evidence he needed to lobby senior managers about the issue, such as a record of sustained patient complaints. Muslim patients were, he said, 'not culturally attuned' to writing letters of complaint. He was looking forward to a situation where his increasing seniority

might enable a review of 'on-call', leading to more equitable arrangements for patients and chaplains alike (fieldnotes, Wellbridge Hospital, December 2009).

By far the most significant financial differential in relation to employment opportunities for Muslim chaplains relates to sector. Compared to the relatively well-resourced Muslim chaplains in the Prison Service, funding for chaplains in higher education, in community chaplaincy or in other sectors (for example Fire Service, Police, airports) is often negligible. Here, the variable economic and social resource of different faith communities in Britain becomes starkly apparent; while the Christian churches support an extensive network of salaried chaplains in higher education, for example (Clines 2008), very few Muslim chaplains associated with HEIs are funded, either by Muslim communities, or institutions themselves. Their work generally remains an extension of an existing institutional or academic role, or is undertaken on a voluntary basis.

Volunteer involvement in chaplaincy is thus an important barometer of the social capacities of different faith communities. So for example, while there are significant numbers of Christians able to support salaried chaplains as unpaid volunteers, one of the interviewees in our study noted the difficulty of finding committed volunteers from Muslim communities. The lack of an established tradition of formal volunteering, combined with the particular demographic of Muslim communities in Britain (disproportionately young), results in an insufficient number of British Muslims able to commit themselves to sustained voluntary chaplaincy roles. The limited supply of Muslim volunteers has been noted internationally. In a largely quantitative study of prison chaplains in the USA, nearly two-thirds felt that more volunteer support was needed in chaplaincy, and among those expressing this view, 55 per cent said that the greatest need was for Muslim volunteers (Boddie and Funk 2012).

Multi-faith 'Teams'

Local and national policies, combined with economic and strategic factors, largely influence the degree to which chaplaincy hours are funded. But day-to-day chaplaincy business, whether carried out by salaried staff or volunteers, is also shaped by the relations within so-called 'multi-faith' teams. In our data many chaplains spoke in generally positive terms about their colleagues of other faiths. Some went so far as to claim that their own practice as Muslim chaplains had been modelled on the example of their Christian colleagues:

> [Musaddiq] first went into the multi-faith room and did a small prayer (du'a). I asked him what this prayer was about, as it is not a conventional practice. He told me that this is something that he picked up from his Christian line manager … that it is good practice to go to the chapel or mosque every day and make a prayer for the sick (fieldnotes, shadowing a full-time male hospital chaplain, July 2010).

One chaplain we interviewed likened his chaplaincy team to a jigsaw:

> I think we all play an important part ... we're these pieces of the jigsaw. A
> Jewish piece, a Hindu piece, a Sikh, a Christian ... a Quaker, you know. And to
> collect all these pieces ... actually creates a picture called the Chaplaincy (full-
> time prison chaplain).

Many chaplaincy departments have now become sites of intensive inter-religious
encounter. So, compared to 'visiting ministers', Muslim chaplains have become
(perhaps more than any other group of Muslim religious professionals in Britain)
important carriers of knowledge about 'other faiths' and the practical and religious
implications of living in a multi-faith society. Furthermore, some chaplains we
spoke to recognised that where chaplaincy services were vulnerable to budgetary
cuts or lack of recognition, it was vital that chaplains worked collaboratively.
The ethos of 'multi-faith' that permeates religion in the public sphere (including
chaplaincy) has tended to exclude those unwilling to subscribe to a 'team'
approach. The kind of collegiality described by many interviewees is therefore
unsurprising; it testifies to the degree to which religious equality, at least in
principle, has become embedded within the structures of many public institutions.
Those unwilling to work in such a way, irrespective of faith tradition, have tended
to leave chaplaincy:

> [Jamil], is a full-time Muslim prison chaplain at HMP [Newtown]. Walking to
> the prison gate after the interview, he described an incident dating from 2003.
> When he first arrived at the prison, the Roman Catholic chaplain asked him not
> to enter the RC Chapel, nor the RC chaplaincy office. [Jamil] was told that the
> sacraments for the celebration of the Eucharist (bread and wine) were stored
> in these locations, and the Catholic chaplain was worried that the proximity
> of a Muslim would 'contaminate' their sanctity. Our interviewee noted that
> no other members of the chaplaincy team had been on the receiving end of a
> similar request. He told us that he was 'ready to leave' when faced with such
> overt discrimination. With support from the Muslim Advisor, he remained in
> post. The Roman Catholic chaplain left his position soon afterwards (fieldnotes,
> HMP Newtown, 21.5.09).

One of the prison chaplaincy administrators we interviewed noted that those people
who had found inclusivity difficult 'are probably no longer around'. He went on:

> I mean one of the questions that I always used to ask of Anglicans on interview
> was, 'how would you feel about a person from a different faith tradition writing
> your annual report?'. And in the early years that caused a few raised eyebrows
> and people scratching their head and thinking, 'well, actually what would it
> mean'? Whereas now when I ask the question people look at me as if to say, well,
> 'why am I asking that question?' ... it's not an issue (chaplaincy administrator).

While this indicates significant progress in the Prison Service, Christian-Muslim relations may be more fragile in parts of the NHS. This might be a reflection of the greater vulnerability of chaplaincy within the Health Service overall, thereby placing a greater strain on working relations as limited resources have to be stretched further. Although very few of our interviewees shared experiences of overt religious discrimination from within their 'team' in the immediate years leading up to our research, we did hear accounts of more subtle forms of marginalisation, some of which appear to reflect Christian anxieties about the growing seniority and influence of Muslim chaplains. Some interviewees told us that they detected a sense of insecurity among some Christian/co-ordinating chaplains, who not only resented the apparent end of a Christian/Anglican monopoly on chaplaincy, but also felt threatened by increasing Muslim leadership in the profession. The converse of this was recognition by some Muslim chaplains that where Christians or Anglicans have led the creation of an effective multi-faith team over time, this can significantly enhance their reputation within the institution.

During fieldwork visits, we saw material signs of subtle tensions which suggest variable and contested understandings about 'multi-faith' working at a day-to-day level. For example, an incident recorded in fieldnotes following a visit to a London hospital points to the difficulties of trying to accommodate different worshipping traditions within a single space, along with the fact that Muslims seem to make disproportionate use of shared worship space in public institutions:

> [Adil] opened the cupboard where copies of the Qur'an and prayer mats were kept. He showed me an arrow on the inside of the cupboard door which had the word 'qibla' written underneath it [to indicate the direction for prayer]. He told me this is the best he can do as his team members would not allow the arrow to be placed anywhere on the walls. This would defy the purpose of a generic worship room. [Adil] told me that he could not understand how a line on the wall would make the room less generic. He raised the issue with his colleagues who said that maybe they should have a compass on the wall with pictures showing the direction towards different faith places such as Makka, Jerusalem, India, Rome etc. [Adil] told them that they were complicating matters and all that he wanted was a small arrow on the wall. He showed me how Muslim service users draw the arrow on the skirting board and how his colleagues delete it with correction fluid. The whole corner is a mess due to the over-use of correction fluid (fieldnotes, part-time male hospital chaplain, April 2010).

But alongside these kinds of tensions, we also heard accounts of inter-religious generosity. For example, a Jewish rabbi was happy that Muslims used the hospital synagogue for Friday prayers, when the Muslim prayer room became too small:

> ... we [had] permission from the Rabbi to use the synagogue, we now from the last two years, and they were happy, they said 'yes, this is a step forward

towards community cohesion, let's do it'. Two years now we are doing it (full-time female hospital chaplain).

Where 'visiting ministers' were once often excluded from chaplaincy events and celebrations, it was notable that a number of Muslim chaplains we interviewed referred to social and professional events in terms which assume inclusion, rather than exclusion. However, these same events have become occasions which test understanding about how chaplains of different faiths can work together:

> I said I would not allow any wine or anything in the building. Well, then the Hindus came up, 'we will not allow any meat in the building'. So, I mean, that sort of compromise we had to reach. I said, 'all right'. That is the sort of compromise we had to reach in the end. All our meals in the multi-faith centre will be vegetarian so that Muslims, Christians, Hindus, anybody can eat there. And there is no alcohol served (part-time male higher education chaplain).

The negotiations which underpin these kinds of dilemmas have nevertheless resulted in some notable examples of inter-religious generosity that would be unlikely to occur beyond a public institution. If the ethos of multi-faith practice has become embedded within many chaplaincy departments to a greater or lesser extent, Muslim chaplains nevertheless continue to experience discrimination and racism from other institutional staff. When chaplains shared stories with us about their struggles and the situations that had distressed them, these tended to involve staff beyond the chaplaincy, not within it. Chaplains felt profoundly distressed by situations they described as racist, or where staff betrayed ignorance of Islam.

External Politics: 'Preventing Violent Extremism'

The variable experiences of Muslim chaplains in different sectors are particularly evident where they feel the impact of external politics, especially policies related to counter-terrorism and so-called 'radicalisation'. Since 2005, a range of government initiatives have been developed with the intention of countering violent extremism, many of which have generated academic critique and research (Birt 2010; Gutkowski 2012; Husband and Alam 2011; Klausen 2009; Kundnani 2009; Lambert 2011; Saggar 2009). Institutions especially associated with so-called 'radicalisation' (such as prisons and universities) have been identified as significant sites that warrant particular attention (Beckford 2010; Dodd 2006; Gallagher 2012; Gallagher and Syal 2011). Our work evaluated the way in which Muslim chaplains have been affected by these developments, both in terms of direct policy interventions, and in terms of the suspicion generated about their work by social policy think-tanks engaged in commentary about their role and influence in public institutions. Experienced Muslim chaplains reflected upon the extent to which their role now encompasses an entirely new agenda, and has become politicised in ways their 'visiting minister' counterparts could never have predicted.

Unsurprisingly, very few health care chaplains had comments to make about the impact of 'Prevent' policy, except those involved in national-level consultations on PVE-funded projects. However, chaplains working in higher education institutions and prisons had much to report. They shared similar worries around the expectation that they should 'spy' on chaplaincy clients for signs of religious extremism. But they differed in other important ways too, principally around the degree of access to, and agency to determine the use of, funds for capacity-building initiatives. Clearly, PVE policy has created both opportunities and problems for Muslim chaplains. The scope to generate positive opportunities, or to manage the more problematic aspects of Prevent, has sometimes been highly dependent upon context, and sometimes upon the agency of individual chaplains themselves. At this point, it is worth considering the experiences of Muslim chaplains working in prisons, in particular. This is because they have been disproportionately affected by Prevent initiatives. Their experiences provide a particularly helpful and vivid point of comparison in relation to Muslim chaplains working in other sectors.

> There is currently an ongoing and widely reported unease within prisons around what is commonly described as the ascendency of the Muslim faith in prisons, and the consequent status, and often resources, afforded to Muslim chaplains (Todd and Tipton 2011: 37).

Muslim chaplains are regarded by some as having undue access to training, resources and attention. Much of this has come through funding associated with PVE, and it has clearly created conditions for 'unease'. While Prison Service rhetoric and policy often stresses that extremist views or behaviour of all kinds is a matter of concern for all staff, Muslim chaplains are often singled out for particular attention and resourcing in relation to what are regarded as extremist interpretations of Islam among Muslim offenders. Senior prison officers are aware of the difficulties that arise when the religious work of Muslim chaplains becomes blurred with their role in counter-terrorism:

> We therefore have to use the role of the chaplain to kind of meet some of the political concerns and pressure prisons are currently facing. We just have to be careful how far we push as the lines that separate, that demarcate those different roles. Losing that neutrality and losing that kind of professional role as a religious leader is a danger (Prison Governor quoted in Todd and Tipton 2011: 26).

Despite the dissonance between policy and practice, PVE initiatives have provided a context for the career progression of some Muslim chaplains. For example, regular residential training courses for Muslim chaplains have often provided a context for the acquisition and deployment of advanced religious knowledge, as well as the chance to reinforce professional and religious networks. Chaplains involved in such programmes are deliberately exposed to leading Islamic scholars who can stimulate new appreciation of classical Islamic texts, or new forms of legal interpretation. Thus the finer points of theological difference are explored and debated, providing chaplains with an opportunity for their work to be less routine and more intellectually rewarding. This is appreciated by many chaplains who often commented to us upon the relatively low level of religious knowledge possessed by many Muslim prisoners. Generally, Muslim chaplains working in the Prison Service appear to have far greater exposure to, and opportunity to engage in, continuous professional development, certainly compared to Muslim religious professionals in other spheres. This reinforces prevalent ideas about chaplaincy as a 'career', as well as a professional vocation.

Muslim chaplains who are involved in approving or screening religious material coming into prisons inevitably find themselves exposed to 'radical' ideas and messages. Deep intellectual engagement with such material provides fertile opportunities for the development of training materials, and an expertise in counter-terrorism that becomes useful to other security agencies. Where Muslim chaplains are involved in the design and delivery of such training, there is considerable scope for their religious and professional standing to increase, within and outside the Prison Service.

Some Muslim chaplains have used anxieties around 'radicalisation' as a catalyst for trying to improve intra-institutional understanding of Islam. In this respect, the confidence and experience of some chaplains becomes especially evident. For example, one chaplain noted that he invited his Governor and other senior prison officers to attend Friday prayers on a routine basis, not only to avoid suspicions around his own preaching, but also to enable new informal conversations about Islam itself. The creation of transparent relationships with key prison staff can ultimately improve, if only indirectly, the experience of Muslim offenders:

> All the security reports that are submitted about Muslims and so on have to go through me … Because we get silly things like officers saying, 'this prisoner's waking up at four o'clock in the morning, he must be an extremist' [laughs], or, 'this prisoner has started to grow a beard, he must be an extremist' [laughs]. So you know, rather than it being logged against the prisoner to say that an officer believes that he's an extremist prisoner, it gets run by me, and I can say 'actually this is perfectly normal behaviour, that's how every Muslim should behave'. So we've got this relationship with the security department and they know, and they know that if I see something out of the ordinary then I will report it (full-time male prison chaplain).

These accounts reflect the cumulative experience of Muslim chaplains, and the degree to which they have become an integral part of the staffing of prisons in a way that was virtually impossible for them as 'visiting ministers'. It also signals an increasing appreciation among prison staff that Muslim chaplains can often provide immediate, trustworthy expertise.

Governors and prison officers are not the only 'observers' of Friday prayers in some institutions. Prisons that are regarded as especially 'sensitive' on account of the offender profile often have to accommodate the presence of police officers working in counter-terrorism. At one of the prisons we visited, a counter-terrorism officer noted that he attends Friday prayers regularly so that he can observe the interactions of prisoners, as well as protect Muslim chaplains from any accusations of 'extremist' preaching. He told us that officers in his position 'worry about what we know we don't know' (fieldnotes, YOI Fellside, November 2010).

The police officer at this particular prison had a full-time counter-terrorism role, suggesting that there were significant concerns about the extent of (or potential for) extremism there. However, interviewing a range of staff during our time at the prison revealed the 'games people play' around perceptions of extremism. Prison staff (including chaplains) noted that it was almost inevitable that the PVE officer would inflate the problem, because his job to some extent depended upon creating perceptions of serious risk. Meanwhile, the police officer noted that prison staff (and chaplains) would be unlikely to admit the extent of extremism in the prison because it would reflect badly on their own offender management. This signals the problem of 'what counts' as extremism – according to the interests of those involved in trying to define it – and the difficulty of creating any meaningful techniques for its measurement or assessment. The Pew Foundation research carried out in the US didn't interrogate these dilemmas in any depth, but does suggest that 'perceptions of the prevalence of extreme religious views tend to vary with the security level of the facility where the chaplains work' (Boddie and Funk 2012: 53). It is also dependent upon the religious identity of the chaplain.

> Those who are Muslim appear less likely than other chaplains to perceive a lot of religious extremism among inmates. Just 23 per cent of the Muslim chaplains say religious extremism is either very common or somewhat common in the prisons where they work, while 43 per cent of Protestant chaplains take that view (Boddie and Funk 2012: 54).

The complexity of the issues associated with religious extremism rarely receives nuanced and informed treatment from social policy think-tanks. The degree to which this can influence the climate in which Muslim chaplains must work makes such reports deeply problematic, and thus worthy of some consideration, if only briefly. For example, a report produced by the Quilliam Foundation in 2009, *Unlocking Al-Qaeda: Islamist Extremism in British Prisons* (Brandon 2009), made a number of assertions about the arrangements for religion in prison and the work of Muslim chaplains that warrant critical evaluation.

The report is typical of many of those produced by think-tanks (such as the Policy Exchange or Civitas) in so far as they are often authored by researchers with no academic track-record in the field about which they are writing. Often they are given the title 'Senior Research Fellow'. But that title loses its real significance and meaning outside a formal academic context, and only serves to obscure the credibility of the author. Many of these reports are methodologically weak, in that they rest almost entirely on secondary and limited sources. Produced in haste, usually without reference to currently available academic literature, and with an almost total reliance on desk research, it is not surprising that think-tanks are themselves becoming a subject of significant critique (Mills et al. 2011).

When it comes to the actual content of *Unlocking Al-Qaeda*, Brandon reveals a certain degree of ignorance about the dynamics of Muslim communities in Britain. To give just one example, he attributes the disproportionate number of Deobandi Muslim chaplains working in prisons to the personal influence of the Muslim Advisor based within the PCS headquarters. He seems to assume that the Muslim Advisor is selecting and favouring chaplains based on his own theological preferences. The reality is however a little more complex, because the Muslim Advisor at the time of writing (Ahtsham Ali) has been strongly associated with the Islamic Society of Britain (ISB) which has in fact emerged from rather different religious roots compared to the Deobandi 'school' of thought. The author appears equally ignorant of the fact that the various Islamic traditions in Britain have different histories of institution-building. So, as noted in Chapter 3, the fact that there are more chaplains of Deobandi background is simply a reflection of migration patterns and the trajectories of institution-building among different Islamic traditions.

At a day-to-day level, some Muslim prison chaplains have become highly sensitive to the risk that their teaching or sermons may be misunderstood. Following an Islamic class that we observed, the chaplain ended by asking the prisoners to return a pocket-size booklet containing Forty Hadith, from which he had been teaching. Although there were large stocks of the (donated) booklet, and despite the fact some prisoners wanted to continue their own private study of the booklet after the class, the chaplain later explained that it was 'too risky' to allow prisoners to remove the booklet from the prison mosque. He qualified this by saying that prisoners might misunderstand particular prophetic sayings without his interpretive guidance, and on those grounds a very basic Islamic source material was being denied to prisoners. In the same prison, a group of Muslim offenders who took part in a focus group discussion in the prison mosque felt that the chaplains were 'restricted' in terms of their teaching. They also pointed to the structural differences that shape the work of mosque-based imams and prison-based chaplains, and the degree to which they can exercise agency within these spaces:

> Prisoner: I see sometimes that the imams in here, I won't name names, but I feel that they're restricted.

> Interviewer: In what way?

> Prisoner: Mainly because obviously this is not. Obviously this is their Masjid but it's not their facility, so if the guv is saying, 'oh, everyone has to go now', they have to listen to that, because it means everyone has to go now – they have to listen to that.

Prisoner: But the thing is, in the mosque it's different, innit? You see, that's the difference in the mosque outside and in the mosque in here. In the mosque in here they are restricted … in the mosques out there they're not.

Prisoner: They're restricted from saying things that they …

Prisoner: And from saying a lot of things as well.

Prisoner: They might take it in the wrong way and then report it.

Prisoner: But even teaching … they are restricted to as well. Like they may not jump on a lot of topics because of the way people might think about them.

Against this perspective, we found evidence that Muslim prison chaplains were prepared to discuss complex subjects, such as 'jihad'. They take the view that such issues are better explained openly rather than privately, and that senior officer presence is even better when such matters are discussed. Consequently, it seems almost inevitable that the sum of staff knowledge about Islam in the Prison Service, regardless of grade, is increasing as a result of the politicised climate that has shaped Muslim chaplaincy work. The role and the teaching of Muslim chaplains has therefore become visible and transparent to non-Muslims in an entirely new way in Britain, and in stark contrast to the relatively hidden role and teaching of many mosque-based imams and religious teachers.

Where Muslim prison chaplains have ready access to support structures, advice and some degree of training, the relatively few Muslim chaplains working HEIs have very limited resources and often work without the benefit of established professional networks. The fluidity of the boundaries around HEIs – certainly in contrast to prisons – makes any assumption that Muslim chaplains can or should 'spy' on students problematic (Brant 2011). Most Prevent funding in relation to higher education has been directed towards the involvement of all categories of staff, not just chaplains. However, both student groups and lecturers have campaigned against the discriminatory implications of Prevent-funded initiatives, with the result that a number of leading UK university unions have refused to work in partnership with Prevent projects.

The discriminatory undercurrents of a Prevent-funded initiative directly targeting the work of Muslim chaplains became evident through the contests surrounding the production of a report produced by an organisation called 'Faith Matters' in March 2010. The report, *The Role of Chaplains in Public Sector Institutions: experiences from Muslim communities*, had a long and troubled pre-history that began five years earlier. Support for the work of Muslims in chaplaincy was identified as an important outcome of 'Preventing Extremism Together' (PET) work done in 2005, following the London bombings of 7/7. As a consequence of PET, an organisation called 'The Experience Corps' was awarded £89,708 (excluding VAT) in February 2008 to 'produce a report based on assessment, collation and analysis of data to establish an evidence base on the existing provision of chaplaincy including standards and recruitment processes, and to develop a draft framework of voluntary standards and recruitment processes for institutions to consider when engaging Muslim chaplains in public service' (Lords Hansard 30th April 2009).[1] Following this report, a second organisation, Faith Matters, was awarded the tender in August 2008, for £80,000 in 2008–09 and for £30,000 in 2009–10, in order to pilot the draft standards and recruitment framework. The combined total invested in these two projects was therefore in the region of £200,000.

The consultations and research that took place for this project suffered from a number of unfortunate shortcomings that ultimately revolved around the political drivers of the project. For example, leading Muslim practitioners who were asked to read and provide feedback on draft documentation (on one occasion at a meeting scheduled over Friday lunchtime) resisted the suggestion that they somehow had a unique responsibility for PVE within their institutions. The very idea that Muslim chaplains should be so directly implicated in such work was regarded as discriminatory. What was important for us to record, however, was the degree to which experienced Muslim chaplains used their acquired knowledge of equality and diversity principles to resist various drafts of the report, so that the final version had a distinctly different tone compared to earlier versions. Furthermore, chaplains were often able to point to well-developed, sector-specific standards and capabilities documentation generated within the public sector (for example Department of Health, HM Prison Service) and by various professional chaplaincy bodies (for example UK Board of Health Care Chaplaincy) which were already in use for the effective recruitment of chaplains from all faith communities (not just Muslims). Not surprisingly, one of the stakeholders interviewed for our project noted:

> I think it's been a particularly unfocused piece of work that has changed its remit and self-understanding a number of times, which has led to frustration not just with ourselves but with our colleagues in health and higher education. Armed forces have pulled out of it altogether. So it just didn't seem to get it right in terms of where it was coming from (chaplaincy administrator).

The degree to which leading Muslim chaplains in Britain were able to exercise a constructive influence on the production and wording of the report was a reflection of their increasing professional socialisation, their acquired understanding of the mechanics of public institutions and their ability to network within and between different sectors, to good effect. Such a concerted effort would have been virtually impossible a decade earlier, while still carrying the title and status 'visiting minister'. Consequently, the production of the Faith Matters report is significant for us, not so much for its content, but as a benchmark by which we can measure the professional career trajectory of Muslim chaplains, and their increasing collective agency.

---

[1]　For full written answer see: http://www.publications.parliament.uk/pa/ld200809/ldhansrd/text/90430w0001.htm.

Chaplaincy and Gender

The involvement of Muslims in chaplaincy provides a unique opportunity for micro-level, critical evaluation of the impact and politics of counter-terrorism policy in Britain as it directly and indirectly affects particular individuals, groups or institutions. But chaplaincy also provides a lens through which a range of questions *within* Muslim communities can be seen with particular clarity. For us, questions of gender relations illuminated a range of contested issues facing chaplains of *both* genders, especially in relation to issues of authority, 'recognition', inclusion and exclusion, dress and the public performance of roles. We explore the gender dynamics of Muslim chaplaincy in more depth at this point, with a particular focus on the experiences of women.

As noted in Chapter 3, Muslim women have come into chaplaincy not so much through 'ulama networks, but rather via the transferable skills derived from their experiences in health care (for example medicine, midwifery), counselling, teaching or voluntary work. Very few chaplains in our sample were qualified religious professionals ('alima), although we made particular efforts to find and include them. Because women have often been sought to cover sessional or ad hoc hours (as opposed to full-time or part-time roles), they have been less subject to openly advertised, formalised recruitment processes. Becoming a chaplain has often been a more 'accidental' occurrence, and has mirrored the kind of diverse and adventitious routes into chaplaincy that were typical for male 'visiting minsters' in the 1990s (Beckford and Gilliat 1998).

Numerous consequences arise from this which directly impact on professional development. For example, with less reliance on 'networks' for getting into chaplaincy there is similarly less mutual support and 'networking' in the job itself, compared to many male chaplains. Because their overall numbers are smaller, and because Muslim women are therefore often more geographically dispersed, opportunities for sharing experiences, or mentoring and supervision become more problematic. This becomes even more significant because of the relatively high turnover of women in chaplaincy. For example, several female chaplains married and/or had children during the life of our research, and for some, this ended their chaplaincy role. Thus, the relative lack of networking among female chaplains both prior to, and within the role, means that their cumulative experiences tend to be lost each time they leave a post. Simultaneously, institutions have to 'start again' in terms of induction and training of new chaplains and relationship-building within the team.

The exception to this general rule seems to apply in relation to the experiences of Muslim women who have formed 'husband-wife' chaplaincy partnership arrangements, either formally via contractually agreed job-sharing, or informally (more usually). We encountered several Muslim women engaged in the delivery of chaplaincy in this way, and it seemed to provide advantageous benefits both for institutions, and for chaplains themselves. Institutions usually acquired 'two for the price of one' (if they were paid at all), while husband-wife partnerships enabled both parties to work within the principles of gender segregation that usually characterise social relations within Muslim communities.

The degree to which Muslim women are able to perform their role according to Islamic principles and norms regarding gender relations can be highly variable, however. While some chaplaincy teams appeared to value the way female Muslim chaplains orientate their work towards women clients exclusively, this was not universal. The principles of 'equality and diversity' that usually shape public institutions in Britain are sometimes interpreted in ways that conflict with the role some female Muslim chaplains wish to perform. In some cases, this betrayed prevailing assumptions within the chaplaincy profession that the execution of religious leadership roles should be measured against Christian (or more usually, Anglican) benchmarks. The degree to which Muslim women feel included or excluded from chaplaincy teams, or feel able to perform their role in a way that is consonant with their faith and beliefs, can still depend on sympathetic line-managers – in much the same way as it did for male 'visiting ministers' in the mid-1990s.

For some Muslim women, their work as chaplains has tested their understanding of Islam in both theological and practical ways. Their relations with male colleagues (Muslim or non-Muslim), their style of dress and the degree to which they are publicly 'visible' are issues which aren't so much contested (because few female chaplains have scope to debate them, together), but which display considerable variety of opinion and practice. This was most evident to us in relation to a small number of women we met who usually wear not only a hijab (headscarf) in public, but also a face covering (niqab). However, while working as chaplains, even in mixed-gender environments, they have chosen to remove the face-veil for the duration of their working hours.

Dress can clearly present challenges for female chaplains, but for many (including male colleagues) the adoption of conservative and overtly pious styles of dress is also an important mechanism by which to secure religious authority within an institution. Conversely, the decision not to wear religious dress can be costly in terms of recognition by clients. One female higher education chaplain we interviewed had chosen not to wear any form of overtly religious dress (including a headscarf). But she went on to lament the difficulties she had faced in building meaningful relations with Muslim students on campus. The fact her role was partly funded via PVE sources probably didn't help.

Given that many Muslim women perform their chaplaincy roles in part-time or sessional hours, they are often indirectly excluded from a range of professional development opportunities. Training courses that involve being away overnight or which involve many hours of travelling can pose difficulties for female chaplains who are juggling chaplaincy alongside domestic responsibilities, or who feel that it would be inappropriate for them to be away from male guardianship for an extended period. In light of these issues, we might have expected professional Muslim chaplaincy bodies to be especially accommodating of their 'sisters' who are working in chaplaincy, but this is not always the case. Muslim chaplaincy manifests its own forms of inclusion and exclusion.

The formation of professional religious associations for Muslim chaplains in Britain has largely depended upon pre-existing religious networks, an increasing and sufficient critical mass of chaplains, and a perceived need to share information, good practice and mutual support. These conditions enabled the formation of the 'Islam Resource Group' within the College of Health Care Chaplains (CHCC) in 2003, the Muslim Chaplains Association (MCA) in 2007 (mainly for prison chaplains) and the Association of Muslim Chaplains in Education (AMC-Ed) in 2009.[2] Many chaplains reported the invaluable support, advice and information they have gained from these associations. However,

> ... faiths can be bad at listening to their women and young people. Where social capital depends upon relationships, as it does, and where many of these are informal and 'soft', as we have observed, forms of sexism and ageism can be rapidly institutionalised at the same time as being obscured by an assumption that they are not happening. Yet we know that the skills required to build social capital tend to be associated with the sorts of networking which accrues to older people and to men ... many women have distinctive experiences of bridging and linking ... our study observed that they are frequently associated with informal roles with less visibility (Dinham et al. 2009: 114).

The direct and more usually indirect exclusion of women from Muslim chaplaincy networks can deprive them of important benefits accruing to males. Their exclusion rarely seems to be deliberate, but the fact that chaplaincy is now a mixed-gender occupation and is conducted in mixed-gender public institutions seems to have been eclipsed by taken-for-granted and perhaps quite unconscious assumptions about gender segregation that often shape social relations within Muslim communities. So while Muslim women are often able to access helpful 'remote' support via email and telephone, the opportunity to attend meetings for more extended discussion and reflection about their work is hampered by what they regard as an 'old boys' network' mentality.[3] This was evident (for some women) in relation to such things as the lack of notice about forthcoming meetings (thereby making organisation of childcare/domestic arrangements difficult), a programme structured around masculine priorities and a lack of willingness to accommodate female views and experiences – even less so when these were critical:

> Interviewer: In terms of support for you in doing your job, like things like the MCA. It sounds as if you, I mean, are you a member of that? Do you find it helpful?

---

[2] An organisation established in 2004 for the graduates of the MIHE course ('The Association of Muslim Chaplains') failed to become a sustainable enterprise, and ceased activities within a few years.

[3] The exception to this general perception of marginality was evident in relation to a *local* Muslim chaplaincy network for those working in the NHS in Yorkshire, which has made particular efforts to accommodate female chaplains.

Chaplain: Yeah, yeah. I've been, you know … I think that it needs incorporating women more. And it's kind of like, I find the MCA … if you kick up a storm or you criticise them, you won't be invited to the next talk (part-time female prison chaplain).

One female chaplain commented that in relation to her male colleagues, 'we're there, but then we're not there' (part-time female prison chaplain). This perception of being on the periphery of chaplaincy (particularly evident among those women working in prison chaplaincy) resonated with the perspective of a male 'visiting minister' from the early 2000s, quoted earlier:

It was hard work to change the attitude of some of the Governors when I first started here … it was very different. An imam wasn't seen as a chaplain really. An imam was an imam, and a chaplain was a chaplain sort of thing. Every other faith was a chaplain, except for the imam [laughs] (full-time male prison chaplain).

On the whole, our data suggested that many Muslim women in chaplaincy are experiencing a similar sense of exclusion from the chaplaincy profession that some of their male counterparts struggled with a decade previously, but this is further compounded by a sense of being marginal to the 'real' work of male Muslim chaplains. There are of course individual exceptions, and some male chaplains were praised for being particularly supportive of their female colleagues, but the overwhelming evidence pointed to structural and professional exclusion.

Female chaplains were by no means the only critics of the MCA, however. While personal relations between office-holders and MCA members were often very positive, some prison chaplains expressed considerable dissatisfaction with the MCA as an organisation. Some had discerned a significant and detrimental shift in focus over time, away from mutual support and networking, and towards greater internal bureaucracy and unhelpful lobbying of the Prison Service Chaplaincy Headquarters. Some chaplains felt that the MCA wasn't sufficiently accommodating of different 'schools of thought', and this perception undoubtedly stimulated the formation of a new body, the 'British Muslim Chaplains' (BMC) in 2010. This organisation (largely reflecting the Barelwi tradition) appears to be defunct (at the time of writing) largely due to a lack of leadership and an insufficient critical mass of members, so the MCA remains the predominant support network for Muslim prison chaplains, to date.

Despite the critical opinions surrounding the MCA, its operational norms reflect the increasing socialisation of Muslims into professional chaplaincy in a number of important ways. Within a relatively short period of time, the MCA has established structures which directly mirror those of HM Prison Service. For example, it has nominated individuals to act as 'Voluntary Area Muslim Chaplains', the informal equivalent of those acting in this formal capacity within the Prison Service. In addition, it has developed an ethos of proactive grassroots 'peer support' which would be decidedly unusual among 'ulama working in community settings. So, in a context where Muslim religious professionals do not have the same kind of hierarchies and structures as Christian churches, these efforts to 'capitalise' on the social capital that Muslim chaplains possess is a significant indicator of professionalising activity.

MCA members have over time also become increasingly aware of professional 'rights' and equality, especially in relation to their Christian colleagues. They are now more willing to actively challenge privilege, especially where this indirectly discriminates against Muslim chaplains. A good example of this surrounds the inequalities that derive from the fact that the Anglican Church makes a formal appointment of a 'Bishop to Prisons' who speaks on criminal justice issues in the House of Lords. The current incumbent of this role, the Rt Revd James Jones, Bishop of Liverpool, 'supports the practical work of the Chaplain General to the Prison Service and the network of three hundred Prison Service Chaplains who share in the front-line care of prisoners' ('Bishop to Prisons announced', Church of England Media Centre, 21.5.2007)[4]. It is very unlikely that Anglican prison chaplains would support the idea that they should hold their meetings with the Anglican 'Bishop to Prisons' in their spare time, or during annual leave. However, Muslim prison chaplains are expressly forbidden to attend MCA meetings during their working hours. In a context where it is one of the few, if only sources of professional peer support, it is not surprising that experienced Muslim chaplains are voicing protest about this kind of disadvantage. Should the Prison Service choose not to appoint an Anglican, or even a Christian as the next Chaplain General, significant consequences will clearly arise for the role of the Anglican 'Bishop to Prisons' in his support for the new Chaplain General.

The direct and indirect exclusions and the internal politics that govern professional Muslim chaplaincy bodies are perhaps an inevitable reflection of the trials and contests that surround the formation of any new profession. But the political acumen that is now evident in the MCA also reflects the emergence of a group of chaplains who have learnt how to 'play the game, avoid the red card, and seemed poised to score'. As an experienced prison chaplain and MCA member reflected …

> Everything is a game. There are two things you need to know in a game, if you don't know this you don't play. You need to know the rules, and you need to know how to score. If you don't know how to play with the rules you'll get a red card in no time [laughs]. So there are two things; know the rules, avoid the red-card. And you have to score, know where the goalpost is. If you know where the goalpost is, you kick once and the goalkeeper will block you two or three times but you will score. Sometimes the goalkeeper will walk away and let you score, you know what I mean? (full-time male prison chaplain).

---

[4]   http://www.churchofengland.org/media-centre/news/2007/05/pr4507.aspx.

Conclusion

Some of the interview extracts cited in this and other chapters indicate the points at which our interviewees laughed. We felt it was important for interview transcripts to indicate these occasions, because of the subtle nuances that are often contained within 'throw away' remarks expressed alongside laughter. Research data coded under a node 'jokes and laughter' yielded interesting insights about the 'politics' of Muslim chaplaincy. Though there were very few jokes as such, in the sense of deliberate efforts to make the interviewer laugh, there was plenty of laughter during interviews which reflected occasions of ambiguity, aggression or embarrassment experienced by chaplains. These occasions often pointed to significant structural, religious or political issues, and so laughter provides a distinctive and unusual lens through which the 'politics' of Muslim chaplaincy can be viewed from a slightly different perspective. If laughter is related to power, then the question of who can laugh at whom, for what reason and with what consequences becomes highly political.

Theories of laughter generally note its communicative functions. It can be a form of aggression, where laughing at people is deliberately intended to make them feel inferior. Laughter can also arise in relation to occasions of incongruity, or ridiculous situations. But laughter can also occur in contexts of equality and friendship where humour reinforces the feeling of group belonging. Feelings of mutuality, expressed through humorous teasing, are a sign of familiarity and a way of strengthening group solidarity. Laughter can be self-deprecating, as well as being critical of others (Pinker 1999). A lot of the laughter heard among our chaplains seemed to be a mixture of all these things. It arises in situations of marginality, where chaplains have felt misinterpreted because their role is misunderstood. Laughter as a form of stoic dissipation is thus an alternative to aggression against others, but often covers very real pain and frustration. Making a joke of things thus becomes a form of minority resistance, and a means by which to rise above the desperation or frustrations of a particular situation.

Very few chaplains reported occasions when they had been laughed at by others, but some did reflect on times when their non-Muslim colleagues confessed that they did not expect Muslim chaplains to smile or have a sense of humour:

> You know, when I went, prison officers admitted to me that they were wary about having a full-time Muslim chaplain, particularly with my beard and my Islamic traditional dress. They were very wary. And later on they said, 'It was so great to see you smiling'. [laughter] And I said, 'Why?' They said, 'You're the first Imam we've seen smiling. We didn't know Imams smiled!' [laughter] (full-time, mixed-sector male chaplain).

If there is a widespread perception that people do not expect Muslim chaplains to smile or have a sense of humour, this might be a reflection of 'political correctness' and concerns not to offend against the norms of religious propriety. But it also reflects that fact that trusting relationships which involve humour or teasing take time to establish; this can take even longer against the background of the wider politics of contemporary Islam, especially counter-terrorism, and the prevention of violent extremism. A chaplaincy secretary talked about the necessity to ensure jokes with 'her boss' were not publicly witnessed:

> Respondent: He has the most wonderful sense of humour, in fact it's naughty, he's got a *terrible terrible* naughty sense of humour [laughs]. Very often I'm at the end of it, I'm the butt of it, but it's fine, it's fine.
>
> Interviewer: But can you tease him back?
>
> Respondent: Oh I can, yes I can, and I do, I do. You know it's simple things that many would take offence at, if you want to be very 'PC', it could be offensive, you know. I don't know if you've noticed it, but he's got a striking resemblance to Osama Bin Laden. He goes out with his rucksack on, and I say, 'What do you have in your bag?' You know, it's little teases like that, really it's just fun between the pair of us, you know, you wouldn't say it in front of other people, they are just our own little jokes. He says things about my great age, and how old I am and we just have great fun. But it's all sorts of things, and you have to laugh because it can be a very sad environment and he deals with so many awfully sad things … (female chaplaincy administrator).

Some chaplains have become adept at using humour as a tool by which to navigate the personal relationships that shape their work. One female prison chaplain used jokes about wearing her veil 'because she was having a bad hair day' as a shorthand way of turning away the aggressive ignorance of prison officers and offering some aggression back … without appearing to be combative. Meanwhile, Muslim chaplains we interviewed were often ready to laugh at themselves. This kind of gentle self-mockery seemed to arise when recounting situations that had gone awry. It was the laughter of experience, often bitter experience. But an ability to self-critically reflect on personal disappointments or weaknesses again reflects a degree of socialisation into chaplaincy. It would be unusual to hear a community-based imam engaging in humorous self-mockery in quite the same way. But laughter in cases of incongruence, embarrassment or rejection seemed to arise where incidents were described in which people do not recognise chaplains for what they are, do not treat them as they should, fail to provide them with what they need, make unreasonable demands on them, project unreasonable expectations on them or would rather they did not do what they do. In these circumstances, laughter allows the chaplain power and distance over difficult and unpleasant situations. It is a kind of laughter of resistance. Cases of 'mistaken identity' and lack of recognition illustrate the point:

> I know lots of people in different capacities. But some of them say to me, 'Are you a taxi driver? I have seen you somewhere before'. [laughs] Then I just

point to that photograph over there on the chaplaincy noticeboard, and they say, 'Oh yes, that's where I've seen you'. It's so funny sometimes (mixed-sector, part-time male chaplain).

I tell you what happened to me, one of my worst experiences. The first day I was going to the prison, there was a shutdown. And I got to the gate and they said, 'You cannot come in'. But I said, 'I'm the Imam'. They said, 'No, you have to go'. [laughs] And I couldn't understand it. I said, 'Well, can I speak to the Governor?' and they said, 'No'. And I was completely confused [laughs]. (full-time male prison chaplain).

The comments used to illustrate this concluding section reflect the experiences of people within a professional group that has come a long way in terms of becoming established, yet have considerable distance to travel in terms of gaining full recognition and equality. Their struggles, as shaped by institutional, external and internal politics in many ways reflect the wider situation of Muslims in Britain, many of whom can probably relate to the idea: 'we're there, but then we're not there' (part time female prison chaplain).

Chapter 6
The Impact of Chaplaincy

Introduction

Chaplains work at the interface of public institutions, multi-faith chaplaincy teams and their own faith communities. Standing at the intersection of these different constituencies they are perhaps uniquely placed to comment upon, and contribute to, the discourse surrounding the place of Muslims in Britain more widely. This chapter surveys the contribution that Muslim chaplains are playing within and beyond their institutions. We shall make extensive reference to the views of Muslim chaplains, using their own words.

We begin by considering the impact of chaplaincy practice on institutional staff. This is because the efficacy of the relationships that chaplains form *within their institutions* often determines the degree to which they can then work for the benefit of clients. Secondly, we consider how and to what extent the employment of Muslim chaplains makes a difference to the experience of being a British Muslim within major public institutions. Based primarily on focus group discussions with Muslim prisoners (adults and young offenders), we reflect on their perceptions of chaplains and their work. Thirdly, how do Muslim chaplains perceive their impact beyond institutions, especially in the wider context of Muslim communities in Britain? What evidence is there for the transfer of their skills, insights and professionalism into mosques and other Islamic organisations, and how are they supported in their work by Muslim communities? Finally, we reflect upon the wider significance of Muslim chaplaincy, and question the ways in which it might be shaping the dynamics of religion in Britain today. How, and to what extent, has the profession of 'chaplaincy' been influenced by the new involvement of Muslims, and how do chaplains reflect upon their broader contribution to society?

In considering the answer to these questions we are conscious of course that any attempt to evaluate or quantify the 'value' of chaplaincy is problematic 'due to the inherently unquantifiable nature of an essentially qualitative role' (Todd and Tipton 2011: 28). However, we have gathered evidence from a range of perspectives which illuminate some of the ways in which the work of Muslim chaplains is valued within and beyond their institutions. In contrast to the material in Chapter 4 which documents the range of tasks Muslim chaplains perform in their institutions – which clearly have a direct bearing on their impact – we examine here the broader significance arising from the performance of these tasks.

The Impact of Chaplaincy Practice on Staff and Institutions

A consistent narrative shaping contemporary chaplaincy discourse relates to the pastoral care that chaplains provide for staff, as well as clients and their families. Chaplains support institutional staff not only professionally, but also personally, regardless of their religious belief. Staff experiencing bereavements, marital problems, stress and family breakdowns turn to chaplains for pastoral care, and it is likely of course that these more personal forms of support are offered as a positive outcome of trusting relationships initially forged around professional issues. For our purposes, the important point to note is that Muslim chaplains are now also engaged in staff support, alongside other members of the chaplaincy team. Our interviewees recalled pastoral stories relating to bereavement, marriage breakdown, sexual abuse and harassment at work, among both Muslim and non-Muslim staff. Their involvement in pastoral care with staff (especially those employed full-time) is an indicator of their evolving role across the breadth of their institutions and a further signal of their transition from 'visiting minister' to 'Muslim chaplain' in the last decade.

While the degree to which chaplains feel they can 'make a difference' is partly related to the hours available to them – especially for achieving short-term practical outcomes – the most significant variables in relation to longer-term impact also reflect experience and/or length of service. Not surprisingly, chaplains who form effective relations with key staff within their institutions over a long period of time are the group most likely to be shaping institutional policies, contributing to staff training and development and undertaking the all-important (but often hidden) work of 'troubleshooting'. Over time, these chaplains have understood where the parameters of their own agency are within the institution's channels of power, and they appreciate how their role intersects with others, as part of a team. Our data also shows that some chaplains have developed their reflective skills over the course of their employment: 'we do not learn from experience as such. We learn only if we develop ways of reflecting upon experience' (Campbell 1985: 76).

Across the various sectors, chaplains have done much to improve knowledge about Islam and Muslims within public institutions, not only in terms of the information they have provided as part of staff training programmes, but also by virtue of their own personalities. They implicitly recognise the fact that general perceptions of Islam and Muslims are shaped by negative stereotypes that they are well-positioned to counter by formal and informal measures:

> I felt that there is a need really to open up to the public and tell them what
> Islam is all about and all that they hear in the media is not true. So I started
> to be more open talking about Islam, for example, we needed to show some
> positive things about Muslims so at Eid I have invited all the staff to have
> some Eid sweets in the staff room. Just to tell them that Islam is not only
> what they hear about violence, also there is sweets [chuckle]. And on the

night it went very well. Now some of those staff when they hear about Islam they remember the sweets not the violence [laughs] (part-time male higher education chaplain).

The novelty of the information that some Muslim chaplains have to share during training sessions can be highly advantageous in terms of engaging staff and winning recognition:

> You always get a very good response because they've never heard this before. We have the advantage of the information that we present, it is very, it's possibly something that they've not heard before and then when you present they do take it very positively, it's, 'Hang on a second, the imam, he speaks like me' (part-time male hospital chaplain).

Chaplains may not be able to achieve significant status or prestige as an outcome of their one-to-one pastoral interventions, but their role in staff training offers the scope to accumulate power of a more subtle kind, based on their intellectual grasp of a body of specialist esoteric knowledge. The complexity of Islamic law in some situations, especially around life and death, can offer Muslim chaplains a distinctive sphere of influence on staff that may not be so readily available to chaplains of other faiths. In the prison context, the involvement of Muslim chaplains in 'advisory' and training roles feeds a rather different agenda however. Our findings concur with Todd and Tipton:

> A change to the role of the chaplaincy recently has been pushing at the boundary of their role through using the chaplaincy team as more a kind of diversity and faith advisor, more and more we are stretching into a world where we use that kind of information to feed into the security world (prison Governor, cited in Todd and Tipton 2011: 24).

Our data show that Muslim chaplains in all sectors make positive contributions to situations that have potential to become difficult in terms of time, staff goodwill and institutional reputation. Sometimes, these interventions are, to use a medical analogy, 'preventative'; in other situations, they reflect proactive crisis management. Minimally, for example, chaplains might work with managers to find ways of accommodating multiple requests from Muslim staff to take extended periods of annual leave during Ramadan or for Eid, while at the other end of the spectrum chaplains may need to deal with management or operational failures that are more serious. In such situations, their capacity to translate across a range of linguistic, religious and cultural boundaries can help in terms of damage limitation.

But very often the input of Muslim chaplains relates to the effective operation of the institution, especially in terms of negotiations that bring potentially turbulent situations into order. For example, when large numbers of visitors arrive to view a recently deceased Muslim patient, experienced chaplains use their authority to quickly manage events:

> What I do with our staff is, I use a technique. If there are so many visitors coming onto the ward I will say, 'Look, I need to talk to the doctor or the nurse in charge and say, is there going to be a post-mortem for this patient?' 'No. Okay, the reason why that crowd is here is because this person had died and they want to come and see this person. Why don't you get the doctor to issue the death certificate ASAP? If the certificate is issued, you are allowed to release the body. If the body goes, the crowd goes, isn't that helpful to you?' And the staff say, 'Yes that is helpful'. I say, 'It's helpful to them because then they can get on with the funeral also', so it works both ways, so it's about using your wisdom sometimes, to help them. Then I will ring the funeral director as a matter of urgency, 'This is a difficult one, can you get here ASAP, because we have large crowds'. They will know when I am serious, and they will come in 10, 15 minutes. In that time I will have prepared the body, I will have done all the wrapping up and everything ... I do all that myself, with the staff, and they are very, very happy, the staff. So it helps the staff, it helps the Muslim community and it solves the problem (full-time male hospital chaplain).

Managers and staff appreciate the employment of Muslim chaplains because they become a point of reference for 'Muslim issues' raised by clients. There is no longer a reliance on Anglican or Christian chaplains to provide answers to questions relating to the needs or questions posed by Muslim clients. The incorporation of 'religion' within equality and human rights legislation can present very particular challenges for public sector managers who may lack expertise in this area. The appointment of a Muslim chaplain adds to the range of expertise that managers can access, if there is a need for advice or 'troubleshooting'. So, when prisoners are refusing to co-operate with security procedures on religious grounds, when female patients are refusing emergency life-saving treatment by male doctors or when Muslim students are refusing to take an exam scheduled over a religious holiday period, Muslim chaplains often have the knowledge and authority to transform a negative to an affirmative, on the basis of Islamic sources. It is their visible embodiment of religious authority that seems to be critical here:

> Even if I wrote it down and gave it to you word by word, or you can have a recording of me doing it, and you give that to the next family, are they going to listen? They're not going to listen. Because it's the authority that they're listening to, it's not the words (full-time male hospital chaplain).

Especially effective chaplains deploy their social and religious capital in ways that enable mutually advantageous outcomes to arise out of complex or potentially volatile situations. Another good example of this became clear to us when we interviewed senior prison officers at a Young Offender Institution:

[The Deputy-Governor] said that at the recent Eid event (held in the sports hall of the prison) there were 185 Muslim young offenders present. He said that the prison could not take the risk of having such a large gathering, were it not for the preparation work done by the imams beforehand and the 'relationship that Faysal and his team have with the boys'. He said this was 'key to the risk assessment' process. The imams had the 'people skills' to work effectively in the prison (e.g. in relation to crowd control), and that they have it 'spot on' in their relations with staff and prisoners. So, they are trusted by both. He noted that in some other prisons, there is a 'fear of Muslims' by staff, but not here. 'It's what they do for their boys' that staff respect (fieldnotes, November 2010).

As one Governor said to me: 'I don't always understand what it is that chaplaincy does but I know when I haven't got it and I don't like it when I haven't got it' (chaplaincy administrator).

The Impact of Chaplaincy Practice on Clients and their Families

The description of practices that underpin Muslim chaplaincy work in Chapter 4 documents the many ways in which chaplains support their clients, both directly and indirectly. Rather than rehearse these again here we consider situations in which chaplains have felt especially appreciated, often in highly sensitive pastoral cases. Before doing so, however, we take a short diversion into the 'material culture' of Muslim chaplaincy, and consider some of the artefacts both used and produced by chaplains as part of their work with clients.

Religious 'things' appear to be relatively insignificant for most Muslim chaplains as part of their role. This is likely to reflect the fact that most chaplains will know important Quranic verses or particular prayers, from memory. In many ways, their practice can be highly portable; there is usually no requirement to have particular artefacts, special dress or religious texts in order to perform much of their role. However, there are some chaplains who are becoming both conveyors and producers of material things. Thus, we came across examples of prison chaplains giving prisoners prayer beads, mats, scarves, dates and other items, usually when chaplains had been able to activate external donations. These are highly significant to prisoners, as an affirmation of their religious identity in a hostile environment. Hospital patients might receive small booklets containing prayers and supplications to provide courage in the face of illness and pain: useful reminders for those Muslims who have lost their connection to Islam over the years, but wish to reconnect in the face of illness. These necessarily become 'gifts' as a consequence of hospital policies around infection control. But among the artefacts of Muslim chaplaincy work we came across, one was particularly striking. *A Gift for the Bereaved Parent* was compiled by Zamir Hussain, a part-time female chaplain at Birmingham Children's Hospital (BCH). Its production

Figure 6.1   Cover of *A Gift for the Bereaved Parent*, written and compiled by Zamir Hussain, Birmingham Children's Hospital

is of profound cultural and religious significance because of the way in which it maps onto a range of existing practices around death and bereavement in British hospitals.

Many hospital chaplaincies organise events to support bereaved parents, usually an annual 'memorial' service in the hospital to which all bereaved families are invited. Condolence cards might be sent on the anniversary of the child's death, and parents might leave the hospital with reading material offering comfort and solace, drawn from Christian traditions. Over time, the chaplaincy team at BCH became increasingly conscious of the lack of suitable material for bereaved Muslim parents. They sought and won external funding for a project that would lead to the *Gift*. Throughout the process, they were concerned that the book should reflect the cultural situation of Muslims in Britain. Thus, borrowing the newsagent 'pocket/gift-book' format, they produced a book, in consultation with Islamic scholars and bereaved families that gave 'death' a new cultural meaning.

The books most associated with Islam are scriptural, and while these may be given as 'gifts', they are intended to be read and used. The *Gift* is also meant to be read, of course, but not in quite the same way, because its format implies far greater agency on the part of the reader. This is a book into which personal meaning can be injected and memories kept alive; it is a book to be treasured for the human bonds that it represents. In this way, the textual content is perhaps less important than the subjective meanings associated with the artefact itself. For our purposes, the production of the book shows the way in which death and bereavement can acquire new meaning for British Muslims (as an occasion for 'gift-giving') and thus resourced in novel ways. The book is now available via a range of UK bereavement charities, and a reader who sourced the book via Amazon.co.uk reviewed it thus:

> I bought this book sometime after the loss of my son … what this book offers is hope and helps to accept what is ultimately decided by Allah. It really did help me on my journey to accept and heal. I can't recommend this book enough, it's refreshing and full of empathy (SJav 22.2.12).

For a range of practical and methodological reasons, much of our client data arises from focus group discussions in prisons and young offender institutions, although some of the more moving stories arise from the work of hospital chaplains. But before examining data from these two sectors, it is important to note that chaplains working in higher education were by no means silent about their value and significance. A number of them described crisis situations faced by individual students, as well as traumatic events on campus that had left other Muslim students shocked and bereaved (for example, sudden death). In such situations, chaplains have been able to intervene to good effect. Higher education chaplains also noted the degree to which their role is seen as beneficial for the public relations of the university, and a 'selling point' in promotional materials. Institutions appear to recognise that there is a distinctive 'religious market' that is likely to respond well to the appointment of a Muslim chaplain (Gilliat-Ray 2000). However, the fact that relatively few higher education chaplains are religious scholars, compared to their prison and hospital counterparts, has a bearing on the degree to which students regard them as religious authority figures. During an interview with the President of the Islamic Society at a university in London, he noted that while the chaplain was a useful ally in the campaign for resources within the institution, he could not be consulted on matters of religious guidance, thus limiting his value. The reverse side of this particular coin came from a chaplain who noted that not being a trained imam was distinctly advantageous. Instead of assuming he would lead Friday prayers on campus students were forced, or rather 'empowered', to exercise or source religious leadership themselves. Seen through the lens of the 'employability' agenda in higher education, the advantages and disadvantages of being an Islamic scholar can clearly be read in various ways.

In light of these reflections on religious qualifications and authority, it is ironic that a female hospital chaplain (not an 'alima) noted that having religious knowledge was irrelevant, and could potentially be unhelpful, if it was not deployed in the right way. She described a particularly memorable situation where she used her pastoral skill to undo the damage caused by an 'alim, but also made hospital chaplaincy relevant to a Muslim family, for the first time. The story she narrated involved a young girl who had given birth to a still-born baby in hospital. Amid her grief, the patient's family asked a religious scholar from their own community to come in to provide pastoral care. What he said was technically correct in terms of Islamic law; he noted that because the baby had not breathed, it was 'pure' and could therefore be buried without washing, without a funeral prayer and with no ritual required. Because she was young and healthy, the scholar conveyed good wishes for more successful future pregnancies. Our interviewee continues the story:

> ... but it was dismissive. His need to make her feel better was so great that he was very dismissive of her pain ... So this woman, she wasn't only dissatisfied, she was *completely, completely* upset, she was so upset that she felt her baby is not even worthy of having ghusl [ritual washing]. Later on, the mother came to the prayer room to offer her prayers and met me coming out of my office. She wondered who I was. I explained and she said, 'We didn't know there was anybody like that here, we didn't know that the hospital had a Muslim chaplain ... please, I need you now'. ... I said, 'Of course, I'll come'. And when I went, first of all I started to listen, empathise, make sure that she said what she wanted to say ... but to end the story, I was aware that some damage had already been done and I have to now undo that damage as well as just do whatever I would have normally done. So I allowed her to speak and she was crying about it, 'This man who came, he's telling me my baby doesn't even get a ghusl just because it was still-born. I can't understand what's happening here, is my baby not as important as any baby that was born alive?' I said, 'Of course it's important ... do you know that the martyrs on the battlefield, they're not given the ghusl because they are so pure, that they are buried as they are'. Then she could see that her baby would be elevated to the ranking of a martyr basically, and it made her feel that self-worth come back, and it made her feel that 'my baby is important and isn't to be dismissed' (part-time female hospital chaplain).

In some cases, chaplains feel their pastoral intuition has saved lives as these two stories both narrated by the same chaplain indicate:

> I've one example that to this day I'm still puzzled about. It happened about four or five years ago. A young girl – a little girl – about eight months or something – I had seen her during the day; her mum asked for me to come to see and pray

with her which I did, a morning meeting about midday. At three o'clock in the morning I got a call that she's dying. The paediatric consultant and I walked through the doors together literally, to call it a day. She was on this monitor, all wired up and he started undoing all the wiring and everything. He had a nurse that was assisting; mum was there, I was there and I just said, 'Can I pray a last prayer before you do that?' And he said, 'Yes'. I started praying and this baby responded. She responded so well that [the doctor] stood back and said, 'Wait a minute, I'm seeing something different'. He stopped the nurse and he started doing his tests and he said, 'Let's carry on with the treatment'. We were there until … like nine o'clock in the morning because we were seeing progression. That baby lived for two and a half years … I still remember that night when [the doctor and I] walked in the doors together – we literally walked in together. And I really feel that there was something there about timing of us both going together. Had he gone in before me, had I gone in before him, it might not have been the same story.

About a year ago in ICU the senior consultant called me and said, 'We've decided to turn off the ventilators for this patient, he's not responding'. I went to see him and it just felt so different. I don't know how he felt, the patient, but I felt different and I came out thinking that I'm going to say to the doctor, 'It's Friday today, give him the weekend. Give him another couple of days; let's see how he goes'. In my mind I was thinking, if he dies today, the registration of death will be difficult – all these things were going in my head. The daughter came up to me and she said, 'Have you been praying with my father?' I said, 'Yes'. She said, 'The doctors have told me that this is it now, but I was wondering if you could ask them for some more time?' I said, 'Why do you say that?' This was only about ten seconds after I was thinking the same, but I wanted a reason and she said to me, 'Because my son is in prison and I need to let the authorities know and I need some time for him to come before they turn off, so Monday would be good, if they'd do that'. And I thought, you know, these are all signs and signals from God. [The doctor] is one of these consultants who always calls me whenever there's an issue and I said, look, 'What difference is it going to make if you give him another 48-hours in terms of your work, your preparation?' He said, 'Nothing much'. And I said, 'I feel, personally, that another 48-hours won't make much difference', and he said, 'Fine'. That was the Friday afternoon. Sunday morning the guy was sat up in bed. And you know, his daughter, she just couldn't believe it and she was thanking me, 'Oh, thank you for stopping the doctor from doing that'. I said, 'I didn't, I just mentioned it to him and they decided to do it'. Funnily enough it was the first ever case that I said, 'Can we buy time?' Normally, every time the consultants call me I say, 'Yes, okay, fine', but for this, for some reason, I thought, no. That guy came out of ICU on the rehab ward. All in all, he was alive for another six months, I just couldn't believe it. So, I'm a firm believer in when the time is right … not a single split second before or after what is meant to be your time on the earth … (full-time male hospital chaplain).

We have deliberately included these lengthy stories, narrated in the words of the chaplains themselves, because they point to some of the ways in which chaplains consider their work to be valuable for clients on the basis of profound spiritual intuition, and distinctively Islamic viewpoints. While the duration and content of such pastoral encounters could clearly be measured in some senses (for example staff time, actions performed, client 'satisfaction') this would of course miss the point entirely. But these accounts also reveal the capacity of Muslim chaplains to narrate pastoral case studies, perhaps one of the strongest indicators of the degree to which they have acquired distinctive identities, as reflective practitioners of chaplaincy.

When we talked to Muslim prisoners about the 'value' of the work done by Muslim chaplains (though male offenders consistently preferred the term imams), they tended to repeat many of the 'qualities' that chaplains themselves recognise as important (and which we documented in Chapter 3). Prisoners talked about chaplains as good listeners, effective teachers, successful facilitators, credible Muslim role models and so on. Our findings also echo those of Gabriele Marranci, who noted that for Muslim prisoners, 'Islam ... was the element through which they asked the establishment to respect them' (Marranci 2009: 116). He notes the myriad ways in which dignity is a

> ... sore point ... Muslims often perceived that their dignity was at best ignored and at worst purposely attacked, both as individuals and as a group. From halal meat to full searches, from offensive jokes to nicknaming ... Muslims in prison at times interpreted the simple mistakes of officers, or certain prison rules, as an assault on their dignity (Ibid. 115).

During our research, we saw evidence of ways in which Muslim chaplains can help to mitigate these negative feelings and restore dignity. The contrasting ways in which officers and chaplains perceive the space of the prison cell is a good example. At a Young Offender Institution, a boy was feeling upset at the way a prison officer had entered his cell without warning just as he was concluding his prayers. His prayer mat was still on the floor, and the officer walked over his prayer mat with his shoes on, thereby 'polluting' the one space within the cell that the prisoner regarded as 'pure'. During our focus group discussion the boy said that the officer could have waited. He said to me '... you should have picked it up, you should have done this, man ... he could have just waited and I could have just picked it up ... obviously I was going to'. We saw, during our fieldwork in this establishment (and others) and we heard prisoners describe to us, the way Muslim chaplains would enter their cells in a very different way. Instead of opening the viewing window, unlocking and just walking in, as an officer would, the chaplain/s knock on the door to signal their presence, tells the prisoner who they are and only then enter the cell. In this way, Muslim chaplains use their ambiguous position within the authority structures of the prison to find ways of conferring dignity on offenders through the simplest form of action.

Prisoners seem highly aware, however, of the ambiguity and tension chaplains must face between being key-carrying servants of the state, and members of a shared religious community (often expressed through the vocabulary of kinship). A group of female offenders seemed to respect the way their chaplain managed this tension: 'I would say she sticks to the rules of the prison, but she's always here for us … she tells you if you are wrong … she is straight with you' (focus group discussion, February 2011). The women felt that the chaplain demonstrated her commitment to them by doing more than simply 'facilitating' religious observance. She had successfully manipulated a range of structures and systems within the prison to bring about institution-wide change, also recognised by a Deputy-Governor:

> What I have noticed is that she is quite proactive in celebrating the fact that there are Muslim prisoners here. And when they celebrated Eid after Ramadan, she was instrumental in organising the feasts; afterwards ensuring that as many of the staff and managers could get there as possible, ensuring that every Muslim prisoner that wanted to be there was there. And that's no mean feat in a prison that's spread out like this one is, and it takes a great deal of hard work. I'm not convinced that we have had that before [Henna] arrived (interview, February 2011).

At the time of our fieldwork, the women were in jubilant spirits in relation to a more recent initiative on her part:

> One good thing she's organised for us, because we aren't able to go to the gym, because there are men there. There are men who hold the classes. So, I mean, she's managed to get one of the female staff here trained up for us, and they've ordered us new kit as well, so that we're fully covered, our legs and arms are fully covered, and they're going to do a PE class for us, just for the Muslim ladies, so I think that's brilliant, because now we can actually go and get some exercise in some sort of class (focus group discussion, February 2011).

Some young male offenders were optimistic that, upon release, their newly acquired understanding of their faith, derived from the example and teaching of the imams, would help them to stay on the straight path because 'they teach you how to stay out of trouble, inside and out' (focus group, YOI, November 2010). In this case, they had been taught that irrespective of whether the criminal justice system was aware of their actions, 'Allah is watching' (Ibid.). Equipping prisoners with the skills to manage their own conduct after release suggests that

> … the reformist or rehabilitative role of the chaplain endures. It now takes the shape of a less aggressive form of pro-social modelling, whereby, through their own performances and relationships, chaplains reflect back to the prison community a way of being and behaving that can be, hopefully, inspirational, educative and thus transformational (Todd and Tipton 2011: 23).

However, Muslim chaplains are under no illusion as to how hard the process of release in Muslim communities in Britain can be:

> But unfortunately in our community the imam, the role of the imam has become very restricted. So they think 'oh, we've got an imam in the prison … it's the same as the imam that we have in our local community' … not realising that, you know, actually the purpose of an imam is to rehabilitate and to reinvigorate society, to re-establish the lost connections with God … I think the role of an imam is under a transformation as a younger generation is rising in our Muslim communities. But I think in terms of a community chaplaincy where we can refer prisoners that are leaving an establishment to a mosque, to an outside community, and for them to continue an effective rehabilitation, I think we are a long way away from that (full-time male prison chaplain).

In light of these comments, some chaplains feel frustrated that their educative and reformist efforts can be wasted when prisoners are released, because of the lack of support within British Muslim communities.

The Impact of Chaplaincy Practice on Muslim Institutions

The degree to which Muslim chaplains are able to exercise an influence upon Muslim institutions in Britain is often determined by the extent to which they have remained connected to, or have explicitly sought to be part of, local religious networks. Although we did not ask chaplains explicitly about these ties and relationships, it is evident that their positioning within the nexus of institutions and religious authority figures in their locality often determines the extent to which they can deploy their social capital and exercise agency between one institution and another.

Although male chaplains by virtue of their gender have relatively unproblematic access to mosques – perhaps the most numerous of Muslim organisations in Britain – female chaplains have nevertheless found their own ways of taking their experiences back into communities, as we shall see. And while we might expect full-time (male) chaplains to have lost their connections to local worshipping congregations – by virtue of their responsibilities within their institutions – some have found important ways of retaining links that provide a channel for exercising a positive influence on communities. These include activities such as leading prayers during Ramadan, serving on national Muslim bodies, or ensuring their inclusion within the local 'council for mosques'. It was clear that chaplains who retain strong community links can often use these to good effect for their clients, and vice versa.

But whatever the precise relationship that individual chaplains have with Muslim communities around them, there are significant tensions and frustrations. Interestingly, these appear to be reminiscent of the accounts of Christian chaplains who often feel that their experiences at the front line of human suffering or endeavour are largely unrecognised and undervalued within the life of the Church (Legood 1999b). Although not referring to chaplaincy specifically, Adam Dinham's observations about this conundrum are relevant here.

> Many faith-based projects, even where they started as initiatives directly arising from congregations, become dissociated, even divorced, from these roots as they grow and expand. Often by the time they have come to the attention of others outside of faiths they have travelled some considerable distance from the community of worshippers whose regular communion is a separate matter (Dinham 2009: 9).

Some chaplains in our study narrated pastoral incidents and aspects of their work with the explicit instruction: 'don't tell anyone'. This conveyed to us a rather nervous awareness on their part of the disapproval they might face if other community members became more fully aware of what their job sometimes involves and the tightropes they often have to walk between the expectations of Muslim communities and the norms of public life and institutions. The line between what is halal and haram is often not only a narrow one, but the boundaries between the two can be indistinct. 'Don't tell anyone' betrays the conservatism that still pervades many Muslim communities (especially in terms of leadership and mosque management structures), and it is indicative of the distance some chaplains have travelled into the world of professional chaplaincy:

> Interviewer: So, I mean, to what extent do you talk about your work in the community?
>
> Chaplain: I can talk to a level about the work that I do, not everything that I do because I don't think everything will be accepted.
>
> Interviewer: Why not?
>
> Chaplain: Because of their lack of understanding. [Gives example]. I don't think I can expose that [example] in the community because they won't understand or I might be criticised for that (full-time male hospital chaplain – example omitted intentionally to protect anonymity).

Many Muslim chaplains feel they have insights and experiences that could be used to benefit British Muslim institutions. In particular, they would like to contribute their knowledge and skills in relation to the professional management of mosques, better use of mosque spaces and facilities between prayer times, more proactive use of relevant Muslim professionals (for example using doctors to speak on health issues), inter-faith relations, ex-offender support, building effective contact with voluntary sector agencies, offering strategies for tackling substance abuse, provision of bereavement support and the question of disaffected youth. Chaplains appear to discern some of the untapped human and material capital that currently resides within Muslim communities. One chaplain noted that the most important thing community religious leadership could learn from chaplains is about pastoral relationships, and the fact that all Muslims, devout and practicing or not, still need the support of religious leaders. Because chaplains generally 'go out' to their clients (to the cells/wings, patient bedside/wards, student corridors), they felt imams should learn how to be more proactive and outward-facing:

> Interviewer: And finally, I mean what do you think community based imams could learn from you, what are the particular skills, knowledge and professionalism that you've learnt from chaplaincy?

> Chaplain: The personal relations with the followers. A person who's not very religious, maybe the imam has no real contact with them, but this thing [chaplaincy] has taught me that if he is not really a practising good Muslim, still he needs your help. And if you stay away from him, he will never return. He is your responsibility. The person who is religious, he will keep in touch with the imam. But the person who is not religious, the imam has no contact with. This chaplaincy service, I learnt from them that the weakest link is important (full-time male prison chaplain).

Many Muslims chaplains feel the conservatism of mosques, especially those that remain under the management of the 'elders' and the religious leadership of overseas imams, constitutes a significant obstacle to progress in shaping more engaged communities:

> I think probably about two years ago there was something going around that they are going to build or use a building that was already there for drug rehab. Because it was in very close proximity to the mosque, there was a big hoo-ha … 'we are not having drug dealers walking around', 'we are not having junkies walking around our streets and our children are going to be at risk'. But to be honest with you, like I said before, I think anybody who says in certain areas that they don't know of anybody in their family or their very close circle of friends that was under the influence of drugs or alcohol abuse regularly, I think they are lying (mixed-sector male chaplain).

> Even today I've been into a masjid and the imam speaks in a different language and he's speaking about how the other group of Muslims are wrong in what they're doing and how we're right in what we're doing. Do we really need to know, does the congregation really need to know about this? Do they really need to know that that group of Muslims over there in the other masjid are doing this right or wrong, is it relevant? It's not relevant. If we carry on talking in our

masajid in a different language about things that are irrelevant, about things that divide us rather than unite us, then the situation is going to get worse (full-time male prison chaplain).

Many chaplains are frustrated by the religious and structural barriers that seem to prevent the exploitation of their skills and experiences. For example, they are conscious of the tensions that could arise if their 'bottom-up' pastorally orientated ways of working were to clash with the rather more 'top-down' authoritative role of mosque-based imams and management. In a context where chaplaincy is generally perceived to be 'high value, high status' work for an Islamic scholar (evidenced by the intense competition for posts), chaplains have to be sensitive to the structural position of their mosque-based colleagues. Perhaps not surprisingly, we heard very few accounts of Muslim chaplains being invited to deliver sermons relating to their work.

The boundaries around prisons can impose particular barriers to the potential outreach of Muslim prison chaplains who, incidentally, have particularly realistic insights into the problems of substance abuse in Muslim communities (often compounded by drug-related gang violence). In comparison, the fluidity of the boundaries around hospitals, the relative transparency of the work that health care chaplains perform and the immediacy of the life-and-death situations they often face means that hospital chaplains seem to have far greater opportunity to undertake tasks and solve problems that can bring them social and religious capital in their locality. Health care chaplains who have established a reputation for their knowledge and effectiveness, especially in relation to the bureaucracy that surrounds death and burial procedures, can often trade on this to good effect in crisis situations of their own. But even the most effective health care chaplains have stories to tell which reveal angst and frustration with the conservatism within their communities. One health care chaplain recounted problems in his community with young Muslim girls having 'one night stands' that resulted in repeated pregnancies, and then hospital terminations:

> [Tahir] told me he had been called in by some of the senior maternity staff who were getting increasingly upset that these girls seemed to show no remorse. They were asking for his help, to see if he could try to get the community to take this issue seriously. He said that he did speak to the 'ulama in the city about it, most of whom he described as being 'in cuckoo land'. He said that at first, they were very keen to address this issue, but then their enthusiasm fizzled out (fieldnotes, full-time hospital chaplain).

Since much of the talk about the impact of Muslim chaplaincy work in Muslim communities that we heard about relates to hypothetical possibilities, rather than actual realities, we are at pains to cite here some examples of where chaplains have been able to 'make a difference' in both short- and long-term ways.

For example, we heard one story about an elderly Muslim who had died in hospital, but appeared to have no relatives to take care of the burial arrangements. His body was going to be placed in the care of social services, which would have inevitably delayed any funeral and burial.[1] Hearing about this, the chaplain intervened and drew upon the 'capital' bound up with relatively high levels of frequent mosque attendance in Muslim communities:

> I went to my local masjid [mosque] and I said, 'This is the situation we have. This person has no funds, no nothing, how can we raise the money for the burial costs and the funeral and everything?' And, alhamdulilah, in zuhr namaz [early afternoon prayer] the announcement was made, and then, Asr namaz [late afternoon prayer], we had £2,200, alhamdullilah (full-time male hospital chaplain).

Initiatives such as this indicate the bridging role that Muslim chaplains can have between different institutions, in this case between the hospital, the social services department and the local mosque. Galvanising the piety of the congregation in relation to the deceased man gave them an opportunity to invest in the efforts of the chaplain (not to mention the spiritual rewards they will have no doubt anticipated), and acquire a greater appreciation of his role. These incidents, like pebbles thrown into water, ripple outwards into communities and make chaplains increasingly identifiable points of contact for advice and information.

Alongside this example which demonstrates how chaplains can initiate practical action within communities, it is clear that chaplains also have important educative roles. A good illustration of this relates to hospital visiting practices and the disposal of bodily remains. Because of the religious merit attributed to visiting the sick, some Muslim patients in hospital receive very large numbers of visitors. This is usually inconvenient for staff, and contrary to hospital visiting policies. However, explaining to staff *why* this practice occurs can circumvent short-term difficulties, while the chaplain undertakes a longer-term educative task within the community:

> It's about educating your own people to say, 'Look, yes, to do the iyadat of a mareed [visiting the sick], to visit, there is reward, there is thawab [Arabic word for reward] in that, but to cause inconvenience to that person, to the staff or other, you know, sick people on that ward, it can lead to a sin. It's no good, so your thawab can change and be ruined. So please take care of the environment you go into ... like, if it means two people per bedside, take it in turns on a visit (full-time male hospital chaplain).

The same chaplain notes his educative work in the Muslim community regarding the disposal of body parts following surgery. Where most hospitals will send these

---

[1]   Muslims prefer burial to happen as soon as possible after death, ideally within 24 hours.

for incineration, he reminds Muslims that these human remains should, according to Islamic law, be buried rather than cremated.

In some cases, the impact that Muslim chaplains have on the wider Muslim community revolves almost exclusively around the relative novelty of their role. A female 'alima working in a prison noted that she was 'blazing a trail' for other traditionally trained Muslim women in Britain. Where many female scholars often tend to work almost entirely with other women and children after their graduation, primarily in teaching roles, she felt her work as a prison chaplain was demonstrating that there are other contexts in which Muslim women can legitimately share their religious knowledge:

> Usually with 'alimas you graduate and you've just got this one career path, you either teach at a madrassa or a school and that's fine … but I'd never heard of a professional role being occupied by an 'alima if you like, well not in the public sector anyway … I wanted something different, I like a challenge. And with prisoners I think there is such a need, that's where an 'alima is probably needed most 'cos a lot of these prisoners are new to Islam and they don't know much about Islam or you know they've just strayed and they want that guidance and I thought, who better than an 'alima to do that … there are lots of 'alima's in my community who are now, because they know what I do, they want the same position (part-time female prison chaplain).

She noted that some male scholars, even those who are highly supportive of Muslim women going into chaplaincy in principle, nevertheless operate by 'double standards' when they go on to express reservations about '*their* women' working within the morally suspect, mixed-gender environment of public sector institutions. She countered this with her own robust views: 'as 'alima's our Imaan [faith] is supposed to be strong [so] that we can go out into a morally corrupt environment and help without having to have a huge worry about our faith being affected'.

We heard examples of other Muslim women educating their communities on a range of issues and through a number of channels, including local radio stations, 'lobbying' of male religious leaders or using their father's or husband's links into the male congregation. In this way, female Muslim chaplains have been able to inform communities about Islamic funeral and burial rites, encourage more Muslim women to undertake hospital volunteering and remind the predominantly male mosque congregation of their duties towards 'sisters'. Muslim women in professional chaplaincy roles also signal to other women that, rather than relying on family networks for support and advice, there are alternative sources of help to which they can turn in times of trouble. Several of our interviewees noted that because of their reputation for chaplaincy work, women in the community seek out their advice and counsel on a range of sensitive issues, especially those which might normally attract 'judgement': 'the chaplaincy role does not end in the hospital, it goes on into the community so you're almost like a pillar of standing in the local community as well, people will refer to you' (part-time female hospital chaplain).

Despite these examples of influence, Muslim chaplains are unlikely to bring about significant structural or social change within Muslim communities, on their own. However, where they are able to work with other Muslim agencies, especially those involving and directed towards young people, their role as catalysts for change becomes apparent. For example, we heard a number of prison chaplains tell us about a project run by the 'Muslim Youth Helpline', a well-established British Muslim charity which had distributed Ramadan 'goodie bags' for prisoners. When a major Muslim organisation visibly supports Muslim offenders in this way, this is likely to help to challenge some of the taboos that currently exist around crime and deviance. Meanwhile, one of the stakeholders we interviewed noted that chaplaincy experience had empowered young British Muslim scholars, and had given them confidence:

> What is happening is that some of the young 'ulama are going back to the mosque occasionally, meeting the young people and saying, 'Look, things are different'. They're avoiding the mosque structure and shuyukh [Islamic scholars] but they are going and engaging with the young people. And this happens because they've become confident enough by engaging in chaplaincy (chaplaincy administrator).

What might be said in conclusion to this overview of the ways in which Muslim chaplains are influencing the wider Muslim community? It would appear that communities are receptive to requests by Muslim chaplains to provide money or material donations (dates, scarves, prayer mats) – things of perhaps obvious, calculable, religious 'merit' – and that communities can be receptive to religious instructions around Islamic etiquette within public institutions (adab). However they appear to be far less inclined to respond well if chaplains raise difficult moral questions, or suggest the internal reform of religious institutions.

The Impact of Muslim Chaplaincy Practice in Wider Society

There are numerous ways by which the work of Muslim chaplains has been recognised in British society today. Awards and honours, training and consultation, media profile, institutional and civic rewards are in different ways indicative of a professional group that has done more than simply 'arrive' on the pitch … they are now beginning to score goals (to continue the footballing metaphor cited by a Muslim chaplain in Chapter 5).

A number of individual Muslim chaplains have been awarded prestigious national level sector-specific awards on account of their work. In the Prison Service, these include Dr Mohamed El-Sharkawy, chaplain at HMP The Mount, winner of the Home Office Justice Shield in 2007, for his work in designing a programme for prisoner rehabilitation. In 2009, Muhammad Abrahams, chaplain at HMP Belmarsh, was awarded the Butler Trust award (Prison Service News, no. 264, April/May 2009, p23). Meanwhile, the Queen's Birthday Honours list in 2012 included recognition for Moosa Gora, the Muslim Chaplain at HMP Full Sutton, awarded an MBE for services to faith and diversity in the Prison Service. In 2010, Yunus Dudhwala was voted NHS Employee of the Year for his work as the Head of Chaplaincy and Bereavement Services at Newham University Hospital in London, while the 2012 London Olympics gave him a platform to contribute to Radio 4's 'Thought for the Day'. These are indicators of entrepreneurialism among Muslim chaplains, and the scope of chaplaincy to provide routes to social mobility. Their upward trajectory implies recognition in key public sector domains in Britain, at the highest levels.

These awards are also, however, a barometer of the strengths and weaknesses of different groups within the professional Muslim chaplaincy population. Thus, women do not figure in among the prize-winners, nor do part-time chaplains and nor do those working in sectors beyond prisons and hospitals. Three out of the four award holders are from the Deobandi school of thought, and of this number, two are British-born/trained. Seen in this light, the internal stratification within Muslim chaplaincy begins to come into relief, and highlights the differential opportunities to achieve social mobility, via employment as a Muslim chaplain. However, these differentials only become evident against the backdrop of a critical mass of Muslim chaplains in Britain today, which is of course an indicator of 'success' at some level.

Besides national level awards, there are other ways in which Muslim chaplains are shaping public life and policy in less visible or high-profile ways. They have been involved in national level consultations on organ donation, NHS uniform policies, counter-terrorism and 'capacity building' within Muslim communities. As they take part in these debates and consultations, they

> ... keep in place fundamental questions about what human life is for. And religions do this not just at an abstract level of intellectual debate. They do this by creating alternative institutions, forging new practices, and sustaining different regimes of life (Bretherton 2011: 362).

Elsewhere, we have written about some of the ways in which the work of Muslim chaplains requires public institutions to consider how changing population demographics might require new ways of delivering public services (Ali and Gilliat-Ray 2012). In this way, Muslim chaplains act as important barometers of social change. But their incorporation into publicly funded chaplaincy has also shifted assumptions about Anglican predominance in this sphere of religious work. The idea that chaplaincy is a multi-faith endeavour is now 'mainstream' and this inevitably shapes perceptions beyond the relatively small world of the chaplaincy profession itself. Thus, some of our interviewees felt their inclusion within chaplaincy had been invigorating for the profession as a whole.

Muslim chaplains have been proactively engaged in negotiations to establish what is 'compulsory' for Muslims within public institutions, and what is merely 'preferable'. The example of 'what counts' as halal (see Chapter 4) is a good example of this. This effort, initially driven by the practically orientated work of 'visiting ministers', has become increasingly political, theoretical and theological with the appointment of 'Muslim chaplains'. This transition has brought about a seismic shift of emphasis within professional chaplaincy more generally. An important outcome of this process has been the accumulation of different kinds of religious and social capital located within the diversity of faith traditions and personalities in chaplaincy teams which, under the right conditions, can be used to support chaplains of all traditions. An example of this growth of collaborative activity can be seen in the way that a Muslim chaplain was able to negotiate a catering issue on behalf of a Roman Catholic colleague.

> Certainly the Roman Catholic chaplain was reassured because he didn't have those same kinds of links that I had with catering and it would have been difficult for him to resolve that issue. So I was ... and vice-versa, there have been issues where my Christian colleagues have resolved issues for me to do with Muslims or Muslim prisoners because they had better relationships with the staff who were dealing with the issue at the time, so it goes both ways (full-time male prison chaplain).

Conclusion

The voices we have heard in this chapter reflect the very different narratives that underpin views about Muslim chaplaincy work. For chaplains, their religious vocation is likely to be predominant. For institutional staff and managers, the value of chaplains is likely to be shaped by more instrumental considerations around 'troubleshooting' and performing the emotional work that other staff might find more difficult, for example breaking bad news, or management of death. For clients, the narrative is about meeting of religious needs, offering services, dignity or comfort. Amid these narratives, chaplains occupy an important intermediate space between private and public realms not least

> because of the manner in which faiths look both ways – inwards to the private interior life of devotion, faith and fellowship; and outwards to the public exterior life of social justice, love, neighbourhood and compassion to which they are often directed, theologically, if not in practice (Dinham et al. 2009: 200).

Irrespective of the narratives at play and the points of intersection between them, the work of Muslim chaplains has reinvigorated the significance of religion in public institutions in Britain. The level of religious adherence within many Muslim communities in Britain, and the degree to which this observance is public and corporate, has challenged prevailing assumptions about religion as an essentially private and individual matter. The boundaries between the state and civil society and between the public, private and personal (Dinham et al. 2009: 14) have been, and continue to be, contested, renegotiated and debated.

Our data also show that Muslim chaplaincy is, in the words of one of our interviewees, 'cultivating a more outward-facing approach to being a Muslim in Britain' (full-time male prison chaplain). And although one stakeholder predicted that it will take 'twenty years' before the full impact of Muslim chaplaincy work is evident in Muslim communities, our research points to some important seeds of change that have been nurtured by the first generation of Muslim chaplains. However, the degree to which future growth will be possible depends to some extent upon broader social, economic and political factors in wider society, and the degree to which reduction in public sector funding impacts upon chaplaincy in general, and Muslim chaplaincy in particular.

Chapter 7

Muslim Chaplaincy in the
United States of America

Introduction

The growth of Muslim chaplaincy in Britain has been paralleled by developments
in other parts of the world, especially the United States, and more recently in
different European countries (Baig 2012; Furseth and Kuhle 2011; Ganley
2012). It is not within the scope of this book to explore these developments in
any great depth, but some degree of international comparison with chaplaincy
developments in the USA will be helpful for throwing development and practice
in the UK into relief.

In Chapter 1, we mapped the 'drivers' for the development of Muslim
chaplaincy in England and Wales since the 1970s. Many of these were distinctive
to a particular political, social and religious period of time. Changing political
currents orientated towards more accountable and inclusive public services
arose as a consequence of the synergy between particular political ideologies
during a particular phase in British political history. The demographic of Muslim
communities in Britain, especially its growth and disproportionately youthful
character, had significant implications for public institutions trying to manage
increasing need for their services, along with the complexity of the religious
issues arising as a consequence. Political and social change was mirrored by
significant developments within Muslim communities, especially the increasing
availability of British-born Islamic religious scholars able to take up newly
created chaplaincy posts. Muslim chaplaincy in Britain has been shaped by the
influence of a particular school of Islamic thought which reflects the distinctive
migration history of Muslims in Britain, and the flow of particular kinds of
economic, social and religious capital. These developments were set in the
context of the more inclusive, 'multi-faith' ethos starting to shape professional
chaplaincy bodies from the late 1990s onwards, enabling Muslims to find new
spaces of belonging and identity. But all these 'drivers' of change reflect the
confluence of a particular set of political, social and religious dynamics in a
specific context.

The migration history and demographic of Muslims in the United States and
in various European countries is obviously quite different to England and Wales,
as is the broader political and social history of these societies. This being the
case, how can we account for the growth of Muslim chaplaincy as a developing
international phenomenon in a range of countries where Muslims constitute a

significant minority? What are the similarities and differences in practice and experience? To what extent are programmes of education and structures for professional accreditation in place? To what extent is chaplaincy practice shaped by varying social, political and religious histories?

The character of Muslim communities in the United States is distinct from the UK, not only because of its diversity, but also because Muslims practise their faith in a society shaped by the First Amendment ('Congress shall make no law respecting an establishment of religion, or prohibiting the free exercise thereof'). By exploring the shape of Muslim chaplaincy in the United States, the distinctiveness of British Muslim experiences come into view, and we can make some evaluation of how the work of Muslim chaplains might be shaped by different political currents, and socio-religious histories.

This chapter draws upon desktop research and a short period of fieldwork in July 2011. It relies mainly on interviews conducted by Mansur Ali at the Islamic Society of North America (ISNA) Annual Convention in Chicago in 2011, where he had the opportunity to conduct interviews, and to present our research to a group of Muslim chaplains attending a fringe meeting. During his time in the US, Ali conducted eight recorded interviews (several of which included more than one interviewee) and in this way, we captured the experiences and views of ten Muslim chaplains from a range of sectors (education, health, prison, military), of both genders, with differing levels of experience and different religious backgrounds. Some of our interviewees were South Asian, some were African-American, some white converts. Muslim chaplains participating in a convention of this kind are not necessarily 'representative', and are perhaps among those with a particular interest in the development of professional Muslim chaplaincy in the US; their voices are thus far from 'ordinary', in all senses of the word. During his time in America, Ali also established contact with key staff, and former and current students of Hartford Theological Seminary in Connecticut, one of the few providers of accredited Muslim chaplaincy training in the US. This data allows us to suggest some broad comparisons between the development and practice of chaplaincy in the US and in England and Wales.

The questions posed during these interviews in the US were very similar to those asked of chaplains and stakeholders in England and Wales, but were nuanced to reflect important differences between the two societies gleaned from initial desktop research. For example, we hypothesised that the politics of Muslim chaplaincy in America was probably shaped in some distinctive ways by the 9/11 terrorist attacks, but to what extent was that evident in the experiences of those we interviewed? How, and to what extent, does the particular significance of African-American history shape Muslim chaplaincy work in the US? How have professional chaplaincy associations accommodated the growing number of Muslim chaplains? These, and other questions, were at the heart of our research in the US.

Muslims and Chaplaincy in America: A Brief Overview

As a matter of government policy, the US does not collect quantitative data about the religious identity of its population. Consequently, there are widely discrepant figures given for the number and socio-economic profile of Muslims in America (Haddad and Smith 1995; Kohut 2007). Numbers vary from as few as two million, rising to eight million, with most estimates at around six million (Hamilton 2006). By now, the heterogeneity of Muslim communities is well known, as is the growth of mosques, Islamic associations and schools that serve Muslim communities.

The Muslims of America are a mixture of immigrants, native-born African-American and white converts and transient sojourners (such as students). The Pew Research Centre report *Muslim Americans* (Kohut 2007) estimated that about 65 per cent of Muslims in America were foreign-born, and 35 per cent native-born Muslims. Within these figures the distinctive character of Islam in America today begins to emerge: about 24 per cent of Muslims in the US are Arabs (from a range of countries) and 20 per cent are African-American (the largest single racial group). There are significant South Asian Muslim communities (Pakistanis, Indians), growing numbers of white converts and well-established centres of Iranian settlement. More recent research estimates that African-American Muslims may now constitute more like 35 per cent of the overall Muslim population (Gallup, 2009, *Muslim Americans*). It also shows that compared to the general population, Muslims have better than average rates of employment, are more likely to be in professional jobs and that well over half consider themselves to be 'thriving' (61 per cent, in contrast to just 8 per cent of British Muslims, based on international comparisons).

In terms of infrastructure, American Muslims have been energetic in establishing schools, mosques and organisations to represent their interests in the public sphere. Among these are CAIR (Council on Islamic-American Relations), a civil liberties organisation based in Washington DC, and ISNA (Islamic Society of North America). ISNA was founded in 1982, but traces its origins to Muslim student associations formed in the 1960s (Haddad and Smith 1995). It is probably the largest Muslim association in the US today. It aims to meet the internal needs of Muslim communities, but also directs its energies towards greater Muslim engagement in public life, and improved understanding of Islam in wider society. In recent years, ISNA has provided a forum for American Muslim chaplains to meet one another to discuss issues of common concern, holding the first chaplaincy conference in 2005. It also has a more formal (if contested) role as a referring agency (or 'endorsing body') for chaplains applying to work in the US Bureau of Prisons (Seymour 2006).

The Muslim population in the United States has evolved as a result of several phases of immigration that stretch back to the late 1800s, and in more recent times, conversion and procreation. In the early 1920s and 1930s, a range of African-American Islamic groups evolved in the US, such as the Nation of

Islam (NOI). Though this group was founded on the idea that Islam was the true religion of African-Americans, its doctrines differed in a number of important respects in relation to orthodox Muslim belief. These centred on the notion of black supremacy, and the need for black people to separate themselves from white subjugation. The idea that black suffering was caused by white oppression was popular in deprived black communities in major American cities (Moore 1995), and it had particular appeal for black prisoners incarcerated in large urban prisons. If Muslim chaplaincy has a history in the US, it begins with the early experiences of NOI ministers and volunteers in the 1930s; this explains the predominance of African-Americans in Muslim prison chaplaincy today.

Despite this relatively long history, when the African-American Muslim convert James (Jimmy) Jones submitted his D. Min. thesis on Islamic prison ministry at Hartford Seminary in 1989, he noted that there was very limited literature on prisons, or 'corrections'. He went on to note that 'the available material on the general topic of prison chaplaincy is even worse, and the limited literature on Islam in prisons was focused either on "how to" meet the needs of Muslim prisoners, or simply rehearsed the contribution of Muslims to prison ministry and rehabilitation' (Jones 1989: 69) His thesis was probably the first reflective piece of writing about Muslim prison chaplaincy, drawing upon his experiences at the Community Correctional Centre in New Haven. Other studies have examined Black Muslim conversion experiences in prisons (Ammar et al. 2004; Barringer 1998), and legal cases brought in relation to the practice of Islam and the work of Muslim chaplains in prisons (Moore 1995; Seymour 2006; Smith 1993). But relatively little sustained academic research has been done with Muslim chaplains themselves that explores their day-to-day practice in-depth across a range of institutions.

However, this situation slowly began to change in the mid-2000s and has been accelerating very rapidly since 2010. For example, several academic projects and research-based articles have explored the work of Muslim chaplains in American higher education (Hamilton 2006; Khoja-Moolji 2011). Doctoral research carried out by a Muslim university administrator in the United States draws extensively on interviews with chaplains in a number of US universities (Kassam-Remtullah 2012). The recent recruitment of a Muslim into a workplace chaplaincy team (Tyson Foods, Tennessee) has not gone without notice (Waller 2012). Important research is now being done around Muslim health care chaplaincy (Abu-Ras 2010; Abu-Ras 2011; Abu-Ras and Laird 2010; Padela et al. 2010; Padela et al. 2012), and new attention is being devoted to the educational role of Muslim chaplains in prisons (Bowers 2009). Alongside these developments, American Muslim chaplains recognise the importance of writing about their work. Prior to our interviews in the US, we identified a number of reflective articles authored by Muslim chaplains, some of which were contained in a special issue of the professional chaplaincy journal *Reflective Practice* (Ansari 2009; Harris 2009; Kowalski 2009; Lahaj 2009; Levine 2009). Fortunately, we were able to interview some of these contributors during our fieldwork.

The fact that our study with Muslim chaplains in England and Wales has occurred in parallel with this upsurge in research and writing about Muslim chaplaincy in the US is probably a good indication of some important commonalities and similar contextual drivers. For example, the Muslim populations in the UK and US have both grown rapidly since the late 1990s (Gallup, Muslim Americans, 2009; Gilliat-Ray 2010b), posing some distinctive challenges to public institutions offering pastoral care services. The recruitment of Muslim chaplains appears to have been a pragmatic response to these demographic changes and new institutional pressures on each side of the Atlantic. Likewise, the needs of Muslim communities in terms of religious leadership appear to be changing as new generations of British and American Muslims begin to explore the ethical, personal and religious challenges of their multi-faith societies, each of which reflect distinctive arrangements for religion in the public sphere. Mosque-based imams are not necessarily best placed to help resolve these issues: 'such modern needs ... have created the institution of chaplaincy' for Muslims (Abdullah 2011: 6). Furthermore, in the US, as in Britain, aspiring Muslim religious leaders appear to be looking at career directions beyond mosques and Islamic institutions. As one of our interviewees noted:

> ... they're choosing not to be imams because they don't know what they're going to face in the mosque, they don't know what the chain of command is, they're not well paid, more than anything they're not well respected. They go into an institution as a chaplain, they know very clearly what their job is, they have good supervision, they have support in case of crises, [and] they have a career path (interview July 2011, chaplaincy administrator/educator).

Meanwhile, both British and American societies have suffered the consequences of extreme acts of terrorism carried out in the name of Islam; these have stimulated far greater attention on the work of Muslim chaplains, and their potential contribution in countering extremist interpretations of Islamic sources. So there are some obvious similarities that help to explain the growth in Muslim chaplaincy in the US, in Britain and various other European societies since the mid-2000s. It is perhaps inevitable that as professional chaplaincy evolves in these various contexts, there will be parallel issues and concerns. We found that questions about qualifications and training, gender roles, accountability, accreditation and endorsement are the subjects of vigorous debate on each side of the Atlantic (Abdullah 2011).[1]

However, because the growth of Muslim chaplaincy in the US and in England and Wales has occurred against the background of very different socio-political and religious histories, these debates can sometimes have different points of emphasis.

---

[1]   The question of the 'accountability' of Muslim chaplains, to their institutions, to the people they serve, to the Muslim community, to the society at large and to Allah was noted in a lecture by Prof Ingrid Mattson at Yale University, 'The Future of Muslim Chaplaincy in the US', 10th March 2012.

These help to explain some noteworthy differences between Muslim chaplaincy in the US and in Britain. A good starting point for this comparative exploration is a brief consideration of the ethos of professional chaplaincy education in the USA. This has shaped the evolution of professional Muslim chaplaincy in America in some particular ways, especially in terms of the question of 'who' becomes a Muslim chaplain. Although American chaplains in some sectors are often called upon to perform very similar tasks as their counterparts in England and Wales, there are some important differences in the educational background, religious formation and action guiding worldviews of many Muslims serving as chaplains today. This appears to have shaped their practice in distinctive ways, as we shall see shortly.

Professional Chaplaincy Education in America

If Muslim chaplaincy in the US has emerged in relation to the distinctive experiences of African-Americans from the 1920s, is has also been shaped by the educational framework and professional structures of chaplaincy that have evolved from the writings of Anton Boisen, a hospital chaplain. In 1925, he founded the 'Clinical Pastoral Education' (CPE) movement, a form of practical theological education that placed an emphasis not so much on academic knowledge, but rather on reflective practice derived from experience. CPE stresses the need to examine pastoral conversations in depth, and to use these as the basis for professional pastoral training (Pattison 2000). CPE is undertaken as part of a supervised internship consisting of 'units' comprising a certain number of hours. This emphasis on lived experience in CPE coincided with the emergence of humanistic psychological theories (for example Carl Rogers, and Eric Berne) and the development of therapeutic pastoral counselling techniques focused on the individual. These ideas and techniques were attractive to theological educators and pastors for a whole host of reasons, and have shaped the ethos of professional pastoral care training in North America for well over 50 years. They remain central today. In 1967, the Association for Clinical Pastoral Education (ACPE) was established in the US, and it remains today the accrediting agency in the field of CPE by the US Secretary of Education and the US Department of Education. It claims to have trained over 65,000 individuals internationally; students come from many different world religions, including Islam.[2] Alongside this emphasis on reflective practice, the growth of religious diversity in American society has stimulated the idea that an appropriately trained chaplain can deliver 'generic' pastoral care, irrespective of their own faith tradition.

> In the United States, chaplaincy services are designed and practiced according to the paradigm of pastoral care or 'spiritual care' for all, regardless of religious affiliation. Chaplains are often trained, paid and credentialed by specific

---

[2]   http://www.acpe.edu/, accessed 20.9.12.

denominational institutions; nevertheless, they frequently serve outside the boundaries of religious affiliation (Abu-Ras and Laird 2010: 55).

In this paradigm, it is assumed that experiences of human suffering are more or less shared, irrespective of belief or culture, and that a reflective practitioner of chaplaincy will be able to discern and meet the spiritual needs of the client, regardless of their faith (or lack thereof). Muslims who are employed as chaplains in American society are required to operate within this paradigm, and recent initiatives have sought to make them more familiar with it. Thus the ACPE established a 'task force' on Islam in 2004, with the goal of 'extending to the Islamic community the spirit and practice of inclusivity that characterizes the Association of Clinical Pastoral Education' (Anderson 2009). This important milestone, itself a recognition of the emergence of Muslim chaplaincy in America, resulted in a special issue of the ACPE journal *Reflective Practice* in 2009 devoted to the work of Muslim chaplains. At the core of this special issue was an article by Rabia Terri Harris, written to support CPE supervisors working with Muslim students. Other contributors to the special issue wrote more personally about their own experiences of undertaking CPE, as Muslim chaplains.

CPE is one defining feature of professional chaplaincy training in the US. But so is the expectation that chaplains will have a relevant academic qualification at Masters level, or above. When Muslims first began to enter professional full-time chaplaincy work, this academic standard often presented a significant obstacle. One of our interviewees noted that:

> … the US military had granted some waivers on some of the requirements for Muslims at the beginning, simply out of an urgency to provide their right for religious accommodation for the Muslims who are in the military. So they did make a waiver for educational requirements for them, but that wasn't going to last forever and didn't necessarily serve the Muslim community very well if their chaplains didn't have an equivalent education (chaplaincy administrator/educator).

This was a catalyst for the development of the Islamic Chaplaincy Programme at Hartford Seminary in Connecticut. The Seminary had a long history of professional Christian ministerial training, especially for those in non-traditional settings or specialist ministries (for example Black Ministries Programme, Women's Leadership, Hispanic Ministries). Furthermore, it had an established reputation as a centre of excellence for academic and professional work in Christian-Muslim relations. It was therefore well placed to develop a new educational programme for Muslim chaplains.

The Islamic Chaplaincy Programme evolved following the appointment of Professor Ingrid Mattson as Director in 1998. Mattson is a Canadian convert to Islam with a PhD in Islamic Studies from Chicago. After several years of 'fact-finding' to establish what the needs of professional Muslim chaplains might be, the new programme was launched in 2000. A strategic decision was made at the outset to pitch the course at graduate level. Mattson recognised that the early cohort of students would need to have sufficient academic capability, combined with experiential understanding based on practice, to generate a new professional Muslim chaplaincy discourse and training materials for subsequent students.

> Many people were urging us, and even my own administration very often said, 'well, why don't we just do a certificate programme?' I felt that for our part we'd make a greater contribution if we had a higher level program, because I felt that we were not only training chaplains, we were simultaneously developing the field. I tell students, 'you are the ones that are going to have to develop the field' (interview, July 2011).

The articles in *Reflective Practice* authored by graduates of the Hartford programme demonstrate the value of this early strategic decision to train Muslim chaplains at graduate level. The articles show Muslim chaplains contributing to professional chaplaincy discourse in a way that seems unlikely in Britain at this point in time. By developing Muslim chaplains via an accredited academic institution with a long track record in theological education, graduates of the Hartford programme have been able to acquire professional recognition on equal terms with their counterparts in other faiths, and are especially well placed to continue contributing to professional chaplaincy discourse into the future. Despite this promising outlook, Muslim chaplains are represented in very small numbers within mainstream professional chaplaincy associations; the Association of Professional Chaplains had 1,600 certified members in 2000, of which one was Muslim. By 2006, only two of its 2,000 members were Muslim (Jones 2007).

The Accreditation and Training of Muslim Chaplains in America

Admission to the Islamic Chaplaincy course at Hartford rests upon academic credentials, most clearly evident through having a BA degree from a recognised university. If this same condition were to be applied to the existing Muslim chaplaincy training programmes in Britain today, it follows from the discussion in Chapter 3 that many traditionally trained Islamic religious scholars would be immediately excluded. Furthermore, if a professionally orientated Masters-level course in Islamic chaplaincy was to become a requirement for Muslims applying to chaplaincy positions in HM Prison Service, in the NHS or in any other public organisation, it would be virtually impossible to fill the vacancies. This is because very few British Islamic scholars with a strong command of Islamic texts, competence in Arabic and a disposition for (or some experience of) chaplaincy work have any recognised academic qualifications. Meanwhile, those British Muslims with the requisite academic profile are usually 'self-taught' in relation to the Islamic tradition, and may lack sufficient competence in classical Arabic and textual interpretation in order to work effectively as chaplains. However, the Hartford course would probably be an attractive prospect for those British Muslims contemplating chaplaincy careers on the back of more conventional academic or community-based roles, such as teaching, counselling, health care professions or voluntary sector work. This would, of course, go on to have a decisive influence on who becomes a Muslim chaplain, and how they practice.

The academic requirements and expectations of the Hartford programme have undoubtedly shaped entry into professional Muslim chaplaincy in the USA in recent years. For example, some of our interviewees in the US had liberal arts degrees, professional qualifications in social work or degrees in Arabic and Islamic Studies from American universities.[3] But these academic programmes in Islamic Studies would be quite different, in both content and ethos, compared to Muslim institutions offering a traditional Islamic curriculum leading to eventual recognition as an 'alim (or 'alima), and usually stressing a strong command of Arabic. The educational bias of the Hartford programme, combined with the emphasis on reflective practice in pastoral education (CPE) in America, has directly affected the approaches to the practice of Muslim chaplaincy in the US, as we shall see.

It is worth noting, however, that neither the entry requirements nor the curriculum offered at Hartford are uncontested among American Muslims (including chaplains and alumni). Perhaps as a consequence of this, the arena of chaplaincy training for Muslims in America is beginning to become more competitive as new providers and training opportunities are developed; this is a situation that is not unfamiliar in the UK. For example, some students of the Hartford course have relished the prospect of training as Muslim chaplains within the inter-religious setting of the Seminary, alongside Jews and Christians. They recognise that Jews (and before them, Catholics) had to fight for recognition and rights as religious minorities in American society, and that Muslims are now engaging with some of the same questions about identity, infrastructure and leadership once faced in these communities. But the value of training within this inter-religious reality has become problematic for some, and the contrasting positions in this debate are clearly evident in these two interview extracts:

> I really enjoyed Hartford Seminary ... it was located in an inter-faith setting, you know, in a setting in which you had to necessarily study with and be in dialogue with, and confront the Jewish and the Christian community. And this is a reflection of the larger reality in which chaplains work. Chaplains don't work in the private sectors usually, even in the closed off spaces; they always work in the public spheres where there is ... where you have to deal with people of all faiths and all traditions. And so studying in that setting I thought, for me, was very hopeful because they constantly made me think, okay, how do I translate this into the broader religiously pluralistic setting of America, you know, so that was one thing I really did like about Hartford Seminary (Muslim chaplain, interviewed July 2011).

---

[3]   Other research notes the combination of academic study and community service as pathways into American Muslim chaplaincy (Khoja-Moolji 2011).

I think it's necessary for chaplains to be trained [but] I think it's a bit problematic if the model for training Muslim chaplains is unlike the model for training Rabbis and Ministers. The model for training ... the primary model for training Rabbis is in the Jewish theological seminary in this country. The primary model for training Christian chaplains is in Christian seminaries. It would be amazing for me if you and I decided to set up a Hindu training, you know, programme for Hindu leadership and see if the Hindus would accept this. And so this is a problem. I think Hartford Seminary is very well intentioned, but the reality is that their focus is on interfaith work. My guess is if we organise a Muslim seminary, interfaith work would be there, but it wouldn't be as far up the line as it is with Hartford Seminary. That's number one. Number two is that Hartford Seminary does not require Arabic facility. It would be hard for us to find a Jewish seminary that doesn't expect a person to read the Torah in Hebrew. I mean ... you expect him or her to at least know enough Arabic to at least recite the Qur'an correctly and maybe do some rudimentary translation? I think it's problematical when the Qur'an is so important to us' (Muslim chaplain, interviewed July 2011).

There are concerted efforts afoot among a number of American Muslims to establish an Islamic seminary offering an accredited programme of learning for prospective Muslim chaplains grounded in a more thorough engagement with Islamic texts and sources via classical Arabic (Abdullah 2011). The proponents of this vision feel that Muslims need to take greater ownership of their professional formation and development. To this end the Muslim Endorsement Council of Connecticut (MECCT) was formed, followed by the Islamic Seminary Foundation (ISF), in 2006 and 2011 respectively.

These developments have not gone without criticism. Some have argued that while Muslim chaplaincy is still under development in the US it is prudent to remain connected to recognised educational institutions, rather than become self-contained and so risk isolation. Meanwhile, the landscape of Muslim chaplaincy training is diversifying. Not only are there increasing opportunities for in-service training (for example those organised by MECCT, and others), new providers and programmes are emerging. For example, the Ecumenical Theological Seminary in Detroit launched a two-year pilot programme in Muslim Chaplaincy in September 2011 as part of the seminary's Urban Ministry Diploma programme. Established through a partnership with local Muslim organisations, the first cohort of students are all local to the institution and can enrol on the basis of a high school diploma. Finally, the Bayan Claremont College (Southern California), a graduate college affiliated with Claremont Lincoln University, offers a range of certificate and MA level courses for aspiring Muslim leaders and chaplains, such as the MA in a Theological Discipline: Spiritual Counseling (Clinical). The impact of these developments remains to be seen, especially in terms of whether there are sufficient numbers of students to make these new courses viable at this point in time.

Muslim Chaplaincy and CPE

At the heart of the debate about the professional training and education of Muslim chaplains in America there appears to be a tension about the degree to which current training programmes place an emphasis on CPE, relative to traditional Islamic sciences and Arabic. Those involved with the Hartford programme tend to stress the former over the latter; this has shaped recruitment to the course and the subsequent chaplaincy practice of alumni. Students at Hartford are encouraged to develop a reflective approach to their work which is very much in keeping with the CPE ethos, not least because most Muslim chaplains have to be able to work effectively with people of all faiths and none. Indeed, many accounts of Muslim chaplaincy practice in the USA note that the vast majority of clients are Christian (or of no faith).

While Muslim chaplains in England and Wales are generally very clear about their willingness to work in multi-faith 'teams' and for the benefit of the wider institution, many of them have been specifically recruited to meet the religious needs of Muslim clients in particular. This would be regarded as unconstitutional in most public institutions in the USA; when a Muslim is hired in a public institution, they are usually hired as chaplains who happen to be Muslim, not as 'Muslim chaplains'. In this section, we hear the voices of American chaplains at length on the importance and value of CPE for Muslim chaplains (and other Islamic religious professionals). This is because many of them have developed a very articulate philosophy of practice that is communicated far more effectively in their own words, rather than our own.

In her article for *Reflective Practice*, Harris advised CPE supervisors working with Muslim students that they might need to be 'stretched' in ways that might be unfamiliar.

> Sometimes it may be necessary for supervisors to help jump-start this process by encouraging Muslim students to articulate what the basic points of doctrine mean for them. How does it actually change you to believe in God? Where do angels fit in your 21st-century life? When on the hospital floor have you met the Divine Decree? Some Muslim students may be startled by questions like these. That cannot be resolved by consulting authorities. Fire away: we need to stretch our theological muscles (Harris 2009: 157–8).

> They need to have thought about things like, well, what is my view on God's love and mercy, does it extent to all people, in what way? What is my understanding of … human spiritual development? (interview, July 2011).

This kind of approach is far less concerned with what is halal or haram, or the necessity to get the 'right' decision on a matter of ethics. Where many British Muslim chaplains who have come into the profession via 'alim training tend to see the world in terms of such binary opposites (permissible/impermissible), this is less the case for American chaplains who have come from a far broader range of backgrounds and have absorbed the CPE ethos. Their practice rarely involves the resolution of complex religious challenges that require a deep knowledge of Islamic law. Three different interviewees stressed the need to understand the real meaning of legal questions posed during pastoral practice:

> I think that's one of the areas that Muslim chaplains, especially if they come from the Imam side, or a scholarship side, you're not always a good chaplain, because you have to really balance what a client is saying to you. It's not always a fiqh issue. And most likely, I mean, the majority of times, it's not a fiqh issue, even if they … if they're asking you a fiqh question, they may have ulterior motives for the fiqh issue, and you have to be able to hear that (interview, July 2011).

> I'd say one of the themes that is emerging is the distinction between fiqh and Islam as a whole. But a chaplain has to have a broader understanding of Islam. Fiqh is a very kind of minimalist approach to Islam and a chaplain needs to understand much beyond that, not just theology but some metaphysics and spirituality, and so that when someone says, 'What should I do?' they're not running to a book of law but they're really looking at the whole person (interview, July 2011).

> Fiqh questions are usually only the tip of the iceberg. I hope I'm not being too controversial when I say that, at least in my experiences, 95 per cent of the time when people come to me with problems it has nothing to do with … when somebody comes to me and says that I'm having a problem with alcohol the issue is not 'is alcohol haram?'. He knows it's haram. I know it's haram. The real question is how do I overcome this, you know? And one of the things that I've learned as a chaplain is that usually the question that people come with, that's not the real question and so then, you know, instead of answering the question, my question always is, 'what makes you ask this question?'. And we start peeling away, peeling away, peeling away, peeling away … as chaplains I think we have to help them step back and sort of unpeel what's going on, you know (interview, July 2011).

These kinds of perspectives are influencing ideas about the skill-set required for community-based religious leadership. One of our interviewees said that she would like to see all imams undertake CPE (especially 'immigrant Imams') because their skills were focused less on human need, and more on law. As a consequence, they stress 'the letter of the law', not the spirit:

> I feel the CPE will help soften their heart to know that Allah won't punish them by bending the rules a little bit by saving a soul, and so that's where I see the need for Imams to really get in tune with more humanity, the spirit of the law rather than the letter. Go back to the broadness of Islam, and make this religion

as easy as Allah meant it to be for us, and not as difficult as us humans keep making it (interview, July 2011).

During our fieldwork in the USA, we were able to interview some Muslim chaplains who described how the CPE ethos had shaped work and practice. Like their counterparts in the UK, they were able to narrate particularly memorable pastoral stories easily, but these accounts clearly reveal the influence not only of CPE but also, for some, the influence of Sufism:

> My heart is like the garden hose: as long as I am shut down if there's any facet of my heart that needs to be cleaned, then I will not give pure water. It's not my water: it's Allah. So when the faucet [tap] is turned on or the connection to Allah is turned on, the water comes through, it's sweet, it's a blessing whomever drinks from there. And the medicine or the water that comes through is specific to each person. I remember being in the Emergency Room and I'm so tired, I feel like I'm going to drop in my tracks or say, 'Allah, I cannot do this'. I go from one patient to the next patient to the next patient. I'm holding people, I'm walking with people, I'm caring for people and I don't want to stop even when it's time for me to go home, I don't want to stop because it's not me. It is not me. Allah is the doer. I am only the vessel. There is no reality but Allah. Behind your face is Allah; behind all of creation is Allah. This is creation. When all of creation is folded up there will only be Allah. Subhanahu wa ta'ala (interview, July 2011).

Muslim chaplains in the States who have undertaken CPE, but not received 'alim training are clear that this can impose limits on what they can do. They feel that it is important to know what their boundaries might be: 'I have to know what I can do and what I can't do, you know, and I have to make alliances with people who can do the things I can't do … I have to have the people I can go to' (interview, July 2011). This comment would resonate with some of the Muslim chaplains we interviewed in the UK, who also relied upon scholarly networks to provide them with particular forms of knowledge. This is especially the case in relation to life-death and other ethical decisions.

Important new research with Muslim hospital chaplains in the US demonstrates that in relation to health care chaplaincy (in particular) qualified Muslim chaplains will be asked to undertake a range of tasks that often require knowledge of Islamic law and sources. This includes religious advice on how to adapt ritual requirements to the hospital setting (for example when disability or the constraints of medical devices make ablution or salat difficult), the specific rituals that Muslims might ask for around birth and death or advice around advanced directives and organ donation (Abu-Ras 2011; Abu-Ras and Laird 2010). Not only do these tasks point to the limitations of health care chaplaincy delivered by Muslims without extensive knowledge of Islamic sources, they call into question the assumptions that underpin 'generic' spiritual care.

American Muslim chaplains who combine an 'alim training with an understanding of CPE (of whom there are very few) are actively engaged in developing an Islamic legal framework that aims to bridge the gap between CPE approaches to chaplaincy and traditional Islamic sciences. For example, in a lecture delivered by the current president of ISNA, Imam Majid (who himself is a chaplain), on the Islamic legal practices in chaplaincy, he explained that there is a need to develop al-Fiqh al-Waqi (contextual fiqh), or al-Fiqh al-Aam wal Khas (particular fiqh, as opposed to general understanding of fiqh).[4] He notes that it is necessary for any chaplain to understand three important realities in their pastoral practice, these being: i) the dominant culture, ii) the sub-culture, iii) individual need. He adds that a chaplain must also have a deep understanding of the institutions in which chaplains serve, and appreciate the influence this might have on the psychology of clients. This is an interesting development, especially when compared to some of the theological 'work' being done by Muslim chaplains in England and Wales. Our data shows that some Muslim chaplains are seeking to resolve legal or pastoral problems by exploring the range of legal opinions within the major schools of Islamic law (Ali and Gilliat-Ray 2012). This process is known as 'talfiq'. In contrast, there appear to be some traditionally trained American Muslim chaplains working to develop entirely new approaches that shift the paradigm from the letter of the law to the spirit of the law (maqasid al-Sharia). This might demand greater interpretive effort, but could be highly significant not only in terms of the outcome, but also because of the methodological potential.

Muslim Chaplaincy Associations

Rather like their counterparts in Britain, Muslim chaplains in America have sought to establish professional associations. A group of Hartford seminary students and alumni founded the Muslim Chaplaincy Association (MCA) in 2006 as a means of sharing good practice, but this appears to have foundered in much the same way as the equivalent initiative the UK, the Association of Muslim Chaplains (AMC), formed by some early graduates of the MIHE course. Postings on the MCA website are now becoming dated, and there are no upcoming events promoted. The postholders for the MCA Board of Directors are listed as 'to be announced' (tba). One of our interviewees reflected:

> ... there is an attempt to create a national chaplaincy organisation, and there are a lot of good intentions there but there's not enough commitment on the part of individuals to focus their work on the collective issue, rather than just, you know, their personal chaplaincy (interview, July 2011).

---

[4]   3 July 2011, 48th annual ISNA convention, Rosemont Convention Centre, Rosemont, Illinois: 'Establishing Best Practices for Muslim Chaplains in a Changing Environment'.

There appear to be some particular reasons why the MCA has struggled to establish itself and appears to have lost momentum. Firstly, it was perhaps established without a sufficient critical mass of Muslim chaplains with the time and resources to direct its work. Secondly, it was probably ahead of its time, relative to the development of Muslim chaplaincy in America, and could not rely upon the kind of networking that is so prevalent among Muslim chaplains (mainly 'alims) in the UK. Thirdly, being an outcome of the Hartford programme, it might have been regarded as 'unrepresentative' or irrelevant for Muslim chaplains unconnected to Hartford. Fourthly, the geographic dispersal of Muslim chaplains in the US makes any kind of physical or virtual meeting problematic; they may be living and working across three different time-zones.

Despite these obstacles, the idea of a professional association for Muslim chaplains in America has remained very much alive, especially in recent years. At the time of our fieldwork, one of our interviewees stressed the importance of such a body, alongside other priorities:

> I'm hoping in the next five to ten years two things will happen … that we in the chaplain profession will organise ourselves so there will be a body for Muslim chaplains to speak as a single voice in this country. There's no such body. The second thing is that there should be an endorsement agency that sets standards for who does Muslim chaplaincy in the public square as well as provide a support network for people who do Muslim service in the public squares. [And] we need to have more robust education programmes (interview, July 2011).

Since our fieldwork in the US in July 2011, we have been following this debate. It appears that some of the individuals most concerned to establish a Muslim chaplaincy association have seized the initiative and a new association was formed in 2012. The Association of Muslim Chaplains (AMC) explains on its website that,

> Between the spring and summer of 2011 (1432 AH), a group of experienced and aspiring chaplains united by a common desire to strengthen the field of Islamic chaplaincy, held a series of discussions to build an organization to serve the needs of chaplains. They recognized the pressing need for an organization that could provide Muslim chaplains with the opportunity to come to know each other for mutual support, nurturing, and encouragement to each other's professional growth in accordance with Qur'anic ideals. These individuals further recognized that such an association must be sincere in manifesting the Prophetic traditions of inclusivity, consultation, and consensus, and that the diversity within the Muslim community and within the profession of chaplaincy must be fully represented (associationofmuslimchaplains.com, accessed 21.9.12).

In March 2012 the group held its first conference or 'National Shura 1433' at Yale University with the aim of providing 'In-Service Training for Chaplains and Imams'. It seems evident, from the range of participants who attended and organisations represented, that this new body has been successful in galvanising the most significant individuals in Muslim chaplaincy in America today (practitioners and educators), and has secured co-operation with bodies most concerned with the professional development of Muslim chaplains, such as MECCT and the Islamic Seminary Foundation (ISF). If this association remains sustainable, it will give American Muslim chaplains a form of professional identity and a collective voice that Muslim chaplains in Britain are yet to establish.

Muslim Chaplains in America Today: A Brief Overview

So far there has been no systematic investigation of Muslim chaplaincy in the US. While there are some important (but isolated) academic studies that focus on particular institutions or sectors (Abu-Ras 2010; Abu-Ras 2011; Abu-Ras and Laird 2010; Ammar et al. 2004; Khoja-Moolji 2011; Padela et al. 2010; Padela et al. 2012), none of this amounts to a developed understanding of Muslim chaplains and their work. However, by combining our interview data with other secondary sources, such as web 'profiles' of chaplains on association websites, newspaper and magazine articles, and even a short film on YouTube, we will complete this chapter by mapping some of the contours of Muslim chaplaincy work in the US today, and in the hope that more sustained research will be undertaken in the future.

Before we look at the experiences of Muslims in particular sectors, we can make some general observations about the demographic profile of those working as Muslim chaplains. Apart from Muslims working in higher education chaplaincy, most Muslim chaplains in the US are considerably older than their counterparts in England and Wales. One only needs to read chaplaincy biographies to reach this conclusion. But this picture is diametrically opposite the situation in Britain where Muslim chaplains tend to be relatively young, apart from those in higher education! Men predominate (as they do in the UK), but chaplaincy is emerging as an important space for women's religious leadership (as in the UK). But how are these dynamics shaping particular sectors of Muslim chaplaincy in America today? In this closing section, we offer a brief overview of the way in which Muslim chaplains are contributing to particular institutions in American society.

Military Chaplaincy

The need to develop Muslim chaplaincy in America was stimulated by the first Gulf War (1990–01), when US forces were stationed in Kuwait and then Saudi Arabia. The value of having a Muslim religious professional within US forces was clear.[5] This was followed by a realisation of the need to provide pastoral care to growing numbers of Muslims in the military (including converts). There are discrepant figures given for the number of Muslims in the US Armed Forces today. Muslim organisations estimate the total to be about 10,000, while a source dating to 2006 puts the figure at 17,000 (Hamilton 2006). There are currently five Muslims in Army chaplaincy, three in the Navy and two in the Air Force.

The first Muslim chaplain appointed to the US Department of Defence was Major Abdul-Rasheed Muhammad, in 1993. He had previously worked as a hospital chaplain, and also served for two years in the New York State Department of Correction. Prior to his appointment there were 'lay leaders' or volunteer chaplains; they continue to have an important role. Abdul-Rasheed stresses the need for Muslim chaplains in the military to have a particularly broad approach to working with soldiers of all faiths and none … more so than any other context in which Muslim chaplains serve (Ahmad 2011: 22).

All the Muslim chaplains in the US military are currently male. However, Muslim women have applied to become Muslim chaplains in recent years, most notably Shareda Hosein, profiled in *The Washington Post* in 2008 (Murphy 2008). She is adamant that there is an important role for Muslim women as chaplains, principally because when male soldiers are deployed abroad, it is the wives and girlfriends who are left behind and may have pastoral need, best provided by a woman who can visit them at home without contravening Islamic norms around gender segregation.

Higher Education Chaplaincy

Muslim chaplaincy in American universities is a new, but rapidly growing field. 'The last two to four years is when you really saw it taking off' according to Omer Bajwa, Yale's first Muslim chaplain, who joined the institution in 2008 (Daneman 2011). There are an estimated 31 Muslim higher education chaplains to date, about a third of them women (Ahmad 2011). Research on Muslim chaplaincy in American universities notes the significance of this sector for the development of public religious leadership for Muslim women (Khoja-Moolji 2011). Consequently, it is also a site where issues about the religious authority of Muslim women, their dress and their role as 'facilitators' rather than leaders of congregational prayer are most evident: 'the lack of the visual symbol of the hijab makes me more approachable for some people; the point being that both wearing and not wearing the hijab can be a hindrance or help, to varying degrees' (Ibid. 17).

---

[5]   Perhaps the most well-known Muslim chaplain to serve in the US Armed Forces was Chaplain James Yee. Yee was assigned to minister to Muslim detainees at Guantanomo Bay, but was later arrested and charged with espionage, spying and sedition, amongst other allegations. He was subjected to extensive periods of solitary confinement and sensory deprivation, vividly described in his memoirs (Yee 2005). All charges against him were eventually dropped.

There are important differences in the employment and contractual status of Muslim educational chaplains, depending on whether they are employed in public or private institutions. The latter are free to hire whomever they wish, but, in order to not to contravene the principles of non-Establishment, public universities and colleges, cannot formally appoint or pay chaplains. In these institutions, Muslim students and alumni must raise funds to support an independent campus ministry. For example the New Michigan Muslim Alumni Association has collected $30,000 to support a part-time chaplain at Michigan University.

Private universities have seen the recruitment of Muslim chaplains as an important responsibility, not only to support Muslim students, but also to have a wider educative role on campus:

> ... it's critical to us at Brown to have a Muslim chaplain at this time of misunderstandings about and prejudice against Muslims in this country and around the world. We need this voice to educate our community not just through our academic programs but through the experience of faith as well (Hamilton 2006).

During our fieldwork in the US, we were able to interview a full-time (male) higher education chaplain, who described some of the contours of his job. His account demonstrates the potential for more full-time chaplaincy positions in Britain; his tasks encompass ritual, pastoral and educational dimensions in ways that are difficult for those restricted to part-time contracts or volunteers. He noted that his first role is 'ministry – organising the religious life of my community' (interview, July 2011). He places a heavy emphasis on Friday prayers, especially 'getting mood and style right'. He does a good deal of preparation around this event, not least because he is trying to support the development of student preachers for the sermon.

However, he estimates that at least half of his job entails pastoral counselling, and there are three distinctive areas which bring students to his door: crises of faith, sometimes brought about as a consequence of academic studies; exposure to different worldviews and interpretations of Islam; and establishing personal discipline and boundaries within the permissive environment of the student campus:

> One of the major issues tends to be about doubting faith, you know. A Muslim takes a philosophy course for the first time and in that philosophy course there's questions about the existence of God – suddenly they're unsure. Sometimes a Muslim might grow up in a very narrow community and they come to college campus and suddenly they're exposed to different ... and suddenly they're like, wow, Islam is much ... you know, wider than I ever thought of it so what do I do with that? How do I operate in that world? And the Islam that I'm practising, is that okay, or do I need to think about the other Islams, you know, so that tends to be another big question. A major issue tends to be identity ... how to maintain the spiritual discipline and the moral regimen as a Muslim on a college campus, in which sometimes the environment isn't always very friendly

to those spiritual or moral qualities. And so how to be integrated whilst also knowing the boundaries – what are the boundaries? How do we figure out what the boundaries are? So just how to live as a Muslim, a faithful Muslim on a college campus, this tends to be another big issue (interview, July 2011).

The question of multiple schools of thought within Islam can present equally challenging issues for higher education chaplains, as for Muslim students. Our interviewee owned to some degree of uncertainty about the degree to which he should be facilitating forms of religious practice that fall outside the boundaries of orthodox Muslim belief: 'when the Ismailis have their special religious observances at a mosque that is maybe 45 minutes away, should I accommodate for that on campus?'. He questions himself: 'who do you think you are a chaplain for?'.

In Chapter 5, we noted the value of Muslim chaplains in higher education working in a husband-wife partnership. Our interviewee confirmed this: 'being married is helpful … my wife is a very active part of the community … they have a relationship with my wife, especially the girls and sometimes they'll go with her for coffee' (Ibid.). The scope for this kind of husband-wife partnership in chaplaincy is probably distinctive to educational contexts.

Hospital Chaplaincy

We have already made reference to a number of studies about Muslim health care chaplaincy in the US (Abu-Ras 2010; Abu-Ras 2011; Abu-Ras and Laird 2010; Padela et al. 2010; Padela et al. 2012). Given their explicit focus on detailing the work of Muslim chaplains and 'imams in healthcare', these studies come close to providing the same kind of rich description of Muslim chaplaincy practice that we explored in Chapter 4. However, these studies map chaplaincy work in particular institutions and localities, and it is very difficult to set their findings into a broader context. We have been unable to locate any sources which provide even approximate figures for the number of Muslim chaplains in American health care today.

This lack of information hints at the possibility that health care chaplaincy is less politicised, less visible and less contested in US society, and is undoubtedly also a reflection of low levels of recruitment:

There are few imams with formal staff positions within hospitals … reasons for the sparse presence of imams in formal chaplain roles may be multiple from lack of time and unfamiliarity with chaplaincy roles on the part of imams to financial limitations or difficulty in ascertaining 'imam' credentials on the part of hospitals … a delineation of core competencies for Muslim chaplains in terms of Islamic law and ethics … remains wanting (Padela et al. 2010: 369).

Prison Chaplaincy

Given the origins of Muslim prison chaplaincy, it is not surprising to find that African-American Muslims dominate this professional field. However, because of the ethnic composition of the Muslim prison population (between 50 and 80 per cent of Muslim prisoners are African-American in state prisons (Bowers 2009)) this means there is a far better 'ethnic' match between chaplains and prisoners in the US, compared to England and Wales. As we saw in Chapter 3, there are significant (and rising) numbers of Afro-Caribbean and Somali prisoners in British prisons, but they are receiving pastoral care from prison chaplains who are often South Asian.

After the 9/11 attacks, the Bureau of Prisons implemented a series of new policies, including a moratorium on the hiring of Muslim chaplains. It was 'the most sweeping curtailment of religious freedom in prisons since the advent of prison litigation in the 1950s' (Seymour 2006: 524). It was symptomatic of a broad 'criminalisation of Islam' (Ibid.) in prisons that seemed unable to draw a distinction between the activities of small numbers of religious extremists, and the pastoral and educational role of Muslim chaplains. Since then, a rather different approach has been taken; one that recognises the role Muslim chaplains might have in counter-radicalisation. Pressure to engage in this effort is felt by Muslim prison chaplains on both sides of the Atlantic.

Judging from the interview we conducted with a Muslim prison chaplain during our fieldwork, combined with secondary sources, it appears that 'despite the sizeable Muslim population behind bars, Islamic programming and leadership in prisons remains underrepresented and underfunded' (Bowers 2009). Muslim prison chaplaincy in England and Wales is therefore probably in a far stronger position at this point in time, given the investment in new posts, training opportunities, and development of Muslim educational programmes since 2007.

Conclusion

The involvement of Muslims in professional chaplaincy in America highlights some of the distinctive features of chaplaincy work carried out by Muslims in Britain. Broadly speaking, the main points of difference centre on the religious qualifications and background of those going into the profession. There are far fewer religious 'scholars' working as chaplains in the USA, and this has meant that their practice is orientated less around questions of Islamic law and belief, compared to their counterparts in England and Wales. Most American chaplains have BA or Masters degrees and are able to articulate ideas about professional Muslim chaplaincy practice in both the written and spoken form; it is clear they are now beginning to engage with a broader professional chaplaincy discourse. At this point in time, few British Muslim chaplains (particularly the 'alims who are currently leading the field) have the educational background that enables them to contribute to chaplaincy debate and discourse, in the written form. The lack of reflective writing about their day-to-day work is frustrating the creation of new training materials for those coming into the profession, and the 'development of the field' more broadly. Despite these differences, however, it is clear that in both the USA, and in England and Wales, the work of Muslim chaplaincy is being pioneered by a relatively small group of individuals, and they are shaping the emergence in each context. Furthermore, their work is exposing some of the same questions about religious leadership and training in Muslim communities that pertain in the UK.

For example, because chaplaincy is providing an important avenue for public religious leadership for women, this is bringing assumptions about gender roles into sharp relief. Women are contesting the assumption that they should be 'relegated to sectors and segments; go talk to the sisters, go talk to the kids ... that needs to shift' (interview, July 2011). Alongside gender, the work of Muslim chaplains in both the UK and the US suggests the need for greater capacity among those engaged in community-based religious leadership. It is becoming apparent that it is unrealistic to expect mosque-based imams to meet a diversity of religious needs, especially given the lack of connection that some Muslims will have to a mosque or imam:

> So creating other spaces in which there are religious leaders, that's very important, and creating religious leaders who have talents that are different than the imam in the Masajid, and particularly I'm speaking about the issue of counselling, and particularly I'm speaking to the issue of, you know, being a youth (interview, July 2011).

But this challenge raises a complex set of issues about how Muslim communities will generate the capacity to create new models of leadership. It depends on a level of social, economic and religious capital that may be underdeveloped at this point in time. But given the socio-economic profile of Muslims in the US compared to Muslim communities in Britain, it seems likely that moves in this direction will be both more likely and more sustainable in America, for the time being.

Muslim chaplains on both sides of the Atlantic appreciate the challenge of their calling amid the socio-economic and religious context in which they find themselves. They recognise that within Muslim communities there are still deep pockets of ignorance about the role of Muslim chaplains, including the terminology itself:

> I think it's very important to keep using the term 'chaplain'. I encourage them [students] to continually use this title because I want it to become so normal for people to hear 'Chaplain Muhammad' so that the awkwardness and the newness of it wears off ... then we understand that it really is a profession (interview, July 2011).

Alongside these challenges, Muslim chaplains have often acquired public prominence in ways that place upon them particular responsibilities and pressures. In many institutions, they have become 'the face of Islam' (interview, July 2011) in ways that rarely parallel the experience of Christian chaplains in relation to their tradition. The terrorist attacks on 9/11 'underscored the need for Muslim religious leaders to be functioning in the public sphere ... [and] chaplaincy is a great way to communicate the universal values of Islam to other people' (interview, July 2011). But at the present time, addressing this responsibility is made harder for chaplains when their role and potential is so poorly understood: 'I think once the community understands how positive we are, in terms of representing Muslims in the public space, I think they will get behind us ... that's our desire, to become more mainstream in our own community' (interview, July 2011). For the time being, questions about educational philosophy, endorsement, skills, accreditation and other matters internal to the evolving world of Muslim chaplaincy still need to reach a point of general consensus, both in American and in Britain. But the outcome of the discussions taking place as part of this process may well be significant, well beyond the world of Muslim chaplaincy.

Chapter 8

Chaplaincy, Religious Diversity and Public Life

Introduction

The Muslim chaplains in our study in England and Wales made frequent reference to a lack of adequate literature to help them to develop their role; there are relatively few specifically Islamic resources that directly address professional pastoral practice. This reality, together with the traditional predominance of Christian involvement in chaplaincy, means that Muslims are susceptible to influences from outside their tradition. Unsurprisingly, therefore, Muslim chaplaincy appears (mostly inadvertently rather than by deliberate forethought) to have ingested a good deal of Christian and secular influence into its practices. Our discussion of Muslim chaplaincy work in the United States (Chapter 7) highlighted some of the distinctive features of Muslim chaplaincy work in England and Wales. Here consideration of the ways in which Muslim chaplaincy has evolved vis-à-vis Christian chaplaincy theologies, practices and models will allow some of the distinguishing features of Muslim chaplaincy practice to become apparent.

To do this, we explore the ways in which Muslim chaplaincy is both similar to, and different from, the work of chaplains of other faiths (mostly Christian), and consider how Muslim chaplains have been influenced by Christian models of pastoral care and the undergirding principles that shape the working of public institutions, such as equality and diversity. We go on to explore the implications of Muslim chaplaincy work as practiced in multi-faith contexts. What kind of social and religious capital do Muslim chaplains acquire as a consequence of their experiences of religious diversity, and how might these various forms of capital have significance for religion in public life and the chaplaincy profession more broadly?

Comparing Christian and Muslim Chaplaincy

Offering a clear understanding of Christian self-understanding, theology and practice in order to enable comparison with Muslim chaplaincy practice is not straightforward. There is no one clear set of ideas, practices, theologies or principles underlying Christian chaplaincy practice in the UK (Legood 1999a; Swift 2009; Threlfall-Holmes and Newitt 2011). It is impossible to outline an agreed and dominant view of how Christian chaplains, even Church of England

Christian chaplains, understand themselves and their roles. The emergence of chaplaincy theory, theology and practice in different institutions has been ad hoc and pragmatic (as perhaps the emergence of Muslim chaplaincy is proving to be). Even now, it is hardly articulate, and certainly not agreed.

Despite this variability and lack of consensus, theologians have sought to explain the various historical traits contributing to the gradual development of Christian chaplaincy models and practices (see 'Health Care Chaplaincy and the Church of England' 2010). Just as there was a felicitous convergence of social and political factors that made the development of Muslim chaplaincy possible in Britain, so, too, a combination of social and theological influences have shaped the evolution of Christian chaplaincy. First, many institutions in Britain, like hospitals and universities, were religiously founded and maintained; Christianity and Christian ministry were integral to their structures from the outset (Bebbington 1992). Secondly, it was gradually recognised that there was a need to provide religious and sacramental care beyond churches and parishes when, for example, people were away from home, or unable to get to church (Legood 1999a). Thirdly, there was a theological realisation that God's concerns are not limited to the churches, but extended outwards into communities and society (Rogers 2000). Fourthly, in a society with an Established Church coterminous with the State, there was an awareness that the Church should minister to everyone within the geographical bounds of the land. All of this was underwritten by a notion of Christendom whereby the incarnational redemptive mission of God through Christ to all people (which embraces concern and care for those in prison, suffering from illness or in other kinds of need) should be made a constant reality.

Within this somewhat vague series of underpinning ideas, Christian chaplains in a range of contexts have adopted various so-called 'theological' models to underpin their chaplaincy work. These include: missionary/evangelist; pastor/ carer; priest/sacramental agent; parish minister/community leader; and agent of prophetic social change (Threlfall-Holmes and Newitt 2011: 118). 'Theological' models can be compared with more 'secular' models of chaplaincy, such as: pastoral care provider; spiritual carer; the 'diversity' model; the tradition/heritage model; and the specialist service provider (Ibid. 118). We will explore these models in more depth shortly. The point to note here is that the role of 'chaplain' has clearly originated in Christianity; it has been shaped by evolving Christian traditions and 'models' over time.

As well as being shaped by Christian ideas and traditions, chaplaincy has also been formed by its institutional contexts. There is a clear set of expectations and practices into which anyone calling themselves a chaplain inevitably walks. So, for example, chaplains are first and foremost expected to be loyal to the managements of their employing institutions as well as to their co-religionists (Burchard 1954). They are expected to abide by the ethos, codes and contractual obligations that govern host institutions. Chaplains must therefore uphold legal obligations to observe and promote equality and diversity and abide by the strictures of the public service ethic in which services should be available to all, without discrimination

(Maxwell et al. 2003). Chaplaincy has been shaped within the ethos of a national church that is available to, and responsible for, everyone. Consequently, there is an expectation that chaplains will be open and available to all who seek their services (Kuhrt 2001). Furthermore, there is an assumption that public spaces and institutions will not be used to evangelise or coerce captive or needy people into particular belief systems. This is accompanied by a strong belief that individuals, together with their beliefs and orientations (or lack thereof), should be respected (Pill et al. 2004).

The effects of these undergirding influences can be seen in both Christian and Muslim practice and understanding. There are, however, some distinctive emphases in the experiences of Muslim chaplains. First, Muslim chaplains have to facilitate a variety of Islamic practices (for example, provision of Friday prayer, ensuring the supply of halal food) that Christian chaplains do not (though Christians similarly have to make arrangements for particular forms of Christian worship and religious rites). Secondly, Muslim chaplains often need to explain both their role (especially to other Muslims) and their faith (especially to non-Muslims) far more widely than Christian chaplains. The latter can assume that people have a better latent understanding of their faith, who they are and the role they perform. Thirdly, Muslim chaplains appear to have more of a focus on family and wider community relations than Christian chaplains; this is largely due to the ways in which Islamic teachings about the family have shaped social relationships in many Muslim communities. Fourthly, the work of many Muslim chaplains in England and Wales (especially those who are 'alims/'alimas) often has a distinctive focus on law and legal interpretation of the Qur'an; for Christian colleagues ideas about 'correct' belief or practice are unlikely to be so significant. Fifthly, there is no ministerial or professional office within Islam that directly corresponds with that of ordained Christian ministry or 'clergy'. Thus, Muslim chaplains have to define their function and role at the point where Islamic traditions intersect with Christian norms and practices and within the ethos and practices of secular public institutions.

Arising out of this background mixture of ideas and practices, how have Muslim chaplains been influenced by the institutional/Christian environment? First, there is an increasing sense that there is a distinctive religious professional role encapsulated in the notion of chaplaincy that allows Islamic scholars (and others) to be regarded as relatively autonomous religious professionals, and to be paid as such. This contrasts with the role of mosque-based imams, for example, who often have little autonomy, and where ideas about 'professionalism' are perhaps less pressing. The degree to which Muslim chaplains are seeking more 'continuous professional development' and training to support their work is in itself a testament to their evolving identity as members of a distinctive group of religious specialists.

Giving weight to pastoral experience and human diversity is an important component of contemporary Christian humanistic, particularly practical theological, discourse (Pattison and Woodward 2000; Pattison 2000). The narratives of Muslim chaplains indicate that many of them have been influenced by this discourse. So while many Muslim chaplains seem to start their chaplaincy careers rooted in Islamic scholarship and with a clear focus on the needs of Muslim clients, we see them ascribing greater value to diversity, within and outside Muslim communities, as they develop their identity as chaplains over time:

> What I tell them is when you meet a boy, if they want to pray, then you teach them how to pray. What you don't do is teach them that this is the correct way and all the other ways are wrong, because we've got to respect the diversity of the theology that we've got here (full-time male prison chaplain).

This experiential challenge is one that appears to be welcomed by many Muslim chaplains, but it often challenges traditional Islamic norms and techniques of religious reasoning, and may require new and rapid interpretation of Islamic sources in the face of pastoral dilemmas.

Alongside increasing recognition of a professional chaplaincy role, and the value of human diversity and pastoral experience, there is increasing emphasis among Muslim chaplains on the care and interests of individuals, irrespective of creed or community. With this has come an adoption of counselling and listening techniques that are commonplace in Christian pastoral care (Pattison 2000). It contrasts strongly with the didactic and normative roles of imams and legal scholars within the Islamic tradition. This adoption of counselling and listening skills among Muslim chaplains, even alongside their concern with 'correct' practice, is perhaps very clear evidence of the influence of Christian pastoral care ideas, themselves influenced by secular norms of helping individuals. The emphasis that the Muslim chaplains in our sample placed on providing non-judgemental care to people of all faiths was marked. Indeed, many Muslim chaplains grow to relish and particularly enjoy their pastoral work, particularly when it comes to being useful and informative to people who are not Muslims. While not a total innovation, this is undoubtedly a striking change of practice and orientation, certainly in comparison to the work of many mosque-based imams in Britain who often have relatively little scope for more outward-facing public or pastoral engagement.

We noted in Chapter 2 that in most Muslim communities over the course of history, 'pastoral care' has consisted of people fulfilling clear Islamic obligations towards their immediate and extended family members. A real innovation in Islamic chaplaincy practice is the visiting of people on hospital wards or in prison cells who are likely to be complete strangers, and, once there at the bedside or in the cell, offering non-judgemental listening. While Christianity, like Islam, has normative and judgemental traditions within it, modern Christian pastoral care in secular settings has emphasised skilled non-judgemental listening to individuals. From our research, it seems that Muslim chaplains, both 'alims and non-'alims, are developing some of the same skills as their Christian colleagues, and are working in ways that institutions value and rarely see as controversial.

Certain Muslim chaplaincy practices seem to have been directly imported or adopted from Christian/secular practice in institutions. First, Muslim co-ordinating chaplains see it as their duty to provide for the religious and spiritual needs of all. Consequently, they adopt a universalist stance to religious need, and are not willing to condemn as erroneous the religious beliefs of others. This clearly follows a liberal Christian paradigm (though one that is contested by some chaplains, both Christian and other). Secondly, the way in which Muslim chaplains set about the organisation of communal prayers and teaching, halal food preparation and so on can be seen as analogous to the work of Christian chaplains who see organisation of formal worship as an important component of their work. Thus Friday prayers are promoted to the authorities in the way that certain kinds of Christian worship would be, such as Catholic Mass, for example. Organising public worship is therefore an important way of being seen to be a chaplain … and this again contrasts significantly with mosque-based imams who have little or no responsibility for facilitating or leading prayers in secular institutions, and would certainly not regard the conspicuous organisation of worship as a performative undertaking to justify their role to non-Muslims. Muslim chaplains have also been influenced by their Christian colleagues in more subtle ways; the use of 'prayer cards' at the bedside of the hospitalised patient being just one example.

To return to the typology of Christian chaplaincy outlined by Threlfall Holmes and Newitt above, what are the most significant aspects of self-understanding and practice among Muslim chaplains (Threlfall-Holmes and Newitt 2011)? Using their models as a comparative benchmark, what can we say about, first of all, the 'missionary' imperative within Islam, and in relation to Christianity? Firstly, both traditions are inherently missionary religions. Christian chaplains generally interpret 'mission' in terms of imitating the life of Christ and exemplifying God's love and compassion within the institution, rather than in terms of overt evangelism and fostering conversion. Muslim chaplains appear to have followed Christians in this general direction, partly to fit in with the secular ethos around them. Like their Christian colleagues, Muslim chaplains see their role as one that requires witness in word and deed, to Muslims and non-Muslims alike. However, in some contexts, especially in prisons, the role of Muslim chaplains in supporting conversion and education into Islam is probably more strongly emphasised than it would normally be in Christian chaplaincy.

The 'pastor/carer' model is essentially alien to traditional Islam. There is no tradition of specially chosen and corporately authorised individual professionals whose job is specifically directed towards the pastoral care of people. While there are strong pastorally and humanistically related traditions within Islam, these do not add up to a mandate for caring for individuals instead of their families, nor do they imply the need to visit strangers, to care for all, whether or not they are Muslim, nor to adopt non-judgemental and listening methods of attending to people's needs. While there may be a broadly pastoral impulse within Islam, this has been implicit. Muslim chaplains have had to make this more explicit, and to find new points of emphasis and interpretations of their tradition, in order to embrace the notion and practices of professionally delivered pastoral care and counselling.

One of the undergirding principles of Christian chaplaincy practice is the idea of priesthood, and the distinctive work of priests as sacramental agents. Martin Luther once wrote that 'God himself will milk the cows through him whose vocation that is' (Campbell 1985: 17). This model of chaplaincy is essentially alien to Islam. There are no sacraments or priests, paid or lay, that mediate divinity to humankind since this would cut across the idea of God's indivisible 'oneness' (tawhid) and the direct unmediated relationship between God and humanity. Though the piety of Islamic scholars is recognised, as is the significance of their authority, neither they, nor Muslim chaplains, are priests. However, during some of our conversations with chaplains we explored as far as possible the idea that they somehow enabled the 'presencing of the divine' in distinctive ways, for example, through practices such as reciting the Qur'an over a glass of water for the client to then consume, in order to acquire its healing potential. In relation to practices of this kind, they indeed spoke about the way in which God might work through them in terms that a Christian chaplain would probably recognise. However, in undertaking such religious practices, there is no sense in which they are supported by sacramental views of ministry, or a distinctive 'priestly' role.

Threlfall-Holmes and Newitt offer a fourth theological 'model' of Christian chaplaincy that centres on the idea of an historical-parish/community leadership role. The emphasis lies upon physical presence in the life of an institution or community, not only to enable pastoral encounters, but also as a means by which the Church validates the experiences of individuals. A ministry of 'presence' makes the sacramental work of priests possible and provides an opportunity to witness to an incarnational view of ministry (Threlfall-Holmes and Newitt 2011: 121). In so far as this model allows for aspects of community leadership and arrangements for corporate worship, there are clear analogies with Muslim community life. However, they refer far more to the work of mosque committees, rather than to that of individual imams/scholars, who may have little scope to shape the organisational context of their work. However, where Muslim chaplains have acquired positions of leadership as co-ordinating chaplains, the work they undertake in overseeing the arrangements for religion in their institution is essentially in imitation of Christian chaplaincy practices and models that draw on the idea of the institution as in some ways equating to 'the parish'.

Both Christianity and Islam are religions based on prophetic witness and teaching and have a concern for the implementation of the will of God so that humans can enjoy conditions of peace and justice. The Qur'an says: 'We have made you into a just community, so that you may bear witness [to the truth] before others and so that the Messenger may bear witness [to it] before you' (surah al-Baqarah 2:143). While a model of chaplaincy as 'prophetic' or critical in the face of institutional injustices is valued by some Christian chaplaincy theorists, it seems to be infrequently practised as part of day-to-day work (Pattison 1994). Some Christian chaplains may from time to time draw matters of concern to the attention of senior managers, but mostly they avoid engaging in difficult conversations with management because the likely outcome might well be alienation and isolation.

Most Muslim chaplains appear to take the same stance. They are working within the norms and rules of their institutions and only take up critical and questioning stances episodically, or when some aspect of the fundamental practice of Islam is in question (for example, when availability of halal food is imperilled). This is not to say that Muslim chaplains are quiescent or indifferent; some are very innovative in their practice, for example in trying to rehabilitate and change views in the wider Muslim community about ex-offenders. But the point is that 'prophetic' witness does not seem to be an important, overt or articulated role for Muslims in public institutions, any more than it is for most Christians. The focus of their work lies with supporting people as they cope with the realities of institutional life, and the challenges of illness, death, imprisonment or other transitions. It may be that as Muslim chaplains become better established and more confident this 'model' will become more relevant and feasible.

Christian chaplaincy is not informed by a consensual or articulate set of ideas and practices. It has evolved over time and in relation to the public institutions in which it is practised. Muslim chaplaincy is similar. Without an established tradition of formal pastoral care, a practical theology of Muslim chaplaincy is emerging, informed to quite a large extent by the influence of models and examples of Christian chaplaincy practised in, and influenced by, the ethos of secular institutions in which it functions. While some models of Christian pastoral care are implicitly fairly isomorphic with traditions and practices within Islam, Muslim chaplaincy has had to take on many practices that are supported by implicit ideologies/theologies of institutionalised Christian chaplaincy. These include things such as absolute respect for individuals, non-judgemental care, non-directiveness and caring for Muslims and non-Muslims alike. Distinctively Muslim practices, theologies and understandings of chaplaincy are at an early stage of development, hindered by a lack of literature and training material from experienced practitioners and scholars. As Muslim chaplaincy develops and gains a stronger identity and voice, it might be expected that not only will it continue to assimilate ideas and practices from institutional/Christian chaplaincy, such as the emphasis on experience and universal inclusion, but that it will also develop a more distinctive set of ideas and practices. It may also become more critical of some of the models and assumptions that it has ingested from outside itself. So, for example, it might regain some confidence in the importance of giving people authoritative Islamic teaching that should be obeyed and conformed to, not just offered as a possible source of insight and information.

How do Muslim Chaplains Change with Experience?

Many, but not all, Muslim chaplains in England and Wales come to chaplaincy as 'alims or 'alima, pious people immersed in the Islamic religious tradition and with the confidence and authority granted to them by their teachers and their faith community. This intense devotional training then meets the experience of working in the secular, multi-faith environments of justice, health care, higher education, and so on. And within those environments, chaplaincy has largely been shaped by historic Christian practices and ideas. So what do Muslim chaplains learn from their experiences?

A chaplain from the United States felt that chaplaincy experiences had required him to

> ... connect theory to practice. I no longer read the great works of people like Imam Al Ghazali and others, just theoretically. Now, whenever I read these great texts or any other book I'm always thinking, okay, so how does that translate on the ground? How does that work in practice? Does it work? Maybe it doesn't work, maybe it shouldn't work, you know, maybe this not the right thing – so I'm always thinking (interview, July 2011).

The complexity of some pastoral and chaplaincy experiences appears to be a catalyst for reflection on the practical and personal meaning of religious texts, signalling some degree of a departure from normative ideas about books and knowledge. Many 'alims and 'alimas have acquired their religious knowledge through the skills of memorisation. Their understanding of Islam is largely grounded on assumptions about the need to 'know' a body of religious knowledge from which certain religious practices will flow in order to be a 'good' Muslim. Chaplaincy practice exposes chaplains to situations and people that seem to prompt a shift in emphasis that requires deeper interrogation of the implications and meaning of religious text. With this there seems to be a move from 'what I need to know' to 'who I need to be'.

Perhaps one slightly unexpected aspect of chaplaincy experience is that it deepens some chaplains' sense of being a Muslim. As one prison chaplain told us: 'working in an environment like this makes you value your Islam' (full-time male prison chaplain). The multi-faith environment makes chaplains very aware of what it means to have distinctive Islamic identity, helping them to see Islam, as it were, from the outside. They also learn the potential for establishing common cause with chaplains of other faiths, and the value of co-operative working as fellow religious professionals. The transition from 'visiting minister' to 'Muslim chaplain' has allowed more committed relationships to flourish within chaplaincy teams; chaplains of all faiths have realised the power to be derived from an ability to act with others through these social relations (Bretherton 2011). One chaplain told us that his Christian line-manager

> ... was Church of England. He's not a Muslim, but we really did get on very well and obviously he didn't teach me Islam, about Islam, but the know-how and the knowledge of how to work within the prison, how to work with people who see differently. Because obviously with him being a Christian priest, the secular organisation sees things differently to the way he does as well, so obviously there were a lot of similarities between myself and him because you have to

remember that the prison service is not a Christian organisation, it's a secular organisation. So a lot of the sticking points that I would have, he would have as well (full-time male prison chaplain).

This account of mutuality pays relatively little attention to the implications that such relations may have for Christian chaplains who, over time, have had to reconcile themselves to the loss of Anglican/Christian dominance and the political and practical consequences of working in a 'multi-faith' society. We shall be exploring this point later in this chapter, as we reflect on the possible trajectory of multi-faith chaplaincy that is now shaped in decisive ways by the predominance of both Muslims and Christians.

As well as deepening faith and commitment for many, some chaplains, particularly in the health sector, gain specialist Islamic knowledge about ethical dilemmas and issues that they would not have developed in other contexts. In addition to rites of passages relating to birth and death, Muslim scholars in health care may need to be able to give advice on complex legal issues related to these rites. This might include for example, ascertaining whether it is permissible to turn off a life-support machine and the circumstances when a foetus can be aborted due to medical complications. With advancing medical knowledge, those Muslim chaplains who are qualified Islamic scholars are acquiring distinctive expertise as they work to find new solutions and interpretations of Islamic sources in order to arrive at the best possible judgements (Arshad et al. 2004). Significant interpretive effort is invested in this process; the scholars are accountable to God for their decisions. At the same time, some 'alims in prisons lament the lack of opportunity to deploy their hard-acquired traditional theological knowledge; the ignorance of many Muslim prisoners about Islam limits the extent to which 'alims can draw upon the range and depth of their knowledge. Different sectors of chaplaincy thus carry different kinds of potential for deployment or development of religious knowledge.

Muslim chaplains working across most sectors learn new attitudes from their experiences. While they often tend to start with normative, didactic approaches that are directed towards co-religionists, their experiences of working with all kinds of people in a multi-faith environment seem to inculcate within them attitudes of empathy, person-centeredness, equality, broad-mindedness, openness, approachability, supportiveness, tolerance, non-judgementalism, non-directiveness, compassion, patience and humility:

Interviewer: To what extent do you feel that your practice of chaplaincy has changed over time?

Chaplain: I think 100 per cent. I think when I graduated as an 'alim, I had never thought that this is the kind of work I would be doing … that I would be sitting down with the Christian colleagues or Buddhist. I think what I've learnt is, over the few years' time … that it's been a lost identity of Islam of how to work with other faiths and other people. And so, I have over a period of time changed my values, my values have changed, code of ethics have changed, my behaviour pattern has changed to accommodate and facilitate this secular organization that you are working, how you need to be working in that organisation as an effective imam (full-time male prison chaplain).

Alongside this, Muslim chaplains seem to feel that they should have a care and concern for those beyond the Muslim community. Some of the most moving stories they tell about their own perceived value are those relating to ways in which they have helped people who are not Muslims. Seen in this light, multi-faith space then seems to become holy and privileged ground, not a place to be colonised for Islam. So those who were used to teaching authoritatively in the Muslim community or in mosques appear to become much less dogmatic and didactic in the chaplaincy context, seeing their role as one of getting alongside individuals and their families so they can arrive at their own decisions to moral and other problems. Perhaps it is because of this apparent profound attitudinal change in relation to others that some chaplains testify to the belief that chaplaincy practice has taught them humility, a fundamental virtue of Islam.

As to practices and habits, a number of chaplains find themselves engaging in activities which would be unthinkable to ordinary 'alims in mosques. These range from shaking hands with, or touching members of the opposite gender, to praying with members of other religions either on their own or at multi-faith acts of worship (one Muslim prison chaplain reads the psalms to Christian prisoners as a halfway house to praying with them), to organising Catholic masses and carol services and distributing Bibles and hot cross buns. While most would steadfastly want to resist any attribution of innovative practice, the nature of the secular environment, pre-existing chaplaincy practices, the ethos of inclusion and the real needs of clients create an experiential environment in which chaplains have to become more flexible and open or they will find themselves uncomfortably isolated. For most, this change is welcome as well as challenging and stimulating. It expands their faith and understanding of their own religious tradition and its possibilities, as well as threatening traditional attitudes and practices in some ways.

Many of these changes in attitude, practice and self-understanding are occurring in the life and practice of particular individuals. It is possible that our interview questions and conversations provoked introspection and reflection which gave voice to these thoughts for the first time. Given the conservatism in many Muslim communities, we may have been among the first to hear stories about such profound personal change and transformation, not least because the development of full-time Muslim chaplaincy is itself a relatively new phenomenon. But what is the significance of these changes? If it is assumed that substantial currents of transformation among a sufficient number of individuals are likely to be cumulative, the likely outcomes warrant some consideration. Indeed, we can already identify some of the implications of Muslim chaplaincy work for Muslim communities, and the place of religion in public life more broadly.

Figure 8.1   Imam Yasar Zaman, Homerton University Hospital (left) with Muhammed
             Foulds (right) Head Chaplain and Imam at HMP Bristol, at the Muslim
             Chaplaincy project conference, Cardiff, September 2011

The Significance of Muslim Chaplaincy for Muslim Communities

The complexity and range of Muslim chaplaincy work can span the mundane
business of facilitating day-to-day religious practice, to highly sensitive, multi-
agency troubleshooting. As chaplains grapple with the demands of their
emerging field of religious work, their distinctive qualities, skills, knowledge
and 'professionalism' are pointing to the need to diversify and develop religious
leadership in Muslim communities:

> Our chaplains are serving as models of Muslim religious leadership generally
> and they're raising the bar, they're raising the standard and it will raise the
> expectations in our community for Muslim religious leaders generally. I gave
> up a long time ago on affecting the dynamics in mosques. But I believe that this
> is the way to actually do that, because communities are starting to see … here
> are these very articulate, passionate, you know, intelligent, service-orientated
> Muslim leaders, mawlana [religious scholars] who are chaplains and then they
> wonder … you know, they see a big gap in those skills and personality and
> training with the imams of their communities. And yes, the imams have some
> other skills, you know, usually they're better trained in the Qur'an and Qur'an
> interpretation and other things, but they're not, you know, they don't have a

lot of the abilities that are needed by the communities so I think this will …
our communities are going to start demanding more of their imams (chaplaincy
educator, United States).

There have been critical voices about religious leadership in British Muslim
communities for many years, often centred around the inability of imams to speak
good English, or engage effectively with young people and wider society (Gilliat-
Ray 2010b; Hussain 2003). The development of Muslim chaplaincy in some ways
accentuates these limitations in community-based leadership still further, because
chaplains provide a model of religious leadership that appears to meet these kinds
of contextual challenges so successfully. A good number of chaplains have gone
into this field because of the frustrations and limitations placed upon them while
working in mosques, but they simultaneously appear to relish the prospect of
working in situations that are often 'complex, liminal and highly charged' (Swift
2009: 152). The needs of British Muslim communities in relation to religious
leadership are becoming more complex; expecting a single individual, the 'imam',
to meet these diverse needs is unrealistic. In these circumstances, differentiated
forms of religious leadership will be more likely to meet the changing needs
of Muslim communities. There is clearly scope for more 'pastoral care' to be
undertaken within mosques and Islamic centres, as well as in public institutions.

> Muslims have problems, and yet there is no one educated to guide the community
> through grief, anger, death, dying and sickness towards wellness. Such guidance
> can be found throughout our sacred sources, which clearly articulate a pastoral
> theology of care based on compassion. That is why I believe that chaplaincy is
> very much an Islamic necessity that someone in every Muslim community must
> fulfil (Ansari 2009: 177).

The question of who might undertake such work, and the resources upon which
they can draw, has been central to our work. However, there is a significant tension
among Muslim chaplains, both in Britain and in the United States, about whether
chaplains should be traditionally trained Islamic scholars ('alims/'alimas) or not.
Those falling either side of this fault-line seem to approach chaplaincy work from
different perspectives. On the whole, religious scholars take Islamic traditions
and laws/shari'ah as their point of departure, but, in the face of pastoral dilemmas,
they are sometimes forced to explore ways of introducing religious flexibility to
meet human need. Meanwhile, those who embark on chaplaincy work from other
professional backgrounds appear to use human suffering and experience as their
starting point; they tend to make less reference to Islamic law and texts to orientate
their response to pastoral issues. Somewhere between these two predominant
approaches there is an echo of a dilemma that is familiar in Christian pastoral
theology about the extent to which professionally provided religious care should
be grounded in textual and/or technical competence.

> If we use professional specialized knowledge as an ideal for all, we fall into an ancient error – that only those who *know* can love God and neighbour. Then pastoral care becomes the captive of the Gnostic heresy. The simplicity of faith is overcome by the complexity of esoteric knowledge (Campbell 1985: 45).

If we extend this quotation to the Islamic tradition, those who do not possess in-depth knowledge of sacred law (shari'ah) might become excluded from professional Muslim chaplaincy. Consequently, what is a communal responsibility, from an Islamic perspective, is in danger of becoming the preserve of the specialist few. The emphasis that many Islamic religious scholars place on the importance of traditional religious training (whether they draw upon that knowledge in practice or not) evidences nascent professional boundary-construction, sometimes via the retrospective categorisation of non-'alims as 'amateurs' (Fournier 2000).

Amid this intense competition as to 'what counts' as necessary spiritual and religious capital for the performance of Muslim chaplaincy, those who have acquired traditional Islamic training are most vocal in articulating the necessity of such knowledge for effective Muslim chaplaincy practice. They exemplify the class and power analysis of Pierre Bourdieu (Bourdieu 1979; Bourdieu 1992). Dinham's discussion of his ideas explores the notion that social (and here we can add religious) capital is a

> … means whereby elites reproduce their privilege through the transformation of interior individualism into collective expressions of perspectives which have hegemony as a result of being most strongly voiced. The strongest network effectively get themselves heard. Indeed, they become the very people who also do the hearing (Dinham 2009: 101).

However, just as Christian chaplaincy and pastoral care traditions in Christianity have been more strongly informed by 'lay' perspectives over time (not least due to a decline in vocations, and the obvious limits of human resources), so, too, the inclusion of Muslim chaplains from a range of educational backgrounds is important for the development of the profession. The only formal 'model' of Muslim chaplaincy that we heard expounded during the course of our research (from a Muslim educator in the UK) recognised the importance of balancing the 'horizontal axis of knowledge ('ilm) with the vertical axis of patience (sabr), spiritual connection to God, and mercy (rahma)'. So, just as it is unlikely that any one single person can meet all the religious leadership requirements of Muslim communities, so, too, the development of Muslim chaplaincy will benefit from the input of those with varying skills, experiences and forms of knowledge along the vertical and horizontal axes of the profession.

Muslim Chaplains and Multi-faith Relations

Muslim chaplains engage in multi-faith dialogue and relationships in many contexts. These include participating in shared acts of worship within the institution (such as ceremonies to support bereaved families in hospitals), offering pastoral support to patients of other faiths, negotiating the use of shared worship spaces, organising the working life of the 'team' and dialogue that occurs as a consequence of a chaplain and client sharing the same mother-tongue. (A patient or prisoner who speaks the same language as the chaplain may be of another faith, but the shared language creates the point of contact for an encounter that happens also to be across different faith traditions.) We did not ask the Muslim chaplains in our study explicit questions about inter-faith relations. However our data reveals a whole spectrum of responses to multi-faith realities, from the conservative to the more ecumenical. The more experienced chaplains become, the more confident they appear to be about the implications of the multi-faith context in which they work:

> It was two years ago, there was a problem at [name of prison] where it was Easter time and hot cross buns were not given to prisoners and there was an uproar to say 'this prison only caters for Muslim needs, look at our Christian needs, our hot cross buns have not been given to us' … so I made it my responsibility, because I have made those links with the catering department, so I told them, the Roman Catholic chaplain and the other Christian chaplains, 'you leave it to me, it's now my responsibility'. So over a number of meetings I resolved the issue and made sure that the following year hot cross buns were given as part of the normal diet, or for anybody who wanted them. So that's an example of how multi-faith chaplaincy teams should be working, where one is supporting the other. I think the biggest shock [was among] the prisoners, when the prisoners realised that it's the imam who's sorting out our hot cross buns. They realised that the imam is not just for Muslims. He's there for everybody; I think that's where they were shocked (full-time male prison chaplain).

Sometimes, Muslim chaplains grapple with the idea of boundaries and when to stop, theologically speaking, to accommodate or facilitate for another religion. One chaplain says that he is able to help and offer pastoral support to a Christian family, despite their religious differences, and his story echoes others that we heard:

> I think the vocabulary is difficult because I can't quote from the Bible and I'm not sure whether it would be right for me to do so from a religious perspective, but I think the pastoral care … you see the family's looking for comfort, the family's looking for support, the family's looking for help, the family's looking for compassion from someone, and I don't think compassion, support, help you know; these attributes aren't difficult for a Muslim chaplain in front of a Christian family. You know, why can't we support or help or feel compassion for a family who have lost a child? (full-time male hospital chaplain).

Pastoral care is thus, in this discourse, separable from something distinctively religious. However, some Muslim chaplains also find themselves working on the doctrinal borderlands of different faiths when they are supporting mixed-faith families. One hospital chaplain told us of an occasion when she had been called by a Christian woman whose Muslim husband was in a coma and about to die. She says that 'it was a wonderful experience because this woman was a clear believer in Christianity and there were so many things that she could share with me that were completely in parallel to my beliefs' (part-time female hospital chaplain). Such occasions require chaplains to make rapid decisions about how to interpret and deploy their religious knowledge, and where the boundaries lie in relation to such activity.

Many chaplains seem to be highly aware of their responsibility to ensure that multi-faith relations are preserved within their institution. This means policing client behaviour, finding ways of accommodating the views and ideas of colleagues, and in some cases 'vetting' the literature that comes into the institution (especially in prisons):

> One of the other things a Muslim chaplain is meant to do … is provide literature, so with the literature comes the vetting of the literature, what's conducive for the prison environment and what isn't. Something that may be good for the local community mosque may not be good over here, and at the same time, because of our interfaith relations, all faith relations nowadays, appropriate respect of my colleagues that talk from a different faith. I would make sure that I don't have any literature which is belittling of their faith communities or their traditions. To give you a very good example, there was a Buddhist that became a Muslim at an open medical conference, and it was a really good [piece of literature] which would be really spot on for our boys. The only reason I didn't bring it in or photocopy or reproduce it is because [in] the last paragraph he talks of how he went to the Buddhist monks to find an answer and he couldn't find the answer, so he found the answer in Islam. I'm very particular. Other people would probably put that in there, but because I feel it's still belittling of Buddhism and their feelings, of their way of life, I could do without that literature over here (full-time male prison chaplain).

The need to work as part of a multi-faith team within an institution characterised by religious diversity is often noted by chaplains as an intrinsic, taken-for-granted part of their role. The description of the multi-faith reality of chaplaincy work may be positive, 'neutral' or negative, but it is clearly seen as part of the wider social context of the institution, and of society more broadly. Muslim chaplains have become carriers of knowledge about how to work in this environment; many of them feel that this aspect of their work has something positive to contribute to social harmony, both within and outside the institution. The fact that it is seen thus seems to be an important observation about the wider significance of chaplaincy as a field of religious activity, and the scope it provides for Muslim religious professionals to acquire a new form of religious capital.

Amid the range of responses to the multi-faith character of public institutions, some chaplains have clearly been shaped by 'equality and diversity' principles. Others found ways of distinguishing general pastoral or spiritual care from distinctively Islamic religious care, or felt confident to draw upon Islamic traditions where this might resonate for clients of other faiths. But some approaches were more strongly informed by Islamic agendas. For example, some felt that chaplaincy was an opportunity for mission (da'wah), though not in an aggressively proselytising manner. Rather, it was about promoting Islam or, at least, the image of Islam. This relates as much as anything to a concern about the societal problems associated with misunderstanding and ignorance of the tradition than to any religious imperative for conversion:

> When I go to the wards initially it is to female Muslim patients. We have a big hospital and I work part-time, [so] I prioritise first in visiting the female wards. But quite often we have bays which have six beds for example and there may be people of other faiths in there, so I will also visit them as well because I think it's not fair on them to see a Muslim chaplain just visiting that person and walking off out of the ward. So I always make an effort just to approach them to see how they are, explain to them what my role is and just offer support and comfort and that works *very very* well again, in sort of promoting community harmony and cohesion, an example of multi-faith work. A lot of times I have been stopped, when I do go to non-Muslim patients, to explain things to them about my religion. Why is it that I have to wear hijab and why we pray five times a day, you know people don't have the understanding. If I were just to visit my Muslim patients and leave the wards and not see them, they would be left without an understanding, 'who was she, why did she come?' and things like that. So I have some *really really* enlightening and interesting discussions and debates with non-Muslim patients as well. I really enjoy that part of the role because I think, again, it's about promoting how beautiful our deen [religion] is and promoting our way of life … because a lot of people have their own misconceptions and the media certainly doesn't help with that at all, so it's beautiful, absolutely wonderful that you can have a civilised conversation with patients as well (part-time female hospital chaplain).

A number of Muslim chaplains also had an overtly Islamic agenda to rediscover elements within their tradition that might promote positive inter-faith relations. An American chaplain made reference to the concept of 'ahl al-kitab' or the 'people of the book', the idea that Jews and Christians are, like Muslims, part of a monotheistic scriptural tradition. Islamic sources accommodate Jews and Christians within an overarching theological (and political/economic) framework. This particular chaplain felt that it provided a unique resource to inform day-to-day working relations in chaplaincy:

I think that one thing that we have that the Jews and the Christians particularly don't have is a concept of ahl al-kitab, [though] they act as if they have it. If you look around the world I think people like to present us as a very monolithic and fascist religion but really when you look at many countries say in sub-Saharan Africa, like Tanzania, East Africa, West Africa, like Senegal, you'll find that Muslims have been co-existing with Christians for many, many years and been electing Christian presidents and electing Muslim presidents. And so I think what we have is within our understanding of the faith is the concept of the people of the book, this is very, very important. I think the challenge over time would be to actualise that concept in the work that we do (interview, July 2011).

Muslim chaplains are clearly influenced by the multi-faith realities that shape their work, irrespective of context. But many go beyond labels and categories to recognise the shared humanity that underpins day-to-day team work. One Muslim chaplain says:

… the way I believe, is that my religion is *very, very* important to me, I'm a Muslim, it's so important to me. But I also believe that somebody else, somebody else's religion is *as* important to them as mine is to me. I call this recognising other particularities (full-time male prison chaplain).

This chaplain has clearly recognised the importance of other religions to their adherents on the basis of his own experience of the importance of Islam. This is subtly different from both the recognition of shared faith and shared humanity, but clearly relates to both. It also reveals a level of reflective practice and self-understanding born out of experience and, to some extent, the influence and ethos of Christian pastoral care traditions of practice and training. At the point where different traditions intersect in a specific grounded context, we can see the way Muslim chaplains are in some sense like their Christian colleagues becoming part of a 'script that they are writing, performing and orchestrating … their public work is a combination of improvisation and compliance' (Percy 2006: 165).

This ability to improvise some aspects of religious practice and approaches within institutional frameworks that require compliance with public sector principles about equality, diversity, respect for the individual and so on is a skill that, arguably, has implications that resonate well beyond the particular institutions in which chaplains work. They provide a role model for clients about the possibilities of inter-religious relations, and demonstrate to managers and policymakers that multi-faith co-operation is possible. A Christian chaplain interviewed elsewhere noted that 'one of the most powerful acts of faith I can be seen to do in this prison is walking on the wings, side by side with my Muslim colleague, having a good laugh' (Todd and Tipton 2011: 23). An American chaplain reflected:

> I think the presence of chaplains is making Islam as an American religion more
> acceptable in a way that is less true of the mosques, simply because some
> chaplains are working every day with the people of other religions. [Chaplains
> of different faiths] have the same problems, they have the same problems with
> administration, the same problems with the people that they're serving and so
> they develop this kind of camaraderie as religious professionals, so I just think
> it's such a critical area (interview, July 2011).

In Britain, the involvement of Muslims as salaried religious professionals in
a wide range of public institutions powerfully signals the fact that Islam is
recognised and supported in very direct ways in public life. Chaplaincy has
provided an opportunity for Muslim religious professionals to inform institutions
about Islamic traditions, while also enabling clients to benefit from the pastoral
and religious care that they offer. This role combines religious, pastoral,
educational and advisory work and an ability to interpret and operationalise
Islamic sources in particular contexts and situations. It was clear in our data that
chaplains have often had to evaluate what is essential for the practice of Islam in
their institution, as opposed to what is simply preferable. This process requires
an ability to undertake informed negotiation with clients, managers, peers and
colleagues of other faiths, against the background of Islamic texts and sources
(such as the Qur'an and hadith), the truths of which are regarded by Muslims
as non-negotiable. To undertake this process successfully requires a significant
effort of 'translation' between different worldviews. Though speaking about
young Muslims in European societies rather than specifically about chaplains,
Pedziwitar's observations are pertinent ...

> Young Muslims in Brussels and London have not fully embraced the values
> inseparably linked with modernity; if they have embraced them at all, they have
> often done so 'on Muslim terms' ... there is a re-drawing of the distinction
> between 'central' and 'peripheral' belief elements. They prove the existence of
> a dynamic that is simultaneously translating the realities of life in 21st-century
> Europe into Muslim terms and translating Muslim dogmas into the terms of life
> in 21st-century Europe (Pedziwiatr 2011: 221).

In a context where there is a 'profound public ambivalence about religion'
(Dinham and Jones 2012: 188) in British society, the work of Muslim chaplains
contributes to more positive, informed understanding of religion in general, and
of Islam in particular. This is because Muslim chaplains have arguably become
a rather distinctive and privileged group of faith actors in public life. Many of
them, especially those with more experience, have acquired a confident grasp
of the language, the concepts and the knowledge to be able to talk confidently
about religious and moral issues in the public domain. Those Muslim chaplains
now serving as co-ordinating chaplains are exercising power to shape the practice
of religion in public life. With this power there comes a sense of ownership of,

and investment in, public institutions more broadly. This is a profound counter-narrative to ideas often promoted in the media about Muslim self-segregation.

Considering inter-faith relations as 'civic practice', Luke Bretherton explores the political, and to some extent the economic, rather than the humanitarian/religious significance, of inter-faith relations (Bretherton 2011). He identifies a number of civic practices that provide a model for inter-faith relations. These include listening, commitment to place and the building and maintenance of institutions as central to the formation of a politics of the common good. If we consider the work of Muslim chaplains in this light, it is clear that they have found ways of making Islamic traditions meaningful in many public institutions, and are contributing to the flourishing of particular places and organisations. The ways in which they are incorporating Islamic traditions and practices into the fabric of British society is in a dialogical relationship to other faiths (especially Christian) and with reference to the principles that shape public life. Chaplaincies have become immensely important sites of religious and social capital that can inform the management of religion in society more widely. Although the Muslim chaplains we interviewed were resistant to occasional expectations that they could be an additional interpreting service, there is a sense in which their structural positioning, between multi-faith public institutions on the one hand, and Muslim communities on the other, gives them a very significant role as facilitators of dialogue across a wide range of cultural, ethnic and religious worldviews.

Figure 8.2   Asgar Halim Rajput, chaplain at Brunel University, London

The Future of Muslim Chaplaincy: Some Indications for the Future

This book has provided a rich description and analytic account of Muslim chaplaincy in England and Wales; it is perhaps one of the most in-depth qualitative studies of a particular group of religious professionals that has been undertaken in Britain for a generation. We hope that it will revive academic interest in the sociology of religious professionals, and will support the recent growth of academic work in the emerging field of 'chaplaincy studies'. We have deliberately quoted the words of our interviewees extensively; to this extent there is a real sense in which this book is theirs, as much as it is ours. We hope that this volume will aid the understanding of professional Muslim chaplaincy, and perhaps also act as a catalyst for more experienced Muslim chaplains to engage in greater reflection about their work and its significance. In this way, this account will hopefully help to structure emerging chaplaincy discourse, and will lead to the development of literature and training materials that can nurture those new to the profession.

Having engaged in such a detailed mapping of the development of Muslim chaplaincy, what kind of tentative predictions can be made about the future? To answer this question, we return to the voices of our interviewees who, at the conclusion of our conversations with them, were asked whether they envisaged staying in chaplaincy or not. Inevitably, the fortunes of Muslim chaplaincy (and indeed chaplaincy generally) will be influenced by public sector economics, but there are ways in which the profession may develop in significant directions. For example, some of the most experienced chaplains currently in post may decide to move on into higher-level management work in their institutions, or direct their energies into shaping the field through academic engagement or policy work. If they take up such opportunities, perhaps as prison Governors, as managers of equality and diversity issues or as civil servants responsible for social policy on religion in Britain, this will not only create opportunities for incoming chaplains, but will see British Muslims making significant contributions to the shaping of public institutions which could have a direct impact on the work of chaplains of all faiths. One of our interviewees said explicitly that,

> … my ambitions are more to be a Governor than to be a chaplain, but as I say, it's a bit late for that. I don't think I'll pass the medical even. But, you know, even the young Imams, I always encourage them to change career, to go into prison management because they can do it (full-time male prison chaplain).

Some of our interviewees were vocal about the need to create resources for Muslim chaplains new to the profession so that postholders were not 're-inventing the wheel all the time' (full-time male hospital chaplain). If such views gathered sufficient momentum, this might see a small number of chaplains move into new spheres that might allow them the opportunity to write and to reflect on the development of the profession. What was most clear, however, was that most Muslim chaplains intend to remain working in chaplaincy, and within their current sector. One prison chaplain predicted: 'I will die in this prison' (full-time male prison chaplain). Because such a significant number of chaplains have entered the profession as Islamic scholars, there are relatively few alternative career paths for them, and their religious motivations inhibit ambitions that might take them from frontline religious and pastoral work.

It is possible that some Muslim chaplains may find themselves assisting with the development of Muslim chaplaincy in other European countries. One of the outcomes of the research upon which this book is based has been invitations to address European conferences and workshops concerned with religious diversity in prisons (Lausanne, September 2010; Paris, September 2011), and the question of how public institutions can manage religious and ethnic diversity (Berlin, 2012). The changes that have taken place in England and Wales since the early 2000s have been noted further afield, and other countries seem eager to learn from the British experience. Recounting the development of Muslim health care chaplaincy in Denmark since the late 2000s, Navid Baig notes the influence of Britain in stimulating the profession there (Baig 2012), not least because some of the first volunteer Muslim chaplains to work in Danish hospitals acquired the 'Certificate in Muslim Chaplaincy' from MIHE in Leicester. This interest and expansion of Muslim chaplaincy in other European societies not only suggests the potential for future international research, but also positions British Muslim chaplains at the forefront of an international development.

Most public institutions currently frame 'Islam' and 'Muslim' as broad homogeneous categories; there is very little recognition of the diversity within the Islamic tradition. This situation contrasts with the way in which Christian diversity is accommodated, so that most larger chaplaincy departments in prisons and hospitals will have Anglican, Roman Catholic and Free Church representation, and usually links to a much larger range of smaller Christian groups (such as independent Pentecostal churches). It is probable that as Muslim communities develop in Britain, there may be calls for the distinctiveness of particular schools of Islamic thought to be accommodated more fully in publicly funded chaplaincy. During the life of our study, evidence to support this possibility came from an approach made to us by a law firm acting on behalf of a Muslim prisoner. Their client felt that his particular Islamic tradition was inadequately supported by the prison's Sunni chaplain.

To some extent, the answer to this conundrum about religious distinctiveness and internal diversity will be resolved by economic pressures. However, it is also likely to emerge as an outcome of a broader debate within chaplaincy as to the advantages and disadvantages of 'one-size-fits-all' approaches to pastoral care in public institutions. There was evidence in our data of the way in which Muslim chaplains could work very effectively within a discourse that promotes the idea that pastoral care need not depend upon chaplains having a particular religious identity:

> I'm not here to invite; in this place you're not here to give da'wah, I'm not here to propagate the deen [the Islamic tradition], I'm here just to be human for anybody who has a need to talk about whatever and if that involves talking

about Allah subhanahu wata'aala [all praise to God] then fine, we'll talk about Allah subhanahu wata'aala. So, being responsive to the human aspect, I think that is 100% Islamic (full-time male hospital chaplain).

However, it is clear from our research that a good deal of the work that Muslim chaplains carry out is valuable precisely because of its distinctiveness. Muslim chaplains embody and manifest the stories, the texts and the language of a particular religious tradition, and understand the practical and religious needs of Muslims in a unique way. Though clearly willing and able to work effectively in multi-faith teams, and to support clients of all faiths and none, there are aspects of their work that sometimes depend upon chaplain and client sharing a worldview that is rooted in a common framework of meaning. Their ability to articulate this perspective within broader chaplaincy discourse could make a profound contribution to professional debate, and could support chaplains of other faiths (at this stage, mainly Christians) who are equally reluctant to be pressured into the delivery of pastoral care that is 'generic'. At the time of writing, this very question is being contested in the Canadian prison service, following a ministerial decision to withdraw funding for those part-time chaplaincy posts that currently support prisoners from minority faiths. In a commentary about the decision the question is posed: 'why not require a chaplain to provide spiritual services for all religions?'. The response is quite simply that 'it becomes an exchange that lacks authenticity and the facts needed for inner transformation'.[1] If chaplaincy services in Britain were to come under similar pressures to become more 'generic', Christian chaplains would find allies among their Muslim colleagues who have become articulate defenders of the distinctiveness and particularity of religion, as opposed to the rather bland notions of spirituality that are often associated with 'generic' pastoral care (Pattison 2001).

It is likely, in view of governmental awareness of the value of 'pastoral' interventions by Muslim chaplains, that, at least for the time being, Muslim chaplains will continue to develop their practice within the distinctive traditions of their faith. In some sectors this will be an overt policy, as with the counter-radicalisation process within prisons. As this book has shown, despite the cumulative and gradual development of a specifically Muslim chaplaincy practice, the role of Muslim chaplains is in some ways at a crossroads. No longer developing in the shadow of Christian chaplaincy, the emergence of Muslim chaplaincy as a novel and significant forum for inter-faith dialogue – for example – is serving to alter the character of chaplaincy overall. The specific requirements of Muslim practice, and the degree to which Muslim chaplains must engage with the management of their institutions to facilitate many of these, is likely to lead to a reciprocal willingness among Christian (and other faith) chaplains to assert the needs of their own constituencies, and to look afresh at how their practices can be both supported and reinvigorated.

---

[1]   http://www.theglobeandmail.com/commentary/one-size-prison-chaplains-dont-fit-all/article4607354/?cmpid=rss1 [accessed 12.10.12].

We have seen how the recruitment of women into Muslim chaplaincy, is not only opening a new door into the profession for Muslim women, but it is also bringing them into the sphere of 'authority discourse' within religious practice in Islam. This may ultimately have considerable future impact, in a context in which religious commentary and authority have until now been an almost exclusively male preserve, particularly in the interpretation of religious texts and doctrines. Muslim chaplains in both Britain and North America can therefore be seen to be 'pushing the boundaries' of Islamic religious practice in a number of spheres, as well as shaping new discourses about religion in public life more broadly.

Glossary

Adab	Etiquettes or manners
Adhan	Call to prayer
'Alim	Male scholar (f. 'alima, pl. 'ulama)
'Alima	Female scholar
Fatwa	Legal opinion
Ghayb	Matters of the unseen
Hadith	Sayings of the Prophet Muhammad
Iftar	Breaking of fast
Iqamah	Pre-prayer call
Jannah	Paradise
Jumu'ah	Friday (referring mainly to the Friday prayer)
Khutbah	Sermon (referring mainly to the sermon before the Friday prayer)
Minbar	Pulpit from which the Friday sermon is delivered
Mufti	Scholar who can issue legal opinions
Niyyah	Intention
Qibla	Direction of the Ka'bah in Mecca towards which Muslims pray
Salat	Daily prayers, performed five times a day
Shahadah	To witness that 'That there is no God but Allah, and Muhammad is his Messenger'
Shari'ah	Principles and practices for Islamic belief, behaviour and worship
Shaykh	An honorific title sometimes used for an Islamic scholar. In its more specific usage it means a spiritual teacher (also spelt 'Sheikh')
Shirk	Polytheism
Sunna	Practices of the Prophet

Surah	Chapter of the Qur'an, pronounced as 'surah' when saying it on its own
Talfiq	To amalgamate opinions from two schools of law
Tarawih	The night prayer in the month of Ramadan
Tasmiya	The saying of 'bismillah' 'In the name of God the most Merciful, most kind'
Tawhid	The indivisible 'oneness' of God
'Ulama	Islamic Scholars (m. 'alim, f. 'alima)
Ummah	Muslim community (mainly referring to the global community
Wudu	Ritual cleansing prior to worship
Zakat	Mandatory alms given out of one's savings every lunar year

References

Abbott, A. 1988. *The System of the Professions*, London: University of Chicago Press.

Abdullah, O.B. 2011. 'Providing Comfort', *Islamic Horizons* 40 (2): 6.

Abu-Ras, W. 2010, 'Chaplaincy Services for Muslim Patients in New York City Hospitals: Assessing Needs, Barriers, and the Role of Muslim Chaplains', New York: Institute for Social Policy and Understanding.

Abu-Ras, W. 2011. 'Muslim Chaplain's Role as Perceived by Directors and Chaplains of New York City Hospitals and Health Care Settings', *Journal of Muslim Mental Health* 6 (1): 21–43.

Abu-Ras, W. and Laird, L. 2010. 'How Muslim and Non-Muslim Chaplains Serve Muslim Patients? Does the Interfaith Chaplaincy Model have Room for Muslims' Experiences?', *Journal of Religion and Health* 50 (1): 46–61.

Ahmad, M. 2011. 'Muslim chaplains play an indispensable role, but community involvement and support is needed', *Islamic Horizons* 40 (2): 20–24.

al-Ghazali, A.H. 1995. *The Ninety-Nine Beautiful Names of God*, translated by David and Nazih Daher, Cambridge: Islamic Text Society.

al-Isfihani, A.N. n.d. *Hilyat al-Awliya*, Beirut: Dar al-Kutb Al-Ilmiyya.

al-Haythami, N. a.-D. 1994. *Majma' al-Zawa'id wa Manba' al-Fawa'id*, Cairo: Maktabat al-Qudsi.

Ali, K. 2006. *Sexual Ethics in Islam: Feminist Reflections on Qur'an, Hadith, and Jurisprudence*, Oxford: Oneworld Publications.

Ali, M.M. and Gilliat-Ray, S. 2012. 'Muslim Chaplains: working at the interface of "public" and "private"', in Ahmad, W. and Sardar, Z., (eds), *Muslims in Britain: Making Social and Political Space*, London: Routledge, pp. 84–100.

Ammar, N., Weaver, R. and Saxon, S. 2004. 'Muslims in Prison: a case study from Ohio State Prisons', *International Journal of Offender Therapy and Comparative Criminology* 48 (4): 414–28.

Anderson, H. 2009. 'Editorial Section III: Islamic Perspectives for Supervision', *Reflective Practice: Formation and Supervision in Ministry* 29 (2): 1.

Anees, M. 1984a. 'Al-Majusi's Observations and Instruction on Medical and Public Health', in Hamerneh, S. and Anees, M., (eds), *Health Sciences in Early Islam*, n.p.: Zahra Publications, pp. 313–31.

Anees, M. 1984b. 'Development of Hospitals in Islam', in Anees, S.H. a. M., (ed.), *Health Sciences in Early Islam*, Blanco, Texas: Zahra Publications, pp. 97–12.

Ansari, B. 2009. 'Seeing With Bifocals: The Evolution of a Muslim Chaplain', *Reflective Practice: Formation and Supervision in Ministry* 29: 170–177.

Arshad, M. Horsfall, A. and Yasin, R. 2004. 'Pregnancy loss – the Islamic perspective', *British Journal of Midwifery* 12 (8): 481–4.

Atkinson, P. and Coffey, A. 2002. 'Revisiting the relationship between participant observation and interviewing', in Gubrium, J. and Holstein, J., (eds), *Handbook of Interview Research: Context and Method*, London: Sage, pp. 801–14.

Atkinson, P. Coffey, A. and Delamont, S. 2003. *Key Themes in Qualitative Research: Continuities and Change*, Walnut Creek: CA: AltaMira Press.

Autton, N. 1969. *Pastoral Care in Hospitals*, London: Hospital Chaplaincy Board/ Free Church Federal Council.

Baig, N. 2012. 'Counseling in the Health Service', in Nielsen, J., (ed.), *Islam in Denmark,* Plymouth: Lexington Books, pp. 219–231.

Barringer, T.A. 1998. 'Adult Transformation Inside Midwest Correctional Facility – Black Muslims' Narratives of Their Conversion', PhD, Illinois, Northern Illinois University.

Bebbington, D. 1992. 'The Secularisation of British Universities', in Marsden, G. and Longfield, B., (eds), *The Secularisation of the Academy*, Oxford: Oxford University Press, pp. 259–77.

Becci, I. 2011. 'Religion's Multiple Locations in Prison: Germany, Italy, Swiss', *Archives de Sciences Sociales des Religions* 153 (Jan–March): 65–84.

Beckford, J. 1998. 'Ethnic and Religious Diversity among Prisoners: the politics of prison chaplaincy', *Social Compass* 45 (2): 265–77.

Beckford, J. 2001. 'Doing Time: Space, Time, Religious Diversity and the Sacred in Prisons', *International Review of Sociology* 11 (3): 371–82.

Beckford, J. and Gilliat, S. 1996. *The Church of England and Other Faiths in a Multi-Faith Society: report to the Leverhulme Trust*, Warwick: University of Warwick.

Beckford, J. and Gilliat, S. 1998. *Religion in Prison: Equal Rites in a Multi-Faith Society*, Cambridge: Cambridge University Press.

Beckford, J., Joly, D. and Khosrokhavar, F. 2005. *Muslims in Prison: Challenge and Change in Britain and France*, Basingstoke: Palgrave Macmillan.

Beckford, M. 2010, 'Chaplains can help fight against Muslim extremism, says Shahid Malik', http://www.telegraph.co.uk/news/uknews/terrorism-in-the-uk/7498615/Chaplains-can-help-fight-against-Muslim-extremism-says-Shahid-Malik.html (accessed, 23/3/10).

Birt, J. 2005. 'Locating the British *Imam*: the Deobandi '*Ulama* between Contested Authority and Public Policy Post-9/11', in Cesari, J. and McLoughlin, S., (eds), *European Muslims and the Secular State*, Aldershot: Ashgate, pp. 183–96.

Birt, J. 2006. 'Good Imam, Bad Imam: civic religion and national integration in Britain post 9/11', *The Muslim World* 96 (October): 687–705.

Birt, Y. 2010. 'Promoting Virulent Envy? Reconsidering the UK's Terrorist Prevention Strategy', *RSUI Journal* 154 (4): 52–8.

Boddie, S. and Funk, C. 2012, 'Religion in Prisons: a 50-state survey of prison chaplains', Washington DC: Pew Research Centre Forum on Religion in Public Life.

Bourdieu, P. 1979. *Distinction: a Social Critique of the Judgement of Taste*, London: Routledge and Kegan Paul.

Bourdieu, P. 1992. *Language and Symbolic Power*, Cambridge: Polity Press.

Bowers, A. 2009. 'The Search for Justice: Islamic Pedagogy and Inmate Rehabilitation', in Haddad, Y.Y., Senzai, F. and Smith, J., (eds), *Educating the Muslims of America*, New York: Oxford University Press, pp. 179–208.

Boyle, H. 2004. *Quranic Schools: Agents of Preservation and Change*, London: RoutledgeFalmer.

Brandon, J. 2009, 'Unlocking Al-Qaeda: Islamist Extremism in British Prisons', London: Quilliam Foundation.

Brant, R. 2011, 'How widespread is campus extremism?', http://www.bbc.co.uk/news/uk-politics-12337531 (accessed, 15.05.12).

Bretherton, L. 2011. 'A Postsecular Politics? Inter-faith Relations as a Civic Practice', *Journal of the American Academy of Religion* 79 (2): 346–77.

Brown, D. 1996. *Rethinking Tradition in Modern Islamic Thought*, Cambridge: Cambridge University Press.

Burchard, W. 1954. 'Role Conflicts of Military Chaplains', *American Sociological Review* 19 (4): 528–35.

Campbell, A. 1985. *Paid to Care? The Limits of Professionalism in Pastoral Care*, London: SPCK.

Clines, J. 2008, 'Faiths in Higher Education Chaplaincy: a report commissioned by the Church of England Board of Education', London: Church of England Board of Education.

Cobb, M. and Robshaw, V. 1998. *The Spiritual Challenge of Health Care*, London: Churchill Livingstone.

Cooper, A.A. 2008, 'Towards a model for the spiritual care of Muslim prisoners in Muslim minority countries', NCEIS Conference 2008: Challenges to Social Inclusion in Australia: the Muslim Experience.

Coxon, A.P.M. and Towler, R. 1979. *The Fate of Anglican Clergy: a Sociological Study,* London: Macmillan.

Daneman, M. 2011. 'Muslim chaplains fill void on campus', *Chicago Sun-Times*, 25th March 2011.

Davie, G. 1994. *Religion in Britain since 1945: Believing Without Belonging*, Oxford: Blackwell.

Davies, C. 1996. 'The Sociology of Professions and the Profession of Gender', *Sociology* 30 (4): 661–78.

Dhalla, M. 1991. 'Doing Time at HM's Pleasure', *The Muslim News*, 21/6/91.

Dinham, A. 2009. *Faiths, Public Policy and Civil Society*, London: Palgrave Macmillan.

Dinham, A., Furbey, R. and Lowndes, V., (eds) 2009. '*Faith in the Public Realm: Controversies, policies and practices*', Bristol: Policy Press.

Dinham, A. and Jones, S. 2012. 'Religion, Public Policy, and the Academy: Brokering Public Faith in a Context of Ambivalence', *Journal of Contemporary Religion* 27 (2): 185–201.

Dodd, V. 2006. 'Universities urged to spy on Muslims', *The Guardian*, 16.10.2006.

Doi, A. R. 1997. *Shari'ah: the Islamic Law*, London: Ta Ha Publishers.

Dols, M. 1983. 'The Leper in Medieval Islamic Society', *Speculum* 58 (4): 891–916.

Dols, M. 1992. *Majnun: The Madman in Medieval Islamic Societies*, Oxford: Clarendon Press.

Dudhwala, Y. 2006, 'Building Bridges Between Theology and Pastoral Care', Lisbon, European Network of Health Care Chaplains, http://www.eurochaplains.org/lisbon06.htm#report, (Accessed: 6/6/07).

Edward Jones, J. 1989. 'Islamic Prison Ministry: Towards an Effective Chaplaincy at Community Correctional Centre-New Haven', PhD, Connecticut, Hartford Seminary.

Eickelman, D. 1978. 'The Art of Memory: Islamic Education and its Social Reproduction', *Comparative Studies in Society and History* 20 (4): 485–516.

Eickelman, D. 1985. *Knowledge and Power in Morocco: the Education of a Twentieth-Century Notable*, Princeton, NJ: Princeton University Press.

Ford, R. 2012. 'Out-of-touch imams responsible for a generation in jail, says cleric', *The Times*, 10 January 2012.

Foucault, M. 1982. 'The Subject and Power', *Critical Inquiry* 8 (4): 777–95.

Fournier, V. 2000. 'Boundary work and the (un)making of the professions', in Malin, N., (ed.), *Professionalism, Boundaries and the Workplace*, London: Routledge, pp. 67–86.

Freidson, E. 1986. *Professional Powers: a Study of the Institutionlization of Formal Knowledge*, Chicago: Chicago University Press.

Fuller, J. and Vaughan, P., (eds) 1986. '*Working for the Kingdom: the story of ministers in secular employment*', London: SPCK.

Furseth, I. and Kuhle, L. 2011. 'Prison Chaplaincy from a Scandinavian Perspective', *Archives de Sciences Sociales des Religions* 153 (Jan-March): 123–41.

Gallagher, R. 2012. 'Counter-terror strategy faces university opposition', *The Guardian*, 16.3.12.

Gallagher, R. and Syal, R. 2011. 'University staff asked to inform on 'vulnerable' Muslim students', *The Guardian*, 29.8.2011.

Ganley, E. 2012, 'France looks at radicalization in prisons', http://www.time.com/time/world/article/0,8599,2111498,00.html (accessed, 11.4.12).

Geaves, R. 2008. 'Drawing on the past to transform the present: contemporary challenges for training and preparing British *Imams*', *Journal of Muslim Minority Affairs* 28 (1): 99–112.

Geaves, R. 2012. 'The symbolic construction of the walls of Deoband', *Islam and Christian-Muslim Relations* 23 (3): 315–328.

Gilliat-Ray, S. 2000. *Religion in Higher Education: the Politics of the Multi-faith Campus*, Aldershot: Ashgate.

Gilliat-Ray, S. 2001a. '*The Fate of the Anglican Clergy* and the Class of '97: some implications of the changing sociological profile of ordinands', *Journal of Contemporary Religion* 16 (2): 209–25.

Gilliat-Ray, S. 2001b. 'Sociological Perspectives on the Pastoral Care of Minority Faiths in Hospital', in Orchard, H., (ed.), *Spirituality in Health Care Contexts*, London: Jessica Kingsley Publishers, pp. 135–46.

Gilliat-Ray, S. 2006. 'Educating the *'Ulema*: Centres of Islamic Religious Training in Britain', *Islam and Christian-Muslim Relations* 17 (1): 55–76.

Gilliat-Ray, S. 2010a. 'Body-works and fieldwork: Research with British Muslim chaplains', *Culture and Religion* 11 (4): 413–32.

Gilliat-Ray, S. 2010b. *Muslims in Britain: An Introduction*, Cambridge Cambridge University Press.

Gilliat-Ray, S. 2011. ''Being There': the experience of shadowing a British Muslim Hospital Chaplain', *Qualitative Research* 11 (5): 469–86.

Gorman, A. 2007. 'Regulation, reform and resistance in the Middle Eastern prison', in Dikötter, F. and Brown, I., (eds), *Cultures of Confinement: a History of the Prison in Africa, Asia and Latin America*, Ithaca: NY: Cornell University Press, pp. 95–146.

Gould, R. 2012. 'Prisons before Modernity: Incarceration in the Medieval Indo-Mediterranean', *Al-Masaq: Islam and the Medieval Mediterranean* 24 (2): 179–97.

Gutkowski, S. 2012. 'The British Secular habitus and the War on Terror', *Journal of Contemporary Religion* 27 (1): 87–103.

Haddad, Y.Y. and Smith, J. 1995. 'United States of America', in Esposito, J., (ed.), *The Oxford Encyclopedia of the Modern Islamic World*, Oxford: Oxford University Press, pp. 277–84.

Halstead, M. 2004. 'An Islamic concept of education', *Comparative Education* 40 (4): 517–29.

Hamilton, K. 2006. 'A Call to Lead', *Diverse: Issues in Higher Education* 23 (7): 28–31.

Hamza, D. R. 2007. 'On Models of Hospital Chaplaincies: which one works best for the Muslim Community?', *Journal of Muslim Mental Health* 2 (1): 65–79.

Haneef, S. 1979. *What Everyone Should know About Islam and Muslims*, Lahore: Kazi Publications.

Harris, R.T. 2009. 'Supporting Your Muslim Students: A Guide for Clinical Pastoral Supervisors', *Reflective Practice: Formation and Supervision in Ministry* 29: 154–69.

Hastrup, K. 1995. *A Passage to Anthropology*, London: Routledge.

'Health Care Chaplaincy and the Church of England', 2010. London: Hospital Chaplaincies Council.

Heelas, P., Woodhead, L., Seel, B., Szerszynski, B. and Tusting, K. 2005. *The Spiritual Revolution: Why Religion is Giving Way to Spirituality*, Oxford, UK and Malden, USA: Blackwell.

Hewer, C. 2001. 'Schools for Muslims', *Oxford Review of Education* 27 (4): 515–27.

Hewer, C. 2006. *Understanding Islam: The First Ten Steps*, London: SCM Press.

Hicks, A. 2008. 'Role Fusion: the occupational socialisation of prison chaplains', *Symbolic Interaction* 31 (4): 400–421.

'HM Chief Inspector of Prisons – Muslim prisoners' experiences: a thematic review', 2010. London: HM Prison Service.

Howe, M. 2007, 'Shifting Muslim Gender and Family Norms in East London', New York, Paper presented at the American Sociological Association, 11th August.

Hunt, S. 2011. 'Testing Chaplaincy Reforms in England and Wales', *Archives de Sciences Sociales Des Religions* 153 (1): 43–64.

Husband, C. and Alam, Y. 2011. *Social Cohesion and Counter Terrorism: a Policy Contradiction?*, Bristol: Policy Press.

Hussain, D. 2003, 'The Need for Home-grown Imams', Muslims of Europe Conference held at the Al-Khoei Foundation, London, 26/1/2003.

Jackson, S. 2009. *Islam and the Problem of Black Suffering*, Oxford: Oxford University Press.

Jenkins, R. 2002. *Pierre Bourdieu*, London: Routledge.

Johnston, R. and McFarland, E. 2010. '"Out in the Open in a Threatening World": The Scottish Churches' Industrial Mission: 1960–1980', *International Review of Social History* 55 (1): 1–27.

Jones, J.J. 1989. 'Islamic Prison Ministry: towards an effective chaplaincy at the Community Correctional Centre – New Haven', D. Min., Connecticut, Hartford Seminary.

Jones, V. 2007. 'A Study in Comfort', *The Boston Globe*, 7.3.2007.

Kassam-Remtullah, A. 2012. 'Islam on Campus: emergence of Muslim chaplaincy in American higher education', PhD, University of Oxford.

Keller, N.H.M. 1994. *Reliance of the Traveller: A Classic Manual of Islamic Sacred Law*, Evanston: Sunna Books.

Kerbaj, R. 2009. 'Muslim population "rising 10 times faster than rest of society"', *Times Online*, 30th January.

Khoja-Moolji, S.S. 2011, 'An Emerging Model of Muslim Leadership: chaplaincy on university campuses', Harvard University: Pluralism Project.

Khuri, F. 2001. *The Body in Islamic Culture*, London: Saqi Books

Klausen, J. 2009. 'British Counter-Terrorism after 7/7: adapting community policing to the fight against domestic terrorism', *Journal of Ethnic and Migration Studies* 35 (3): 403–20.

Kohut, A. 2007, 'Muslim Americans: Middle Class and Mostly Mainstream', Washington DC: Pew Research Centre.

Kowalski, M. 2009. 'Names of God: Practical Theology for Muslim Chaplains in CPE', *Reflective Practice: Formation and Supervision in Ministry* 29: 178–86.

Kuhrt, G. 2001. *Ministry Issues for the Church of England: Mapping the Trends*, London: Church House Publishing.

Kundnani, A. 2009, 'Spooked! How not to prevent violent extremism', London: Institute of Race Relations.

Lahaj, M. 2009. 'Making It Up As I Go Along: The Formation of a Muslim Chaplain', *Reflective Practice: Formation and Supervision in Ministry* 29: 148–53.

Lambert, R. 2011. *Countering Al-Qaeda in London: Police and Muslims in Partnership*, London: Hurst.

Lane, E. 1863. *Arabic English Lexicon*, London: Williams and Norgate.

Legood, G., (ed.) 1999a. *'Chaplaincy: the Church's Sector Ministries'*, London: Cassell.

Legood, G. 1999b. 'Introduction', in Legood, G., (ed.), *Chaplaincy: the Church's Sector Ministries*, London: Cassell, pp. ix–xv.

Levine, S.E.J. 2009. 'Muslim Chaplains in America: Voices from the First Wave', *Reflective Practice: Formation and Supervision in Ministry* 29: 142–7.

Lindholm, C. 2002. *The Islamic Middle East: Tradition and Change*, Oxford: Blackwell.

Lucas, S. 2011. '"Perhaps You Only Kissed Her?" A Contrapuntal Reading of the Penalties for Illicit Sex in the Sunni Hadith Literature', *Journal of Religious Ethics* 39 (3): 399–414.

Macdonald, K. 1995. *The Sociology of the Professions*, London: SAGE.

Makdisi, G. 1981. *The Rise of Colleges: Institutions of Learning in Islam and the West*, Edinburgh: Edinburgh University Press.

Marranci, G. 2009. *Faith, Ideology and Fear: Muslim Identities Within and Beyond Prisons*, London: Continuum.

Maxwell, G., McDougall, M. Blair, S. and Masson, M. 2003. 'Equality at work in UK public-service and hotel organizations: inclining towards managing diversity?', *Human Resource Development International* 6 (2): 243–58.

Metcalf, B. 1982. *Islamic Revival in British India: Deoband 1860–1900*, Princeton: Princeton University Press.

Metcalf, B. 2002. *'Traditionalist' Islamic Activism: Deoband, Tablighis, and Talibs*, Leiden: ISIM.

Mills, T., Griffin, T. and Miller, D. 2011, 'The Cold War on British Muslims', London: Spinwatch.

Mogra, I. 2004. 'Makatib Education in Britian: a review of trends and some suggestions for policy', *Muslim Education Quarterly* 21 (4): 19–27.

Mogra, I. 2011. 'On Being a Muslim Teacher in England', *American Journal of Islamic Social Sciences* 28 (2): 34–62.

Mohammad, R. 2005. 'Negotiating Spaces of the Home, the Education System, and the Labour Market: the case of young, working-class, British Pakistani Muslim Women', in Falah, G.-W. and Nagel, C., (eds), *Geographies of Muslim Women: Gender, Religion and Space*, New York: The Guildford Press, pp. 178–200.

Moore, K. 1995. *Al-Mughtaribun: American Law and the Transformation of Muslim Life in the United States*, NY: State University of New York Press.

Mughal, F. 2010, 'The Recruitment of Muslim Chaplains Within Key Institutions in England: developing the recruitment process and framework of standards', London: Faith Matters.

Mukadam, M. and Scott-Baumann, A. 2010, 'The training and development of Muslim Faith Leaders: Current practice and future possibilities', London: Communities and Local Government.

Murad, A.H. 2009. *The Mantle Adorned*, London: The Quilliam Press Ltd.

Murad, K. 2005. *Interpersonal Relations: an Islamic perspective*, Leicester: Islamic Foundation.

Murata, S. and Chittick, W. 2000. *The Vision of Islam*, London: I B Tauris.

Murphy, C. 2008, 'Soldier of Faith', http://www.washingtonpost.com/wp-dyn/content/article/2008/01/16/AR2008011603131.html, (accessed, 28/1/2008).

Nasr, S.H. 2004. *The Heart of Islam: Enduring Values for Humanity*, New York: Harper Collins.

Noblett, W. 2002. 'Prisons: a developing chaplaincy', in Jones, C. and Sedgwick, P., (eds), *The Future of Criminal Justice*, London: SPCK, pp. 89–102.

Norwood, F. 2006. 'The Ambivalent Chaplain: negotiating structural and ideological difference on the margins of modern-day hospital medicine', *Medical Anthropology* 25 (1): 1–29.

Padela, A., Killawi, A., Heisler, M., Demonner, S. and Fetters, M. 2010. 'The Role of Imams in American Muslim Health: perspectives of Muslim community leaders in Southeast Michigan', *Journal of Religion and Health* 50 (2): 359–73.

Padela, A. I., Killawi, A. Forman, J. DeMonner, S. and Heisler, M. 2012. 'American Muslim Perceptions of Healing: Key Agents in Healing, and Their Roles', *Qualitative Health Research* 22 (6): 846–58.

Padwick, C. 1969. *Muslim Devotions: A Study of Prayer-Manuals in Common Use*, London: S.P.C.K.

Pattison, S. and Woodward, J., (eds) 2000. '*The Blackwell Reader in Pastoral and Practical Theology*', Oxford: Blackwell.

Pattison, S. 1994. *Pastoral Care and Liberation Theology*, Cambridge: Cambridge University Press.

Pattison, S. 2000. *A Critique of Pastoral Care*, London: SCM.

Pattison, S. 2001. 'Dumbing down the Spirit', in Orchard, H., (ed.), *Spirituality in Health Care Contexts*, London: Jessica Kingsley Publishers, pp. 33–46.

Pedziwiatr, K. 2011. 'How Progressive is "Progressive Islam"? The Limits of the Religious Individualization of the European Muslim Elites', *Social Compass* 58 (2): 214–22.

Percy, M. 2006. *Clergy: the Origin of Species*, London: Continuum.

Phillips, E. 1970. 'Research Ministry: A New Concept for a Hospital Chaplain?', *Journal of Religion and Health* 9 (1): 218–32.

Pigott, R. 2012, 'Church of England could lose key prison chaplain role', http://www.bbc.co.uk/news/uk-17020294 (accessed, 30/3/2012).

Pill, R. Wainwright, P. McNamee, M. and Pattison, S. 2004. 'Understanding professions and professionals in the context of values', in Pill, R. and Pattison, S., (eds), *Values in Professional Practice: Lessons for Health, Social Care, and Other Professionals*, Oxford: Radcliffe Press, pp. 13–28.

Pinker, S. 1999. *How the Mind Works*, London: Penguin Books.

Priestly, P. 1985. *Victorian Prison Lives*, London: Methuen & Co. Ltd.

Quraishi, M. 2008. 'Researching Muslim Prisoners', *International Journal of Social Research Methodology* 11 (5): 453–67.

Rahman, F. 1989. *Health and Medicine in the Islamic Tradition: Change and Identity*, New York: Cross Road.

Robinson, F. 2009. 'Crisis of authority: crisis of Islam?', *Journal of the Royal Asiatic Society* 19 (3): 339–54.

Rogers, D. 2000. *Politics, Prayer and Parliament*, London: Continuum.

Rose, N. 1996. 'Psychiatry as a political science: advanced liberalism and the administration of risk', *History of the Human Sciences* 9 (2): 1–23.

Russell, A. 1980. *The Clerical Profession*, London: SPCK.

Saeed, A. 2006. *Islamic Thought: an Introduction*, London: Routledge.

Saegert, S. Thompson, P.J. and Warren, M.R., (eds) 2001. '*Social Capital and Poor Communties*', New York: Russell Sage Foundation.

Saggar, S. 2009. 'Boomerangs and Slingshots: Radical Islamism and Counter-Terrorism Strategy', *Journal of Ethnic and Migration Studies* 35 (3): 381–402.

Schneider, I. 1995. 'Imprisonment in Pre-Classical and Classical Islamic Law', *Islamic Law and Society* 2 (2): 157–73.

Scourfield, J., Gilliat-Ray, S., Khan, A. and Otri, S. 2013. *Muslim Childhood*, Oxford: Oxford University Press.

Seymour, S. 2006. 'The Silence of Prayer: an examination of the Federal Bureau of Prisons' Moratorium on the Hiring of Muslim Chaplains', *Columbia Human Rights Law Review* 37 (2): 523–88.

Shils, E. 1965. 'Charisma, Order, and Status', *American Sociological Review* 30 (2): 199–213.

Siddiqui, A. 2007, 'Islam at Universities in England: meeting the needs and investing in the future', London: Department for Innovation, Universities and Skills.

Siddiqui, A.R. 2001. *Lift up your Hearts: A Collection of 30 Khutbah for Friday Prayer*, Leicester: Islamic Foundation.

Smith, C. 1993. 'Black Muslims and the Development of Prisoners' Rights', *Journal of Black Studies* 24 (2): 131–46.

Snape, M. 2005. *God and the British Soldier: Religion and the British Army in the First and Second World Wars*, London: Routledge.

Spalek, B. and Wilson, D. 2001. 'Not Just 'Visitors' to Prisons: the experiences of Imams who work inside the penal system', *The Howard Journal* 40 (1): 3–13.

Speck, P. 1988. *Being There: Pastoral Care in Time of Illness,* London: SPCK.

Swift, C. 2009. *Hospital Chaplaincy in the Twenty-First Century: the Crisis of Spiritual Care in the NHS*, Aldershot: Ashgate.

Tarleton, P., Kazi, K. and Jenkins, K. 2003. 'Multi-faith Chaplaincy: spirituality and shared values in prison', *CJM (Centre for Crime and Justice Studies)* 52: 8–9.

Threlfall-Holmes, M. and Newitt, M. 2011. *Being a Chaplain*, London: SPCK.

Tjora, A. 2006. 'Writing small discoveries: an exploration of fresh observers' observations', *Qualitative Research* 6 (4): 429–51.

Todd, A. and Tipton, L. 2011, 'The Role and Contribution of a Multi-faith Prison Chaplaincy to the Contemporary Prison Service', Cardiff: Cardiff Centre for Chaplaincy Studies.

Waller, S. 2012. 'Workplace Chaplaincy', in Rothwell, W., (ed.), *Encyclopaedia of Human Resource Management*, Chichester: J. Wiley & Sons, pp. 443–9.

Watt, W.M. 1968. *Islamic Political Thought*, Edinburgh: Edinburgh University Press.

Winkelmann, M.J. 2005. *From Behind the Curtain: a Study of a Girl's Madrasah in India*, Amsterdam: Amsterdam University Press.

Yee, J. 2005. *For God and Country: Faith and Patriotism Under Fire*, New York: PublicAffairs.

Zaman, M. Q. 2002. *The Ulama in Contemporary Islam: Custodians of Change*, Oxford and Princeton: Princeton University Press.

Index

Ahmed, Maqsood 8, 101–2; *see also*
    Muslim Advisor
Ali, Ahtsham xvi, 13, 112; *see also* Muslim
    Advisor
'alim 19, 21–2, 25–6, 46–7, 49, 53, 56,
    58–61, 63, 79–81, 83, 90, 92–4,
    130, 153–4, 157–9, 164, 169–170,
    173–6, 178–9, 191–2
'alima 19, 21–2, 26, 45–6, 59, 61, 72, 92,
    115, 130, 139, 153, 169, 173–4,
    178, 191
Arshad, Mohammed 16, 83

Baig, Navid 187
Beckford, James xvi, 6–8, 11, 15, 76, 95,
    100–102, 115
Birmingham Children's Hospital vii,
    127–8; *see also* Hussain, Zamir
birth 27–9, 94, 130, 157, 175
    adhan 28, 89, 191
    naming babies 89
    pregnancy 51, 90
Bourdieu, Pierre 23, 179
Bretherton, Luke 185

Cardiff Centre for Chaplaincy Studies 67
chaplain, Christian 8, 15, 20, 52–3,
    56, 65–5, 83, 100–102, 104–7,
    116, 119, 126, 134, 142, 167–9,
    170–175, 180, 183, 188; *see also*
    Christian churches
    Anglican 5–6, 14, 99, 101, 106–7, 116,
        119, 126, 141, 175, 187
    influence of 3–4, 10, 43, 48, 64, 83,
        85–6, 105–6, 128, 167–175, 183, 188
    Roman Catholic 49, 103, 106, 142,
        171, 176, 180, 187
chaplain, definition of, 5
chaplaincy, Christian
    history of, 5, 43, 168–9, 173, 179

models of, 25, 85, 167–174, 178–9
chaplaincy, in Muslim societies
    Indonesia 39
    Malaysia 39
    non-institutionalisation 25, 40–43
charity 27
    donations to chaplaincies 127, 140
    Muslim Youth Helpline 140
Christian churches 5, 105, 119
community chaplaincy 89–90, 94, 105,
    134
confidentiality 41, 56
converts 1, 20, 51, 80–81, 85
counter-terrorism 8, 13, 108–11, 115, 121,
    141
crowd-control 86, 126–7
    hospitals 86, 126
    prisons 127

dars-i-nizami 46
dar ul-uloom 9, 19, 45–7, 66
da'wah 30, 52, 182
death 26–8, 50, 53, 58, 60, 66, 80–82,
    86–7, 89–90, 104, 125–7, 129, 131,
    137, 142, 157, 175
    bereavement 82, 85, 87, 124, 128–9,
        136, 141
    burial 28, 30, 58, 86, 137–9
    death certificates 58, 89, 126, 131, 137
    foetal death 53, 90, 127–9, 175
    funerals 28–30, 58, 81–2, 86, 89, 97,
        104, 126, 130, 138–9
    Gift for Bereaved Parents 127–9
    graves 27–9, 53, 82,
    still-birth 90, 130
    suicide and sudden death 66, 129
    washing corpse 28, 30, 130
Deobandis 9–10, 19, 21, 45–6, 51, 62–3,
    112, 141
dignity 7, 79, 132, 142

Dinham, Adam 63, 135, 179
dress 59–60, 73, 84, 92, 100, 115–116,
    120, 161
    authority of 59–60, 73, 116, 161
    hijab 88, 116, 161, 182
Dudhwala, Yunus xvi, 141

Eid, *see* Ramadan
equality and diversity 4, 56, 77, 87, 94,
    104, 106, 114, 116, 119, 126,
    167–8, 182–3, 186
ethics 25, 40, 59, 87, 155, 176
    abortion 28
    life-support machines 60–61, 90, 175
    medication regimes 78–9, 90
    organ donation 40, 141, 157
extremism, *see* Preventing Violent
    Extremism

Faith Matters 113–4
families 29–30, 33, 40–41, 60–61,
    78–9, 82, 85–7, 89, 94, 97, 124,
    126–130, 136, 139, 169–171, 176,
    180–181
    mixed-faith 181
fasting, *see* Ramadan
fiqh xiv, 59, 82, 156, 158
Friday prayer xiii, 8, 34, 37, 60, 65, 71–5,
    88, 107, 110–111, 114, 129, 169
    hospitals 74–5, 107
    preaching 73–4, 88, 110–111
    prisons 8, 34, 60, 65, 72–5, 88,
        110–111
    universities 75, 129
funerals, *see* death

gender 2–3, 16, 19, 22, 52, 65–6, 68, 71–2,
    83, 87, 91–3, 176
    female chaplains 3, 17–18, 21, 28, 46,
        49, 53, 72, 92–95, 100, 115–118,
        134, 139, 141, 189; *see also*
        'alima
    husband-wife chaplaincy 115, 163
    professional development 65–6, 68,
        115–118
    recruitment 46, 53, 93, 115
    female chaplaincy clients 72, 94–5,
        89–90, 116, 133

Governors, in prisons 77, 79, 102, 109–11,
    118, 122, 125, 127

Hadith xvii, 25, 29, 32, 44, 59–60, 96
    pastoral practice 32, 59–60, 82, 112
Hafiz, Imam Asim vii, xvi, 17
halal food 7–8, 41, 75–9, 100, 132, 135,
    141, 169, 171, 173
Hindus 16, 34, 81, 103, 106, 108
hospitals, in Muslim societies 33–36,
    39–40
Hussain, Zamir vii, 127–8

iftar, *see* Ramadan
imams
    British-born 19, 21, 62, 141, 145
    mosque-based 7–8, 47, 58, 112–113,
        121, 134, 136–7, 149, 169–171, 178
    overseas 19, 21, 39, 136
    role 26, 29, 35, 38–40, 43, 51, 55, 79,
        81, 134, 136, 170–171, 178
    training 35, 44–6, 93, 129
infection control 43, 83, 127
inter-faith relations xiii, xiv, 135, 180–185

Jewish chaplains 5, 106–7
Jumu'ah *see* Friday prayer

language
    Arabic 29, 36, 38, 59–60, 81–3, 85, 92
    community 9, 58, 83, 88–9, 180
    interpreting and translating 58, 80,
        88–9, 104, 125, 185
laughter and smiling 79, 94, 97, 102, 110,
    119, 120–122, 125, 183

Madinah, University of 19, 45–6
madrasah 47
Markfield Institute of Higher Education
    xiii, xiv, xvi, 12, 64–6
    Certificate in Muslim Chaplaincy 10,
        12, 64
    placements xiii, xiv, 10, 13, 50, 65
    trainers 62
Marranci, Gabriele 79, 132
medieval Islamic
    hospitals 33–6
    prisons 36–7

universities 37–8
mosques 4, 11, 23, 26, 29, 31, 33–5, 49,
    53–5, 79, 86, 105, 123, 134–140,
    172, 176–8
    prison 9, 73, 112–113
    Wandsworth, HMP 9
material culture 127–8
muftis 26, 60–1
Muhammad, Prophet 1, 26, 30, 79
    medicine of 33
    role model for chaplains 3, 25, 31
multi-faith spaces 105,
    sharing of 107, 180
multi-faith teams 1, 3, 15, 93, 101, 104–8,
    123, 174, 180–185, 188
Muslim Advisor, HM Prison Service xvi, 8,
    13, 55, 77, 101, 106, 112
Muslim chaplains
    administrative work 62, 73, 87
    age profile 18, 21
    awards and prizes 140–141
    career path 3, 9, 11, 15, 43, 48–55, 63,
        65–6, 95–6, 109–110, 114, 139,
        170, 186–7
    continuous professional development
        xvi, 9–10, 12, 15, 51, 64–9, 95,
        102, 109–10, 115–116, 164, 169
    educational background 44–48
    job titles 48–9
    mentoring 68, 91, 115
    numbers, in England and Wales 16
    payment and salaries 95
    personal qualities 55–58, 132; *see also*
        non-judgemental
    place of birth 18, 21
    previous roles 47–8
    professionalisation xiii, 4, 13, 43, 46,
        60–63, 66–7, 69, 99, 114, 119, 169
    recruitment 49–52, 99, 101, 114–115
    staff training 80, 85, 87–8, 96, 113,
        124–5
Muslim Council of Britain (MCB) 9, 16,
    67, 102
Muslim News, The vii, 9–10, 102

National Health Service (NHS) 7, 13, 16,
    60, 68
Noblett, William 101

non-judgmental 31, 56, 85–6, 90–91,
    170–171, 173, 175

pastoral stories and cases 124, 130–132
Pathan, Sikander xvi
Patients' Charter 5
prayer 26, 81–3, 105, 127, 131–2, 171; *see
    also* Friday prayer
    arrangements for 7, 41
    washing before 26, 42
preaching, *see* Friday prayer
pregnancy, *see* birth
'Preventing Violent Extremism' (PVE) 4,
    6, 66, 99, 100, 108–114, 116, 121
Prison Service, in England and Wales
    6, 8, 16–17, 20, 48, 50, 55, 60,
    62–3, 66–8, 72, 77–8, 99, 101–2,
    105, 107, 109–10, 113–114, 119,
    140–141, 175
    Prison Act 1952 5
    Prison Service Chaplaincy (PSC) xvi,
        8, 11, 13, 16, 21, 50, 55, 62, 77,
        101, 112, 118–119
    Prison Service Orders 76
prisons, in Muslim societies 36–9
professional associations for Muslim
    chaplains (UK) 2, 4, 10–13, 17, 39,
    50, 62, 99, 117–118
    Association of Muslim Chaplains 10,
        64–5
    Association of Muslim Chaplains in
        Education 11, 67, 117
    College of Health Care Chaplains
        Islam Resource Group 11, 117
    Muslim Chaplains Association 11,
        117–119
proselytism 8, 52, 80, 182

Quilliam Foundation, *see* think tanks
Qur'an
    pastoral practice 32, 81–3
    healing power 26, 32–3, 172
    memorisation of 39, 44, 83, 127, 174
    Surah Yasin 28, 82

Rajput, Asgar Halim vii, xvi, 185
Ramadan 3, 26–7, 74, 78–80, 87, 94, 125,
    133–4, 140

Eid 27, 78–80, 84, 124–5, 127, 133
    iftar 27, 79
Religion and Society Programme xv, 12
Religion in Prison: Equal Rites in a
    Multi-faith Society 8, 101; *see also*
    Beckford, James
research, Muslim Chaplaincy Project 11–22

Sajid, Imam Jalil xvi
scholars, *see* 'ulama
Siddiqui, Ataullah xiv, xvi, 12; *see also*
    Markfield Institute of Higher
    Education
shari'ah 1, 25, 178–9
spirituality 37, 48, 156, 188
substance and drug abuse 9, 74, 81, 136–7
    dog-searches, in prisons 67
    rehabilitation 136

think tanks 108, 111–112
    Quilliam Foundation 111
troubleshooting and crisis management 89,
    96, 124–6, 129, 137, 142, 177

'ulama 1, 19, 25–6, 45, 51, 65–6, 82, 115,
    119, 137, 140; *see also* muftis
United States of America

Clinical Pastoral Education (CPE)
    150–151
Hartford Seminary, Connecticut 10,
    146, 148, 151–5, 158–9
Islamic Seminary Foundation 154, 160
Islamic Society of North America
    146–7, 158
Mattson, Ingrid 149, 151–2
Nation of Islam 147–8
Yale University 149, 159, 161

'visiting ministers' 6–8, 11, 13, 15, 46,
    48–9, 60–61, 64, 68–9, 74, 95,
    100–103, 106, 108–110, 114, 116,
    118, 124, 142, 174
volunteers
    Muslim chaplains as xiii, 11, 20, 49,
        67, 187
    supporting Muslim chaplains 87, 105,
        139

Warwick, University of 6, 13
Woodhead, Linda xv
wudu *see* prayer

Young Offender Institutions 15, 20, 72,
    123, 126–7, 129, 132